The Modern Confessional
Jon C. Jenkins

Originally written for the completion of a D.Min, 2013
Published by Nashotah House Press, 2014

The research and content are copyright of Jon Jenkins SSC
Permission for use must be obtained from the author and
Nashotah House Theological Seminary

Formatted and designed as a book by
Ben Jefferies
Editor-in-Chief, Nashotah House Press

Cover:
Confessional, Drawing
*William & Robert Chambers Encyclopaedia - A Dictionary of Universal
Knowledge for the People (Philadelphia, PA: J. B. Lippincott & Co., 1881)*

Coffeshop, photograph
by soopahtoe on freeimages.com

BISAC: Religion / Christian Rituals & Practice / Sacraments

ISBN-10: 0979224330
ISBN-13: 978-0979224331

THE MODERN CONFESSIONAL

The Modern Confessional

A Study of the Sacrament of Reconciliation for use in the Anglican Church, along with practical "How-to" advice for the novice confessor.

Rev. Jon C. Jenkins SSC

D.Min., M.Div.

A NASHOTAH HOUSE THEOLOGICAL SEMINARY

D.Min. Thesis

published by

NASHOTAH HOUSE PRESS

CONTENTS

PART III:
HEARING CONFESSIONS

LIST OF FIGURES

ABSTRACT

It seems "The Modern Confessional" is mostly empty these days, gathering dust, and reminding us of a seemingly dim dark past, in which confessions were heard, penances were prescribed, and penitents were made to feel miserable about their sins, without offering any real healing or guidance. But is this a true assessment of the confessional? Did confession ever have anything to offer, and does it potentially have something greater to offer now for a modern audience?

History teaches us that we have a constant need for reconciliation with the Lord, and that the means of this reconciliation has changed and evolved over time. The problem with confession in the 21st century is that it appears to be following a Reformation model that was responding to a uniquely Medieval spirituality, which simply does not exist in the culture of today. As such, the clergy and laity need to be trained in more modern means of attending to the spiritual needs of their souls, and to be wary of the cult of autonomy in modern culture that teaches us that our sin is really no one else's business and that it is possible to solve our own problems without the love and support of our Church's leadership and community.

Within these pages, the reader will discover the history of confessional practice and atonement from the Bible to now, take a glimpse of our current culture's surprising response to the confessional, and demonstrate how the confessional practices of old may be amended or even resurrected so to adopt a truly Anglican model of confession that will offer modern confessors potential for greater success in guiding penitent souls back to God in an age that is desperate for answers and remedies to sin.

ACKNOWLEDGEMENTS

I wish to offer my most humble and grateful thanks to those who assisted me in the production of the dissertation project that led to the publication of this text, in particular:

The Rev. Dr. Steven Peay, who advised and supported me along the way of this study, and offered limitless encouragement, support, and rabid enthusiasm.

The Rev. Dr. Jack Gabig, who was a tremendous help to me in the preparation of this study, particularly in preparing my surveys and focus groups, and in encouraging me to write the "done doctorate," and to save the "perfect doctorate" for later; and who also served as a second reader to this project.

The Rev. Dr. Arnold W. Klukas who has been my dear Father in the field of Ascetics since my M.Div. days, and who also participated in the formation of this project.

The Very Rev. William Crary, who has been a fine mentor in the world of ascetics, and who has been a supportive guide in my ministry and in this study.

The Rev. Dr. Karl C. Schaffenburg who served as a final editor for the source material of this text.

My wife Claire, for her loving support, and who by marrying me in the final year of my doctoral studies provided me an adequate excuse to put off this project for a year so to gather more data and more time to write, and who also helped me discover my many faults through proof-reading this tome.

The people of Christ the King Episcopal Church, Fort Worth, Texas, for granting me time away to study in the summers, and for supporting my studies financially by their magnanimity.

To the clergy of the Diocese of Fort Worth who participated in this study and gave me honest data to crunch for the benefit of the Church and our diocese.

To the laity and youth of the seven parishes who sacrificed their time and perspectives for the sake of future souls to be won for Christ.

And finally, to the staff of Nashotah House, particularly those without titles or preferments who manage the grounds, clean the guest apartments, cook the meals, shelve and order the books, manage the bookstore, and send me bills for the copious copies I produced. You have been a tremendous support to me throughout my seminary career, and your love will not be forgotten.

—Jon Jenkins SSC

INTRODUCTION

Problem and Rationale

It is assumed that while a few confessions are heard in confessionals, most modern pastors likely hear more confessions while sitting on a barstool, eating in a restaurant, sitting on a park bench, drinking coffee in a Starbucks or other coffee-shop, waiting for lift-off on an airplane, or while tending to someone in a hospital bed, and so on. Furthermore, it appears that even those faith traditions that do make use of confessionals only see a fraction of their parishioners taking advantage of the practice, leaving a majority of those in the pews without spiritual direction or any real opportunities beyond a general confession to really purify themselves of sin; and, more importantly, to be guided on how to avoid their particular sins in the future. However, it seems that most clergy who can be identified as clergy in public are often approached in a casual way by people who want to ask them something pertaining to their lives or their faith. These casual conversations are, in my experience, almost always about something sinful, or something they are neglecting in their spiritual lives, and are therefore perfect material for a proper confession. Most confessions I hear, as an active clergyman, are at our diocesan youth camp, in a pub, or in some other casual context in which someone asks for advice or vaguely addresses me to "ask me something they are curious about," which again tends to be something pertaining to their sin or neglect of the soul.

Since it appears, from various sources, that most pastors or priests of this age encounter more opportunities for spiritual direction and confessions in public or casual settings than in a confessional booth, pastors of this age may need to develop a deliberate technique in which to guide these moments of private counsel into a formative confessional process, including teaching them to have contrition, guiding the penitent to formally define their problem, and thereby to make a confession of fault, and then assist them into implementing methods of change so to amend their lives, and hopefully actually remedy their habitual problems. Shaping these moments, usually instigated by the would-be penitent, into a healthy confessional process would certainly do them the most good, and advance the work of the church into an area that is most critically necessary for our people to obtain spiritual progress.

Therefore, the purpose of this text is to demonstrate the history of confessional practice, evaluate these methods in light of our current culture's response to and use of such practices as demonstrated by a recent survey of the usage of said practices among the clergy and laity of the Episcopal Diocese of Fort Worth, and based on these data points, to then review a recent study of laity on confession in a number of different parishes spread across the spectrum of available demographics, so to conclude where confessional practices should be amended to adopt a model in which will foster greater success in guiding souls to God, and restoring sinners to holiness for the greater Church.

Premise

Everyone sins. There is generally very little debate on this point. In fact, if you do not believe this is true, then this book will either be of absolutely no use to you, or it will drastically change your world-view, hopefully for the better. So, if everyone sins, and we all agree that getting rid of sin is the first step to reconciling our personal relationships with God, we must find a means of putting sin away, and hopefully, with a lot of practice, conquering our habitual sins, which are usually the ones that overtake us in the end.

Every classic spiritual resource on spiritual direction, the holy life, or living at one with God, all begin with this common premise: until you get rid of sin first, you cannot move forward into holiness.

Whether it's *The Book of Pastoral Rule* by Gregory the Great, *The Ladder of Perfection* by Walter Hilton, *The Cloud of Unknowing* by an unknown, probably Cistercian author, *The Introduction to the Devout Life* by Francis deSales, *The Spiritual Exercises* of St. Ignatius, or any number of modern resources including *The Purpose Driven Life* by Rick Warren— all of these spiritual authors begin by stating, in one way or another, that in order to move forward toward holiness, we must first begin by diagnosing where we are in relation to God's commandments, and eliminate sin, if we are to then take step two, three, four, and etc. Simply stated, How can we move on to step two, three, four, or five, unless we take step one? One cannot climb a ladder to heaven by starting in the middle. It's just not possible.

As such, this study was undertaken as a result of a series of conversations among regular confessors whom I consider mentors, the youth who are always eager to learn more about the Sacraments, and others (largely strangers) who from time to time ask me about the life of a Priest while in a public setting. All of these groups have a natural curiosity about confession, although from differing perspectives.

The clergy who are regular confessors have an interest based on the perception that confession is the very best thing one can do for their own soul, second only to and subservient to the concept that true discipleship is rooted in submitting oneself to the will of Christ. And the first step toward discipleship seems to be in getting the sin out of our lives. The confessors all wonder why more people do not take advantage of the confessional, as it has been a tremendous positive influence on our own lives and ministries, and we have all witnessed the tremendous potential for change in a person's life when exercised regularly by the laity.

The youth seem to be curious about confession, but mostly from a perception of fear of the practice. Our modern culture teaches them that either sin does not exist, or if it does, it is surely no-one's business—unless of course you can make a reality television program out of it, and then make millions off of showcasing their sins to others, while pretending no one notices their blatant sins. This perception is not only common among the youth, but it is likely the prevalent perception of modern society in America at the beginning of this 21st Century, particularly among those who are 45 and under.

The other conversations I have regularly with strangers about confession mirror closely what the youth seem to think of confession. However, the youth I refer to are youth from the Church Camp who actually seem to have some root in the Church (although some of your youth camp kids come from various denominations or various strata of the Anglican world we live in today), where the average person who engages me in public rarely seems to be a church-goer. Therefore, it seems that the average person's perception is therefore only informed by what they see in movies or on television. There are a select older few who claim to have "grown up in the Church", or more specifically "grown up Catholic," and as such have a perception of confession from a largely pre-1960's (Pre-Vatican II) view of the confessional. They tell me that they are largely afraid of it because for them it was used as a threat to attempt to keep them out of trouble, much the same way parents threaten that if children aren't good, Santa Claus won't be visiting this Christmas.

So, that was the origin of a need for a study of this magnitude. The perception was that active clergy might need to develop the skills necessary to turn these "Starbucks" moments of casual conversations into opportunities to guide souls towards putting away their sins, and making a fresh start. The questions people ask clergy in public settings almost always have to do with their own sin in some way, and so this project began as a "Manual on Hearing Barstool Confessions." In fact, that was the first proposed title for this study. Data were then gathered from the people, the clergy, and from history, to support this idea, and to see whether this sort of thing was truly the next evolution in confessional practice. What was found, however, was quite the opposite. The people are actually very interested in making a confession in the church, but feel mostly that the opportunity simply is not there, or it is not being advertised, utilized, and taught as a necessary thing within their churches. Rather, it seems that confession is one of the things our Churches have put on the library shelf, or behind glass in the museum, as relics from a dim dark era that are no longer of any real use anymore.

So what can we do to resurrect this sacrament of our Church that has become largely un-used? Is it still relevant? Do the people have an interest? Do the clergy know how to administer it as a sacrament? These questions, and more, will be answered in the pages to come.

Now, to briefly discuss the pedigree of this study, the first step toward developing this project was a simple four-question survey conducted at a clergy retreat in which they were simply asked whether they sat for confessions, whether they did so regularly, did anyone come, and how often they were approached in public about confessional subjects? The results of this first candid survey revealed that this was a pertinent subject, and one that had more questions to ask. From that first survey, the data revealed that most clergy do not sit to hear confessions because they say that no one comes, and as a result they stopped offering regular confessions at all. However they all reported that people often came to them in public to ask spiritual advice, and that they heard more confessions while sitting at a lunch counter, than at the Church. I found this true of my own ministry, in that I tend to hear more confessions at our youth camp than anywhere else. Each year I continue to hear more confessions in public than in the Church, and I too had (at the time of that first survey) stopped offering regular confessional hours at my parish because all I ever did was sit there and read books, with no penitents in sight. It seemed to me that people still have a hunger for good spiritual advice, and to conquer the things that trouble them, but they have a fear of the Church setting. As a result of all of these things, I came to a singular goal: to determine what needed to change in our confessional process to make it more accessible to the people who truly need some way of getting sin out of their lives, and to receive good and godly counsel.

It may also be of note to later readers concerning who I am, and where I am in my ministry at this time. I am a thirty-four-year-old priest in the conservative, traditional, and largely Anglo-Catholic Anglican Diocese of Fort Worth. I was ordained in 2006, and at this point I have been a Priest for nearly seven years. I have served all of that time in the same Diocese. I am also a regular penitent myself, and I have a true heart for the value of confession in one's spiritual life, as it has been a great positive influence on me as a Christian foremost, but also as a Priest. My confessional relationships with confessors have changed over time. As a result of my studies and discussions, I have come to be regarded among my peers as more of a colleague than a penitent, which has led us to discussing my own sin on a different level. Although I admit that I prefer to be treated as a penitent than a Priest, or a penitent-Priest, than a priest alone. I prefer to maintain a level of submission to my confessor in which I submit my life to his spiritual guidance, and follow his advice with utmost diligence. I was trained to hear confessions at Nashotah House Theological Seminary in the context of an Ascetical Theology course under The Rev. Dr. Arnold Klukas and The Rt. Rev. Dr. Donald Parsons, which was solid; however the most useful training I have received has been in the reading I have done since seminary while waiting to hear confessions. I tell most new priests who feel inadequate as confessors to read a few books I suggest while waiting to hear confessions, and by the time they hear their first, they will have become an expert. The suggested reading list for those interested in this kind of training is at the very end of this book.

The context of this study was in the Diocese of Fort Worth where I minister, but which is also more open than others to sacramental confession, and which is home to only a few regular "confessional priests," whom I label this way because they sit to hear confessions absolutely every week without fail. We are fortunate here to have many regular confessors who are not only available, but who are truly excellent spiritual directors and confessors. This diocese is largely Anglo-Catholic, but many of our clergy do seem to have more Western theological or Catholic leanings than anything else. However, we do have several more Protestant-minded clergy who have no real aptitude or desire for confession, and who truly do not see a need for it in the life of the Church. These will be discussed more fully in the clergy study, but it is safe to say that the diocese is not of "one mind" when it comes to such things.

As for the nature of this research, my philosophy was simple: to be as honest as possible with myself by submitting my own mind to a thorough theological study of the history of the confessional to determine whether my tradition was really built with the proper "DNA" (as it were) to make sacramental confession a successful practice. This meant opening my mind to being wrong about my own perceptions of "how it's always been done." Likewise I could not rely on my own opinions for the "clergy perspective" for a study of this magnitude, so I endeavored to get all of the clergy of my diocese to complete an honest and anonymous survey of their confessional practices, to determine if I was alone in my practice, or rather if I was simply one among many who had come to the same conclusions. Then, in order to keep the clergy honest, I asked the lay-people in eight focus-group studies whether they were participating in the confessional life of the Church, and specifically, what they were hearing from the clergy. To keep this as honest as possible, I chose two urban churches, two rural churches, and three suburban churches, in order to get an honest spread among the laity of what was going on in our Diocese. In choosing these churches, I attempted to find clergy who were both in favor of confession, as well as those who were not as in favor of confession. Finally, my goal in gathering these data was to be as honest as possible about potential solutions concerning this confessional problem and to answer a few key questions: is confession something we should be doing? Are the lay-people interested? Are the lay-people or the clergy responsible for increasing awareness and interest for their own spiritual care? And what could we be doing differently to make this process more successful?

So, having now covered the context, purpose, and philosophy behind this research, we need to address the direct question: what are the prevalent problems with confession? As will be demonstrated in later data, the first problem appears to lie in the negligent use of the confessional. A process that was once in widespread use has fallen out of practice in the last fifty years, although there are pockets of the Church that still maintain regular confessional hours, with or without any penitents. A second problem has become evident in that the clergy of the Diocese of Fort Worth admit to a lack of training in hearing confessions or offering spiritual direction. As such, one goal of this study will be to identify possible remedies to this problem, and even suggest a potential course of study for immediate use, as well as beyond that which lies in these pages. Lastly, there seems to be a lack of faith traditions outside of the Anglican Church that maintain the use of confessionals, and as such, when ministers come to our diocese from these other traditions, many of them come without proper training in the use of the confessional within our tradition.

Although this study will be focused solely on the practices of the Anglican Diocese of Fort Worth as of December of 2012, those of other traditions may use this study to draw their own conclusions about the practice. It should become evident that where the teaching on the confessional model or spiritual direction model is lacking, so also the praxis of any such program is also lacking. We will also address the need that remains evident, that lay-people still acknowledge a need to confess their sins and to be guided in remedying their habitual sins so to achieve atonement, peace, and comfort in their relationship with God. As this need remains, I shall also present my own conclusions on the use of the current practice, as well as suggestions of potential means of providing a new model for pastors who are willing to try another approach so to bring their people closer to the healing power of absolution, and to more adequately meet the needs of the people in their various contexts.

As such, our road-map will be as follows: we will review the history of atonement from the Bible until now and witness the evolution of atonement into confessional practice and the varying ways that process was handled and evolved over time. We will then hear from the clergy concerning their own training, practice, and implementation of a confessional model, if any. Then we will hear the first-hand voices of laity from all different ages and demographics concerning their perceptions of confession, and what they would like to see improved. Then from these data we will extract some potential model of confession, or other modes of teaching to help them bring themselves closer to God, and closer to living a life of holiness. In the end, the hope is to arrive at the very best of what the Church has to offer in confessional practice and spiritual direction, and to make this our aim as well-intentioned disciples of Jesus Christ.

The
Modern
Confessional

PART I: THEOLOGY OF CONFESSION

Biblical Theology

CHAPTER ONE
Confession And Atonement In The Bible

The scriptures contain examples of millennia of broken interactions between God and man, as well as various means of restoration. It is too broad a statement to say that "there was an Old Testament way of doing things, and a New Testament way of doing things, " or that, "In the Old Testament days, we made animal sacrifices, and in the New Testament Jesus is our only mediator and sacrifice." Although these statements are true, the means of reconciliation between God and man has changed shape and form over the years, and consistent patterns can be seen throughout the Bible concerning sin and reconciliation. As sin remains a constant, so does a need for reconciliation. In some cases, this involves restoration through sacrifices as payments or offerings. In other places the scriptures emphasize a greater need for contrition, sorrow, and genuine intentions beyond the prescribed sacrifices. Sometimes sacrifices are represented by actual animal oblations, while at other times the Bible speaks of the sacrifice of the heart. However these sacrifices come about, a common theme associated with reconciliation between man and God is "repentance," which is to say, a re-orientation of the current trajectory in order to move forward in a right direction.

In Hebrew, the primary language of the Old Testament[1], two words are used for the word repentance. The most common Hebrew word is נָחַם (naw-kham) which has many shades of meaning including:

---

[1] Note: For the purposes of this dissertation, the term "Old Testament" will be used to refer to the Hebrew Scriptures, as this text is written from a Christian perspective, in evaluation of a Christian practice. No offense is intended toward those who may use this text among any other religious communities.

to be sorry, to console oneself, to repent, to regret, to comfort, be comforted, to be moved to pity, and to have compassion. The second most common Hebrew word for repentance is שׁוּב (shoob) which can mean: to return, to turn back, go back, come back, to apostatize, to turn away, to repent, to restore, refresh, repair, or to lead away. The former emphasizes more of an interior or emotional change, while the latter focuses more on the actual physical act of movement towards or away from the things that draw man away from God. Much of the Old Testament speaks to us in the context of various journeys taken with God, and when the people fail, it is often because they have gone away from the path God has set for them.

The Old Testament also speaks of righteousness in this way. When someone is said to "walk with God," this is an idiom describing their righteousness or faithfulness. For example, in Genesis, Enoch is taken by God because he walked with God: "Enoch walked with God; then he was no more, for God took him."[2] Yet another example, "Noah was a righteous man, blameless in his generation; Noah walked with God."[3] David is spoken of in this way by his son Solomon while in prayer at the dedication of the new temple in Jerusalem:

> And Solomon stood before the altar of the LORD in the presence of all the congregation of Israel, and spread forth his hands toward heaven: And he said, LORD God of Israel, there is no God like thee, in heaven above, or on earth beneath, who keepest covenant and mercy with thy servants that walk before thee with all their heart: Who hast kept with thy servant David my father that thou promisedst him: thou spakest also with thy mouth, and hast fulfilled it with thine hand, as it is this day. Therefore now, LORD God of Israel, keep with thy servant David my father that thou promisedst him, saying, There shall not fail thee a man in my sight to sit on the throne of Israel; so that thy children take heed to their way, *that they walk before me as thou hast walked before me.*[4]

Moses' guidance to Israel speaks in this same idiomatic way:

---

[2] Genesis 5:24

[3] Genesis 6:9

[4] 1 Kings 8:22-25 (Emphasis added)

Ye shall observe to do therefore as the LORD your God hath commanded you: ye shall not turn aside to the right hand or to the left. *Ye shall walk in all the ways* which the LORD your God hath commanded you, that ye may live, and that it may be well with you, and that ye may prolong your days in the land which ye shall possess.[5]

The Greek language primarily uses one form for the word repentance, which is μετανοία (metanoia) which means to change one's mind, or repent. However there is a separate word for turning which is στρέφω (strepho), the parallel to the Hebrew "stroob," having almost identical meanings and usage to describe a change in physical direction. So we see in both biblical languages that the primary usage of the word repentance in both the Old and New Testaments emphasize repentance as an act of the mind first, usually followed by a physical act of change, sometimes involving an actual change in direction, but more often indicating a change in behavior. We find this pattern consistently when the Bible speaks of repentance. For example: when John the Baptist preaches, "Repent for the Kingdom of God is at hand,"[6] we are then told what happened as a result of his preaching this message: "Then went out to him Jerusalem, and all Judaea, and all the region round about Jordan, and were baptized of him in Jordan, confessing their sins."[7] Here, the repentance of sin involved a change of the mind, followed by a physical act—in this case: the verbal confessing of their sin along with a physical act of washing in the Jordan River, which was also to represent an inward cleansing.

Another important word to examine prior to an in-depth study of reconciliation is the word confession. Confession comes from the Latin language, meaning *to agree, to acknowledge, or to give consent.* The most frequent use of this word describes the oral action of professing one's thoughts or beliefs, and in this act we either affirm or deny our actions and positions as we see them in the light of God's commands. In the Latin use of the word confession there is a synthesis of the two

---

[5] Deuteronomy 5:32-33 (Emphasis added)
[6] Matthew 3:2
[7] Matthew 3:5-6

meanings used above for repentance, in that there is an acceptance of a need for a change in the mind, and simultaneously a recognition of the responsibility to move and act in a different manner or direction. From all three languages we discover that confession and repentance begin as an act of the mind, and also usually result in an actual change of behavior to fulfill the act of repentance.

Sometimes in the Bible God acknowledges moments when the people were actually acting as they were supposed to act, such as fulfilling the law by making sacrifices. And yet the sacrifices they offered were at times considered by God to be "empty," because of poor intentions or because they were offering tainted sacrifices. This was the primary message preached by the prophet Malachi in the last book of the Old Testament. The people were offering sacrifices, yet they were offering polluted sacrifices, which was Malachi's way of saying that they were offering to God sacrifices of animals that met the code in one respect, such as being the right animal, yet they were not offering their first-fruits, their best, or animals "without blemish." Rather, they were offering animals that were born blind, lame, or otherwise blemished and had no real value to them, which is to say that sacrificing such animals really didn't cost them anything as they were likely to be discarded anyhow. This was contrary to the intent of making sacrifices to God, which was to show our trust and dependence upon Him.

This was also a message preached by Jesus to the Pharisees who constantly challenged him on the "letter of the law" and yet he frequently taught them that they did not have their hearts in the right place. For example, the twelfth chapter of Matthew begins with Jesus doing and performing acts that were presumed forbidden on the Sabbath:

> At that time Jesus went through the grain-fields on the sabbath; his disciples were hungry, and they began to pluck heads of grain and to eat. But when the Pharisees saw it, they said to him, "Look, your disciples are doing what is not lawful to do on the sabbath." He said to them, "Have you not read what David did, when he was hungry, and those who were with him: how he entered the house of God and ate the bread of the Presence, which it was not lawful for him to eat nor for those who were with him, but only for

the priests? Or have you not read in the law how on the sabbath the priests in the temple profane the sabbath, and are guiltless? I tell you, something greater than the temple is here. And if you had known what this means, 'I desire mercy, and not sacrifice,' you would not have condemned the guiltless. For the Son of man is lord of the sabbath." And he went on from there, and entered their synagogue. And behold, there was a man with a withered hand. And they asked him, "Is it lawful to heal on the sabbath?" so that they might accuse him. He said to them, "What man of you, if he has one sheep and it falls into a pit on the sabbath, will not lay hold of it and lift it out? Of how much more value is a man than a sheep! So it is lawful to do good on the sabbath." Then he said to the man, "Stretch out your hand." And the man stretched it out, and it was restored, whole like the other. But the Pharisees went out and took counsel against him, how to destroy him. Jesus, aware of this, withdrew from there. And many followed him, and he healed them all, and ordered them not to make him known.[8]

It is interesting, within this discussion, that rather than bringing up the law, Jesus speaks about mercy, guilt, and sacrifice and says, "Something greater than the temple is here." This series of events not only challenged and infuriated the Pharisees, we are told that they then took counsel on how to destroy him.

In any case, repentance always involves a change, sometimes physically, sometimes mentally, and often both, if one is to successfully "walk with God." The emphasis should be that repentance involves bringing into harmony both our faith and the actions that properly express that faith into synthesis with the will of God for our lives. And this change usually begins with self-reflection, which becomes as much a part of the process of repentance as the actual moment of repentance or atonement.

Old Testament Texts

Beginning in Leviticus, the Old Testament acts of reconciliation are largely a communal act. In the teaching on the "Day of Atonement" from Leviticus 16, the sins of the whole nation were to be confessed

---

[8] Matthew 12:1-16

at a single time and place, and on an annual basis. This ritual sacrifice was called the "Sin Offering." Leviticus does prescribe a "guilt offering" in chapters five through seven for those whom had committed an individual sin, but we do not see many instances of a guilt offering being offered in the Bible outside of the inaugural teachings in Leviticus, with two peculiar exceptions: when the Philistines returned the Ark of the Covenant to Israel in 1 Samuel 6, they returned it with a guilt offering; and in Ezra 10:19 the Bible speaks only in passing of a guilt offering being offered for those who had married foreign women during the exile, but we do not witness the actual guilt sacrifice. This is not to say that guilt offerings were not practiced, as we see reminders to perform guilt offerings in Numbers 6:12, and 18:9, and Ezekiel speaks of the places where the guilt offering were to be offered in Ezekiel 40:39, 42:13, 44:29, and 46:20. However, this is to say that most of what is seen of the practice of sin offerings has to do with the sins of a whole community, which, early-on in the book of Numbers, followed a fairly predictable pattern: the people begin to lose hope in God's provision for them, they grumble and long for better days, and their lack of faith and sinful backsliding into old ways of idolatry led them into danger. God's wrath is then expressed, and their repentance follows in a cultic fashion, following the prescribed sacrifices outlined in Leviticus. Before entering the Promised Land, Moses reminds the people of their regular rituals, and we can observe from several other Old Testament texts that this pattern continued in the life of Israel many generations later, particularly in Isaiah 63:7-64:12, Daniel 9:4-19, and Hosea 6 and 14. In addition to these instances of cultic reconciliation, we also observe certain actions that accompanied repentance, such as fasting, sitting in ashes, donning sack-cloth, and tearing one's clothes. All of these actions reflected a need for reconciliation and repentance, and are often a sign given by the priests to the people that something has gone terribly wrong. In the first chapter of Job, Job makes these signs signifying to himself, to those around him, and to God, that he recognized that something was going terribly wrong, and as such he made signs of repentance without really knowing why the evils around him came about. At the arrest of Jesus the high priest rent his clothes as a sign to the crowd that he believed Jesus had uttered blasphemy (Matt. 26:65). Many of the prophets are sent by God to remedy not only the sin of Israel, but also their means of sacrifice. The use of idols was a continual burden throughout the generations as they mingled cultures with foreign nations. With each perversion, the atoning sacrifices lose more and more meaning, until such as time as Israel either abandons their ritual for reconciliation, or kept the ritual without the contrition and repentance that were meant to accompany the ritual acts. Hosea famously spoke of Israel as a "harlot" who had profaned herself with the foreign idols. In every case, the prophets call the people and priests of Israel to repent, and to return to the pure religion as outlined for them in the Law. The means of restoration in each case did not change; rather, the prophets speak the voice of God calling them to repent and return to Him in the same cultic ways prescribed to them in the Pentateuch.

The Psalms also served a significant role in the liturgical life of the people. Annemarie Kidder, writing on this subject says, "The Psalms are enlisted in worship to be sung, enacted, and used for meditation and thanksgiving, and they serve as an ongoing mnemonic tool for day-to-day reflection and exhortation."[9] We know that many of the Psalms were used liturgically as coronation hymns or liturgies at the gate of the temple to gain entrance. For example, the "Psalms of Ascent," Psalms 120-134, were used as hymns along the journey leading up the mountain to Jerusalem, and certain psalms in this collection were virtually passwords to gain admittance, and to literally demonstrate one's worthiness to enter the temple.

The aptly called "Penitential Psalms" offer us a personal insight into the struggles of David, a King who was usually very righteous and "walked with God," and yet despite his many occasions of faithfulness, also struggled with sin, and wrote about the process necessary to seek atonement with God. These Psalms express his lamentation, feelings

---

[9] Making Confession, Hearing Confession: A History of the Cure of Souls by Annemarie S. Kidder. Minnesota, Liturgical Press, 2010. 5.

of sorrow, contrition, and repentance, and were also used by Israel in confessing their sins. Kidder speaks of these Psalms in this way: "Later, during the post-exilic period, it is individual confession that takes on a more prominent role. Litanies of confession, which are personal and individualistic, include Psalms 22, 33, 34, 40, 55, and 116."[10] Many others have also made lists of what they believe to be the "penitential psalms." Kidder also points out that others in the Bible use Psalms, or portions and echoes of Psalms, to express their penitential needs. The cries of Jonah in the belly of the whale (Jonah 2:2-9) resound the refrains of several psalms (18:6, 120:1 ,88:3-12, and 42:7). The Song of Hannah (1 Sam. 2:1-10), which some scholars believe may have been added later, seems to reflect the same familiar refrains from the Psalter (Psalms 18:2, 28:1, and 62:2,6). Mary's song, the Magnificat (Luke 1:46-55), shares these same attributes. These few examples demonstrate the power of these Psalms to convey many thoughts beyond their original context, not the least of which are penitence and sorrow for sin. Some of the penitential psalms begin as laments with the psalmist lying in sin and depravity, and end with a song of thanksgiving proclaiming to us that God hear their pleas, and restored them to Himself. For example, Psalm 6 begins "O LORD, rebuke me not in your anger, nor chasten me in thy wrath. Be gracious to me, O LORD, for I am languishing; O LORD heal me for my bones are troubled."[11] Yet by the end of the Psalm, we hear: "The LORD has heard my supplication, the LORD accepts my prayer."[12] The psalmist then prophesies about his enemies: "All my enemies shall be ashamed and sorely troubled; they shall turn back and be put to shame in a moment."[13] Psalm 130 follows a similar pattern, beginning: "Out of the depths I cry to thee, O LORD! Let thy ears be attentive to the voice of my supplications!"[14] Yet by the end of the psalm, the psalmist teaches the people to repent and to act

[10] Kidder, Making Confession, 5.

[11] Psalm 6:1-2

[12] Psalm 6:9

[13] Psalm 6:10

[14] Psalm 130:1-2

and pray as he has so to achieve the same reconciliation: "O Israel, hope in the LORD! For with the Lord there is steadfast love, and with him there is plenteous redemption. And he will redeem Israel from all his iniquities."[15] In this case, the Psalm itself is both a plea for forgiveness, and an instructional example of how to achieve reconciliation by the means of repentance.

Alfred Mortimer identified seven "Penitential Psalms," and attached each of them to a "Deadly Sin." These Seven Deadly Sins, posited to have originated from the penitential psalms, would first appear in the writing of John Cassian and Gregory the Great, but continue, particularly in the Medieval Period, to be a standard of diagnosing sin. Mortimer classified these sins as follows: Psalm 6 he attributed to anger, 32 to pride, 38 to gluttony, 51 to lust, 102 to avarice, 130 to envy, and 143 to sloth. Some Medieval authors also attributed the origin of the Seven Deadly Sins to the Psalter. Whatever the enumeration, it is clear that the content of the Psalter serves in many places as a model for a confessional process, including repentance, and often a conclusion of praise teaching us how God responded to their petition for forgiveness and restoration. In particular, Psalm 51 has long played a significant role in the prayer life of the Church, particularly in the liturgies for Ash Wednesday. Following the imposition of ashes, the congregation kneels together to pray Psalm 51 together as a corporate act of contrition. Such is the nature of the penitential Psalms. They demonstrate an example of contritional prayer, and exhort the reader to repentance.

New Testament Texts

Prior to the ministry of Jesus, John the Baptist preached a message of baptism and a confession of sins as a sign of repentance. Kidder argues in her book that this action of being baptized in the Jordan was an example of "penance and self-humiliation."[16] This act of penance

---

[15] Psalm 130:7-8

[16] Kidder, Making Confession, 6.

was to reflect an inner state of repentance, and also as an indicator of an outward change of behavior in preparation for the coming Messiah. John actually preached against the mindset of the Pharisees and Sadducees who came to see the work he was doing in the Jordan River:

> But when he saw many of the Pharisees and Sadducees come to his baptism, he said unto them, O generation of vipers, who hath warned you to flee from the wrath to come? Bring forth therefore fruits meet for repentance: And think not to say within yourselves, 'We have Abraham as our father:' for I say unto you, that God is able of these stones to raise up children unto Abraham. And now also the axe is laid unto the root of the trees: therefore every tree which bringeth not forth good fruit is hewn down, and cast into the fire. I indeed baptize you with water unto repentance: but he that cometh after me is mightier than I, whose shoes I am not worthy to bear: he shall baptize you with the Holy Ghost, and with fire: Whose fan is in his hand, and he will thoroughly purge his floor, and gather his wheat into the garner; but he will burn up the chaff with unquenchable fire.[17]

After Jesus' baptism and temptation in the wilderness, he begins to preach a similar message of repentance with a sense of urgency. In Mark 1:14, Jesus preaches, "The time is fulfilled, and the kingdom of God is at hand: repent ye, and believe the gospel." We should note that very early on, Jesus' message is one of personal repentance, rather than corporate repentance. Jesus' message is singularly focused on the individual. Nowhere do we hear him speak of the sacrifices of Leviticus, although the New Testament texts clearly reflect a life in Judaism that continued to maintain their pattern of ritual sacrifices such as the prescribed feasts and offerings. This can be observed in the prayer life of Jesus, and in the criticisms he receives from the temple leaders who question his leadership based on a seeming lack of adherence to the ritual code. However, the life and ministry of Jesus challenges their understanding of their ritual, and even supersedes it on various occasions, with Jesus saying things such as: "For the Son of man is Lord even of the sabbath day;"[18] and "The sabbath was made for man, and not man for the sabbath."[19]

---

[17] Matthew 3:7-12

[18] Matthew 12:8

[19] Mark 2:27

Just as John preached, "Bring forth therefore fruits meet for repentance,"[20] so Jesus preaches, "Either make the tree good, and his fruit good; or else make the tree corrupt, and his fruit corrupt: for the tree is known by its fruit."[21] Further emphasizing the failure of the Pharisees as regards the inner nature of repentance, Jesus says,

> Woe unto you, scribes and Pharisees, hypocrites! For ye make clean the outside of the cup and of the platter, but within they are full of extortion and excess. Thou blind Pharisee, cleanse first that which is within the cup and platter, that the outside of them may be clean also. Woe unto you, scribes and Pharisees, hypocrites! for ye are like unto whited sepulchres, which indeed appear beautiful outward, but are within full of dead men's bones, and of all uncleanness. Even so ye also outwardly appear righteous unto men, but within ye are full of hypocrisy and iniquity.[22]

The emphatic nature of Jesus' teaching on repentance continues in his preaching about removing all obstacles that get in the way of our good progress, including family and personal goods. Jesus says dramatic things such as, "Who is my mother, or my brethren? And he looked round about on them which sat about him, and said, Behold my mother and my brethren! For whosoever shall do the will of God, the same is my brother, and my sister, and mother."[23] Speaking in similar fashion about possessions to a wealthy young man who came to him asking how to inherit eternal life, Jesus told him to keep the commandments. When the young man said that he had done so since birth, Jesus responded:

> One thing thou lackest: go thy way, sell whatsoever thou hast, and give to the poor, and thou shalt have treasure in heaven: and come, take up the cross, and follow me. And he (the young man) was sad at that saying, and went away grieved: for he had great possessions.[24]

In such dramatic fashion, Jesus emphasizes the need to put away all things which keep us from inheriting the kingdom, as many of these physical things and relationships often keep us from doing the things

---

[20] Matthew 3:8

[21] Matthew 12:33

[22] Matthew 23:25-28

[23] Mark 3:33-34

[24] Mark 10:21-22

we know we must do to be righteous. Perhaps this is why the largest portion of his audience and followers were to be found among the poor, the marginalized, and the sick. These were largely examples of individuals who did not have the access to the corporate sacrifices as they were deemed unclean or unworthy to enter the temple. Another way of looking at this might be that Jesus brought repentance to those who had no means of obtaining it, and he furthermore criticized those who had exclusive access to the temple and the atoning sacrifices, and yet were inwardly corrupt and sinful. Therefore, in Jesus' ministry, repentance is not limited to the temple sacrifices, but is spoken of on an individualistic basis in addition to His reformation of the temple practices.

Jesus' preaching on the understanding of repentance continues, particularly in the Gospel of Luke. In the parable of the lost sheep, Jesus concludes that story saying, "I say unto you, that likewise joy shall be in heaven over one sinner that repenteth, more than over ninety and nine just persons, which need no repentance."[25] In the parable of the prodigal son, we see aforementioned characteristic of the shift from mind to action illustrated by Jesus in the actions and thoughts of the son who was lost.

> And when he came to himself, he said, How many hired servants of my father's have bread enough and to spare, and I perish with hunger! I will arise and go to my father, and will say unto him, "Father, I have sinned against heaven, and before thee, And am no more worthy to be called thy son: make me as one of thy hired servants." And he arose, and came to his father.[26]

Here we see a repentance of the mind of the prodigal son, when Jesus says: "And when he came to himself..." The son has a moment of self-awareness, self-diagnosis, a repentance of the mind, which is followed by a change in behavior: "I will arise and go to my father...I have sinned against thee..." and we know from the rest of the story that

---

[25] Luke 15:7

[26] Luke 15:17-20a

the son followed through, and the resulting message of the parable is that of the great mercy of God towards those who repent and return to the father with contrition and humility. The son was not seeking honor, only to apologize, admit his fault, and to be treated as one of the hired servants.

Jesus also speaks of the value of the prophets who came before preaching repentance, including Moses, in the parable of Lazarus and the rich man. At the end of that Parable, the rich man calls out to Abraham to send a messenger to his brothers that they might repent, saying: "Father Abraham: if but one went unto them from the dead, they will repent."[27] But Abraham responded, "If they hear not Moses and the prophets, neither will they be persuaded, though one rose from the dead."[28] This style of preaching on repentance continues right up to the end of the Gospel and the Great Commission, where Jesus preaches: "Repentance and remission of sins should be preached in his name among all nations, beginning at Jerusalem. And ye are witnesses of these things."[29] Jesus' preaching of the good news of the kingdom involved repentance of the heart and will—far beyond the keeping of the ritual atoning sacrifices. He in fact was to become the atoning sacrifice, and we maintain this language in the Church, calling Jesus: the paschal lamb, the Passover, the sacrificial lamb, and so on.

In the Acts of the Apostles, the Church takes in a new audience. Repentance in the scriptures is no longer limited to the Israelites through the atoning sacrifices. Gentiles also become members of the new covenant of Jesus Christ. In Acts 11, Peter contends with the circumcision party about the Gentiles and says,

> Forasmuch then as God gave them the like gift as he did unto us, who believed on the Lord Jesus Christ; what was I, that I could withstand God? When they heard these things, they held their peace, and glorified God, saying, Then hath God also to the Gentiles granted repentance unto life.[30]

---

[27] Luke 16:30

[28] Luke 16:31

[29] Luke 24:47-48

[30] Acts 11:17-18

Paul also proclaims this as a significant part of his ministry in chapter 20, saying, "I kept back nothing that was profitable unto you, but have showed you, and have taught you publicly, and from house to house, testifying both to the Jews, and also to the Greeks, repentance toward God, and faith toward our Lord Jesus Christ."[31]

Paul spends much of his ministry ministering primarily to a Gentile audience, and repentance is the most common theme of his writing. Almost all of his letters are written to churches because he heard something of the troubles they were experiencing, so Paul writes to them to repent, amend their ways, and to aim towards righteousness. We actually hear the effect of his first letter to the Corinthians in his second letter to the church at Corinth:

> For though I made you sorry with a letter, I do not repent, though I did repent: for I perceive that the same epistle hath made you sorry, though it were but for a season. Now I rejoice, not that ye were made sorry, but that ye sorrowed to repentance: for ye were made sorry after a godly manner, that ye might receive damage by us in nothing. For godly sorrow worketh repentance to salvation not to be repented of: but the sorrow of the world worketh death.[32]

Here, we hear that Paul's letter worked into them a spirit of sorrow for the proper season, until it brought them to repentance. In writing to Timothy to teach him how to be an effective apostle, Paul instructs him on encouraging repentance:

> And the servant of the Lord must not strive; but be gentle unto all men, apt to teach, patient, in meekness instructing those that oppose themselves; if God peradventure will give them repentance to the acknowledging of the truth; And that they may recover themselves out of the snare of the devil, who are taken captive by him at his will.[33]

Perhaps one of the most pivotal teachings in the New Testament scriptures on the subject of repentance is found in the sixth chapter of the letter to the Hebrews. This text is significant because of the

---

[31] Acts 20:20-21

[32] 2 Corinthians 7:8-10

[33] 2 Timothy 2:24-26

effect it would have on the early Church, particularly until the rise of monasticism. This is one of the few texts that speaks to the problem of post-baptismal repentance. Here, the author of Hebrews spoke of repentance as a limited commodity:

> Therefore let us leave the elementary doctrine of Christ and go on to maturity, not laying again a foundation of *repentance* from dead works and of faith toward God, with instruction about ablutions, the laying on of hands, the resurrection of the dead, and eternal judgment. And this we will do if God permits. *For it is impossible to restore again to repentance those who have once been enlightened,* who have tasted the heavenly gift, and have become partakers of the Holy Spirit, and have tasted the goodness of the word of God and the powers of the age to come, *if they then commit apostasy,* since they crucify the Son of God on their own account and hold him up to contempt. For land which has drunk the rain that often falls upon it, and brings forth vegetation useful to those for whose sake it is cultivated, receives a blessing from God. But if it bears thorns and thistles, it is worthless and near to being cursed; its end is to be burned.[34]

This text, which speaks of the impossibility of "restoring to repentance those who have once been enlightened," had an enormous impact on the early Church, in that repentance was readily open to those who were new converts, however, once baptized and made a part of the Church, a higher level of scrutiny was placed on those who apostatized and fell back into their old ways. This further conveys the sense of urgency taught by Christ and embraced by his disciples in the early days of the Church's life.

The Epistle of James is another significant text in the life of the New Testament, particularly in the use of the term "confession," as opposed to repentance. James, like the author of Hebrews, also expresses a concern for post-baptismal repentance, and even establishes an order to such confessions. For James, the health of the body is intimately tied to the health of the soul, and it is in this context that he speaks of confession in the fifth chapter of James:

> Is any among you afflicted? Let him pray. Is any merry? Let him sing psalms. Is any sick among you? Let him call for the elders of the church; and let

---

[34] Hebrews 6:1-8 (Emphasis added)

them pray over him, anointing him with oil in the name of the Lord: And the prayer of faith shall save the sick, and the Lord shall raise him up; *and if he have committed sins, they shall be forgiven him. Confess your faults one to another, and pray one for another, that ye may be healed.* The effectual fervent prayer of a righteous man availeth much.[35]

In the context of illness, James speaks to the matter of sin as a root cause of illness, adding into the equation the anointing with oil "in the name of the Lord" at the hand of the elders of the Church. The effect of this anointing is said to be the result of "the prayers of the faithful," and the net result is also the forgiveness of sins. James then emphasizes the need for prayers for healing, and further emphasizes that "the prayers of a righteous man availeth much." Some have inferred from this text that the "righteous man" is the elder called upon to administer the anointing, as James then likens this individual to Elijah:

Elias [Elijah] was a man subject to like passions as we are, and he prayed earnestly that it might not rain: and it rained not on the earth by the space of three years and six months. And he prayed again, and the heaven gave rain, and the earth brought forth her fruit. Brethren, if any of you do err from the truth, and one convert him; let him know, that he which converteth the sinner from the error of his way shall save a soul from death, and shall hide a multitude of sins.[36]

James upholds the office of those who bring others back from sin as one who will cover a "multitude of sins." This entire text has been held as one of the chief cornerstones in the practice of repentance and anointing the sick, which, as we will see, will be bound in two of the Church's sacraments.

At this point, it is important to mention another key phrase in the practice of confession, which is rooted in the words of Christ to the disciples during his appearance to them in the first week after the resurrection:

Then the same day at evening, being the first day of the week, when the doors were shut where the disciples were assembled for fear of the Jews, came Jesus and stood in the midst, and saith unto them, Peace be unto you.

---

[35] James 5:13-16 (Emphasis added)

[36] James 5:17-20

And when he had so said, he shewed unto them his hands and his side. Then were the disciples glad, when they saw the Lord. Then said Jesus to them again, Peace be unto you: as my Father hath sent me, even so send I you. And when he had said this, he breathed on them, and saith unto them, Receive ye the Holy Ghost: Whose soever sins ye remit, they are remitted unto them; and whose soever sins ye retain, they are retained.[37]

Having breathed on the Disciples, Jesus gives them a power that was controversial in his own ministry, which is the power to forgive sins. When Jesus heals the paralytic in the ninth chapter of Matthew, he says, "Son, be of good cheer; thy sins be forgiven thee."[38] The scribes then immediately accuse Jesus of blasphemy. Jesus then responds by offering the paralytic forgiveness and saying to the scribes, "But that ye may know that the Son of man hath power on earth to forgive sins, then saith he to the sick of the palsy, 'Arise, take up thy bed, and go unto thine house.' And he arose, and departed to his house."[39] We then hear the response of the crowd in the next verse which reports: "When the multitudes saw it, they marveled, and glorified God, which had given such power unto men."[40] Now, in this passage from John, after the resurrection, Jesus bestows this power and authority upon the apostles. This verse will be used, along with the verses from James, as the foundation for the absolving power of the priesthood in the centuries to come.

As a suitable "bookend" to this section, the Revelation to John concludes the New Testament with an overwhelming message on final judgment and our need for immediate repentance. In the vision of the Revelation John is offered a view of the last judgment and of the victory of Christ over all of his enemies. As a result of this vision of the future the angel has charged John to write to seven churches in order to call them to repentance. The word repent appears ten times in the text, most prevalently in the second chapter, in which the angel bids

---

[37] John 20:19-23 (Emphasis added)

[38] Matthew 9:2

[39] Matthew 9:6-7

[40] Matthew 9:8

the hearers to repent of their evil and idolatry, although with gentleness and expectation that this repentance will come to pass. "Remember therefore from whence thou art fallen, and repent, and do the first works; or else I will come unto thee quickly, and will remove thy candlestick out of his place, except thou repent."[41] And again,

> *I gave her space to repent of her fornication; and she repented not.* Behold, I will cast her into a bed, and them that commit adultery with her into great tribulation, *except they repent* of their deeds. And I will kill her children with death; and all the churches shall know that I am he which searcheth the reins and hearts: and I will give unto every one of you according to your works.[42]

As in the Epistle of James, we hear of sin being bound to illness, and even death. However the overarching theme of the Revelation is the instruction to "repent while there's still time." The sins of which they are guilty are consistent with the Old Testament sins: apostasy, idolatry, sexual immorality, and pride. However the remedy in this case is fortitude—to be faithful to that which they believed at their conversion, and to repent of the deeds of which they are accused. This repentance, as prescribed, is significantly easier than the Christians of the next few centuries would enjoy.

---

[41] Revelation 2:5

[42] Revelation 2:21-23 (Emphasis added)

Historical Development

CHAPTER TWO
Early Patristic Penitential Discipline

From all accounts, the rigor of early Christianity in the centuries following the age of the apostles was far more rigid than what we witness in the scriptures. Some have speculated that the persecuted Church of the early centuries led to more exacting expressions of the faith due to the multi-faceted martyrdom of the first three centuries. In particular. R.S.T Haslehurst wrote in his text on patristic discipline,

> The outbreak of the Decian persecution in A.D. 250 marks a new stage in the development of the penitential discipline. Coming at the end of a 'thirty years peace' it found the Church unprepared. Persecution made many martyrs, but caused the fall of many as well. The latter were of two kinds: those who had actually sacrificed or burnt incense, and those who had received libelli or certificates to that effect.[43]

Among the early patristic writers such as Tertullian and Origen, the consistent teaching of the Church seems to have been that baptism was the primary source of repentance for Christians, and all of the sins committed prior to baptism were forgiven and put away. However, there was a great division over how to handle post-baptismal sin. Although the Epistle of James spoke of confessing sins to one another, Hebrews had painted a different picture altogether. This led to two significant practices in the early Church: first, the practice that those who had apostatized were not to be re-admitted without significant scrutiny; and secondly, that many held off their baptisms until as near death as possible.

Clement of Alexandria, writing from the end of the second century into the third century, addressed two types of repentance: the

---

[43] Some Account of the Penitential Discipline of the Early Church in the First four Centuries by R.S.T. Haslehurst. London, S.P.C.K., London. 1921. 71.

first being that obtained in baptism, and the second which is described as "the fear of the Lord." "He, then, who from among the Gentiles and from that old life has betaken himself to faith has obtained forgiveness of sins once. But he who has sinned after this, on his repentance, though he obtain pardon, ought to fear."[44] Origen supported this teaching, emphasizing that the sins needed to be recent, and repented of before too much damage was done. However, for major sins, he believed that there was no repentance, leaning upon the foundations of the letter to the Hebrews which reads: "For if we sin willfully after that we have received the knowledge of the truth, there remaineth no more sacrifice for sins."[45] Kinner states in her book that Hippolytus, a Bishop of the late second to third century, was equally rigid in his administration of this rule, although this was not consistent among all of the bishops: "His fellow presbyter Callistus, on the other hand, not only retained members, but kept adding to his flock those who had been previously excommunicated by Hippolytus."[46] With Callistus as a model, more and more churches began to relax their standards of reconciliation in the interest of growing their Churches, however simultaneously instituting new modes and models for confession. One of the most popular models for repentance was what came to be known as the practice of "the Order of Penitents." Those who committed major sins were to be admitted after a trial period in the Order of Penitents, a process of readmission involving making a public confession, segregating oneself from the faithful worshippers for a time, and going through a period of fasting, almsgiving, and prayer. Then, after years if not even decades of penance, one might be enrolled back among the faithful and allowed to receive the Eucharist.

This model of readmission also involved, at times, public humiliation, which allowed the community to be made aware of one's sins. The Greek term used by the early Church was *exomologesis,*

---

[44] Anti-Nicene Fathers, Vol. 2, eds. Alexander Roberts and James Donaldson. Peabody, Massachusetts. 1999. 360-61.

[45] Hebrews 10:26

[46] Making Confession, Kidder, 13.

typically referring to the minor sins of a community expressed together at the Eucharist, but also for the system of humiliation and public penance which went along with more grievous sins requiring public penance. Concerning exomologesis, John McNeill writes:

> The Greek word "exomologesis" was used alike for this routine public confession of minor faults and for the humiliating procedure followed in the confession of offences involving discipline and penance. Exomologesis involved so much self-abasement that the word itself came to embrace the idea of an act of penance and to be used with reference to works of satisfaction. Tertullian employs the same word in Latin, with an exposition which offers the earliest circumstantial description of penance itself. He calls it a "discipline of man's prostration and humiliation requiring a behavior conducive of mercy." It involves the wearing of sackcloth and ashes, engaging in fasts, and uttering groans, prayers, and outcries to God. The penitent is, moreover, enjoined to "bow before the feet of the presbyters and to kneel to those who are dear to God, to enjoin all the brethren to b his ambassadors to bear his deprecatory supplication" before God.[47]

This humiliation served several functions, among them to make the public aware, so to assist the sinner with resisting his/her particular sin in the future, but also to make the Church members aware that one was excommunicated and undergoing a period of repentance so to be restored. These acts of humiliation likely served several purposes for the penitent as well, both encouraging the penitent to be faithful in his/her act of repentance so to be restored, as well as to shame them, and to serve as an incentive to not sin again, while also serving as an effective example to others of what would happen if they were to sin as grievously. It is difficult to gauge the success of such programs, as records were not kept as to how many repented versus those who fell away, but it does stand to teach us of the rigor with which the early church attempted to maintain purity among the faithful and to provide a means of repentance to those who had fallen away after baptism.

Between the years A.D. 250 and 300 Cyprian, the Bishop of Carthage, wrote extensively on the struggle between those clergy

---

[47] Medieval Handbooks of Penance by John T. McNeill and Helena M. Gamer. Columbia University Press, New York. 1938. 6.

under his cure who kept a more rigid stance, versus those who were more lenient. Those whom he referred to as the "Puritan Party," such as those under the leadership of Novatus, who had once been a supporter of leniency toward the lapsed, refused pardon to those who had lapsed from the Christian faith by offering incense to other gods rather than being martyred. Others, whom he called the "Lax Party", actually insisted on the readmission of those who had received labelli certificates, particularly those given to them by martyrs and confessors. Once Novatus joined forces with Novatius in Rome, Cyprian found himself in a position to write epistles to the Church so to offer a public teaching on this subject. Hastlehurst cites Cyprian's ninth epistle, in which he complains of this struggle:

> For although in smaller sins sinners may do penance for a set time, and according to the rules of discipline come to public confession, and by imposition of the hand of the Bishop and clergy receive the right of communion: now with their time still unfulfilled while persecution is still raging, while the peace of the Church is not yet restored, they are admitted to communion and their name is presented; and while the penance is not yet performed, confession not yet made, and the hands of the Bishop and clergy not yet laid upon them, the Eucharist is given to them, although it is written, 'Whosoever shall eat the bread and drink the cup of the Lord unworthily shall be guilt of the Body and Blood of the Lord.'[48]

Hastlehurst continues in his own words:

> Cyprian's own bias was towards leniency: 'Our patience, our facility, our humanity are ready for those who come. I entreat all to return to the Church. I remit everything. I shut my eyes to many things, with the desire and the wish to gather together the brotherhood. Even those things which are committed against God I do not investigate with the full judgment of religion. I almost sin myself in remitting sins more than I ought. I embrace with prompt and full love those who return with repentance, confessing their sin with lowly and unaffected atonement (Ep. liv. 16).' But he had to school himself to administering discipline, in spite of the veneration which the confessors and martyrs who had pled for restoration of the lapsed necessarily commanded. Cyprian's policy was to wait until the tyranny should be overpassed, and then formulate a definite policy.[49]

---

[48] Penitential Discipline, Hastlehurst, 72-73.

[49] Ibid, 72.

With the passage of more time and persecution, Cyprian was surprised to discover that the beliefs of the various parties turned out to be quite the opposite of what he had expected. While he expected a certain severity from the clergy and a laxity on behalf of the laity, and expected himself to be the mediator, he found instead a laxity among the clergy, and a severity demanded of the lapsed by the laity.

At the end of A.D. 250 there came a relief in the persecutions. This temporary peace allowed for two councils to be held in 251 and 252. At the first council, Hastlehurst reports,

> The libellatici who had received the certificates from the persecutors were to be examined, and the lapsed were to be granted communion if on their death-beds. Those who had lapsed without sacrificing, i.e. the libellatici, were to be restored on doing penance. The discussion on the lapsed who had sacrificed was deferred. The second council was held in 252, and its synodical declaration is contained in [Cyprian's] Epistle liii. 'Now, under the compulsion of necessity, we have decided that peace is to be given to those who have not withdrawn from the Church of the Lord, but have not ceased from the first day of their lapse to repent, and to lament, and to beseech the Lord.'[50]

In this, we can see a struggle between mercy and discipline in the words of Cyprian, and in the discussions among the clergy and laity of his cure. While he wanted to be merciful, the bishop restricted this mercy to those who were outwardly penitent and eagerly seeking forgiveness. Writing about this Council, John Henry Hopkins wrote:

> It does not appear that any precise times of public penitence were yet appropriate to particular sins, but it was left at the discretion of the Church, under the council of the bishop and the clergy, to determine each case as it occurred, according to the best judgment which they could form of the intensity of the penitent's sorrow for his guilt, and the signs which he exhibited of a true conversion.[51]

As Hopkins points out, to this point penance was entirely a locally controlled practice, and no uniform declaration of the whole Church

---

[50] Ibid, 74.

[51] The History of the Confessional by John Henry Hopkins. Harper & Brothers Publishers, New York. 1855. 163.

was available to guide sinners back into the fold after lapsing from the faith.

The shift toward relaxation of the rigor of public penance seems to have come around the time of St. John Chrysostom (ca. A.D. 347-407) in Constantinople. As mentioned before, smaller sins were more readily forgiven, but at this time the major sins were to be forgiven only once, and only after years of penance and a long system of restoration. Chrysostom was known in his day for the shortness of the penances he prescribed. His predecessor, Nectarius had abolished the practice of having an official "Office of Presbyter of Penance" around the year 391, supposedly following a scandal of abuse related to a deacon-confessor using the contents of a confessional relationship to obtain money from a female penitent. Such offenses, we will see, are repeated in the confessional in later centuries. Chrysostom, without the benefit of the offices of official confessors, assumed his authority as Bishop and made a shift toward offering leniency rather than exacting years of prolonged penance.

Leo the Great

By the mid fifth century in the West, the influence of the writing of Leo the Great (d. A.D. 461) demonstrates a continuation of the relaxing of the penitential rigor of the earlier centuries, as well as a step towards a more formal process of offering penance. Although early in his ministry he had maintained that those who committed sins post-baptism were to be examined, he also allowed for some charity towards those who were in imminent danger of death. Concerning this earlier portion of Leo's episcopate, Trevor Jalland wrote:

> First of all, he [Leo] points out that Penance provides a remedy for sin committed after Baptism, adding that God's pardon can only be obtained by the prayers of the Bishops. Then he describes the method by which forgiveness is imparted: "For the mediator of God and man, the man Christ Jesus, entrusted this authority to the leaders of the Church, so that they might assign not only the performance of Penance to those who confess

their sins, but also when these have been cleansed by salutary satisfaction, admit them by means of the gate of reconciliation to sacramental communion."[52]

Here we see that confession and penance are seen by Leo at this time as the means of restoration to the Church, and that the administration of this process was to be handled by the bishops. Leo did allow for reconciliation to take place for those who were in urgent need of absolution, such as those with a grave illness, although should they survive they were still required to perform their penances. Leo further argued that forgiveness did not come by the long duration of penance, but rather as a matter of true conversion. Jalland cites Leo on this subject: "We ought not, therefore, to be hard-hearted in dispensing the gifts of God, nor to ignore the tears and groans of those who accuse themselves, believing as we do that the desire to do Penance has been formed by the inspiration of God."[53]

Jalland also firmly stands on the belief that Leo may have also established what would later become a "classic model" of atoning for sins through the sacrament of reconciliation. Jalland identifies a three-step process by which Penance was performed, with a fourth and final stage serving as a public recognition of the penance having been satisfied:

> It is clear from Leo's treatment of the subject that he contemplated four essential stages in Penance of any sort, whether public or private.
>
> (a)   Penitence. Frequent emphasis is laid on the fact that no human can claim to be without sin. Yet there can be no forgiveness without penitence. "Happy, O holy Apostle, were thy tears, which for the remission of the guilt of denial had the virtue of holy Baptism." Penitence, however, must include real sorrow for sin. The penitence of despair only brings ruin.
>
> (b)   Confession or the acknowledgement of sins committed delivered the penitent from condemnation. It must be full and sincere, for an untrue confession cannot obtain remission; even the most intimate secrets of the heart are known to God. Such confession is to be made normally in private to the Bishop.

---

[52] The Life and Times of St. Leo the Great by Trevor Jalland. S.P.C.K., New York. 1941. 141.

[53] Ibid, 142.

(c)   Satisfaction is a normally indispensable part of the whole process. It is often spoken of as "penance" and is assigned by the bishop to the penitent, who is said to request "penance." Satisfaction includes the performance of such exercises as prayer, fasting, and almsgiving. In fact an outstanding importance is assigned to the latter as a means to obtaining forgiveness. On the negative side the penitent is required to undergo a number of serious privations. He may not undertake any part in the civil service not any litigation nor trading for profit, nor may he engage in marriage.

(d)   Absolution or reconciliation is the final stage. This is accorded by the bishop, normally only after the penitential exercises have been performed. Those who accept a penance in sickness are required to perform it, should they recover, and a condition of absolution. Yet while those who die before their penance is accomplished are to be left to the judgment of God, should a penitent on his deathbed desire absolution it should not be refused to him, although the requisite penance has not been performed. Equally in the case of one at the point of death, who is physically unable to express himself, the testimony of others as to his sincerity is to be accepted.[54]

Although, at this time, the sacramental status of confession or penance had not yet been established, we see in the writing of Leo the direction of a bishop instructing his clergy in how to formally re-admit those who had fallen away after baptism, as well as an increased measure of charity towards those who were contrite, yet unable to perform the public penances.

Towards the end of his life, in 459 Leo wrote a letter to three bishops in Campania, Samnium, and Picenum on the subject of abuses in their practices of penance. Concerning this letter, McNeill wrote:

Here he [Leo] sternly condemns as 'presumption' the practice of compelling penitents to read publically a "libellus" containing a detailed confession of their sins. The practice has, he observes, no apostolic sanction, and it may needlessly inculpate Christians before their enemies and so subject them to legal punishment. Leo is here dealing with cases of secret offenses. He does not forbid public confession in such cases; he regards it indeed as "praiseworthy." What he does forbid is the compulsory reading of a written declaration of sins. This he regards as an innovation fraught with serious possibilities. In rejecting it, however, he goes so far as

---

[54] Ibid, 482-484.

to pronounce unnecessary any public acknowledgement in detail of secret sins. He recommends as sufficient a "confession first offered to God and then to the Bishop." He fears that a continuance of the custom will cause many to avoid penance altogether.[55]

McNeill continues in the next paragraph to demonstrate that many scholars have used this passage to argue various sides of the nature of private confession at this time in the West.

H.C. Lea suggests that Leo here inaugurated the practice of 'private confession of sins.' B. Kurtscheid states that this letter conveys the first clear and unambiguous authorization for secret confession and strict silence on the part of the confessor. J. Tixeront uses the passage to support his contention that sacramental confession had always been secret. Such also is the view of Vacanard in the article cited above. Poscmann find in the utterance evidence of the fact that for secret offenses public penance was practiced with secret confession. Watkins uses it to corroborate his opinion that detailed public confession of private sins was probably never obligatory. As negative evidence on open confession for secret sin, it is impossible to take Leo's words too seriously. That which he definitely states to be contrary to "apostolic rule" is the public reading of the statement. Certainly there is no evidence to the use of such a written catalogue of public confession heretofore, and the introduction of such a procedure was in itself a startling departure from earlier practice... It is a mistake, then, to regard Leo's statement as sufficient evidence for the prevalence of secret confession at this time. Nor can it be regarded as legislation by which the practice was established in the West. Lea, indeed, notes that 'centuries were to elapse' before the medieval secret penance system emerges, and indicates that libelli for public confession were in later ties approved, even by popes.[56]

As such we do not see a formalized nor unified system yet in place, however we can witness from this period a relaxing of the rigor of the earlier centuries, and efforts to manage the system of public penance in a way that protected the penitents from further attack or harm.

---

[55] Medieval Handbooks of Penance by John T. McNeill and Helena M. Gamer. Columbia University Press, New York. 1938. 12.

[56] Ibid. 12-13.

CHAPTER THREE
Late Patristic Developments

With the turn of the fourth century several factors combined to make yet another shift in the paradigm of penance among early Christians. First, the "Peace of Constantine" brought about by the Edict of Milan issued in A.D. 313 allowed for Christians to express their faith without the rigor brought about by the persecutions of the first few centuries after Jesus' resurrection. Secondly, with more than a few generations of Christians having practiced the faith and dying before the "second coming of Christ," the sense of immediacy for Christ's return began to wane, and with it, the urgency on the teaching on repentance was relaxed. Third, the fourth century also gave rise to the first codifications of the Bible into a single canon, rather than multiple collections of autonomous letters. With them came a more consistent teaching on the nature of repentance between the teaching of Christ in the gospels, the letters of guidance in Paul, and the now centuries-old practice of the Church in re-admitting lapsed sinners. Fourth, the beginning of conciliar discussions through general councils on practices within the Church and codification of doctrinal creeds and statements began a movement toward more accountable consistency in the praxis of the whole Church. And finally, with the rise of monasticism from the fourth to sixth centuries, spiritual direction began to evolve and clergy made a shift in their teaching toward the guiding of souls emphasizing the pursuit of righteousness rather than merely shaming their people into repentance. The spirituality of the desert fathers had a significant impact on the manner in which penitents were restored, primarily by doing away with public penance and public confession, and taking confession and reconciliation behind closed doors, but also by increasing the education of clergy, specifically in the guidance of souls.

Constantine

The "Peace of Constantine" brought about a significant shift in the practice of the Christian faith. This peace meant not only a cessation of widespread persecution of Christians, but also a tolerance and even encouragement of the Christian faith through the official endorsement of Constantine, making Christianity the official religion of the empire. What was previously a largely underground religion was now free to not only go public, but to also begin building public churches and more publicly teach the content of the faith. Along with this peace, the relief of persecutions, and the passing of several generations, the anxiety over the immanent second coming of Christ was relaxed, and so was the rigor of penitential discipline during the previous centuries under persecution.

Codification of Scripture

Although we have already discussed the content of Holy Scripture on this subject, it is worth mentioning the results of the Council of Nicaea on the codification of Scripture. At the Council held in Nicaea in A.D. 325 requests were made among the Bishops for a list of the books or letters being used elsewhere in Christendom. The result of this discussion was the open exchange of the biblical texts and the eventual codification of the Bible as we now know it, according to the list of texts given by St. Athanasius to the Church in A.D 367. in his *Thirty-Ninth Festal Epistle*. Although there is not any specific writing on this subject as pertains to spiritual direction and confession, the increased citation of Holy Scripture in the writings of the fathers of this period demonstrates the increased access to the biblical texts among the whole Church following the fourth century.

Conciliar Accountability

Another benefit of the Conciliar Period was the increased accountability of the Church gathering to discuss matters of discipline and doctrine. Although it is primarily true that the councils were called to discuss Christological concerns, other topics were discussed, among them the discipline of the church toward the lapsed. We have already mentioned above the councils of A.D. 251-252 at Carthage, however there were others between that time and Nicaea. The Council of Carthage, although a gathering of Bishops, did not produce anything doctrinal beyond letters written by the bishops stating their opinions. The first example of a council that did produce canons of discipline was held in A.D. 313 in Elvira, Spain, in which six separate canons were produced addressing penitential discipline:

> Canon I: It pleased the Council that if anyone, after the faith of saving baptism, and being of full age, should go to the temple for the purpose of playing idolater, and should do so; for this principle crime, which is the highest weakness, he shall be deprived of the communion to his life's end.

> Canon VII: If any faithful, after having committed adultery, and fulfilled the appointed time of penitence, shall again become a fornicator, let him be deprived of the communion to his life's end.

> Canon VIII: In like manner, those females who shall leave their husbands without any sufficient cause, and connect themselves with other men, shall be deprived of the communion to his life's end.

> Canon XXXII: If anyone shall pass from the Catholic Church to heresy, and shall again return, penitence shall not be denied to him, forasmuch as he acknowledges his sin. Let him, therefore, perform penance for ten years. After ten, he ought to be admitted to communion. But if infants have been thus led away, they ought to be received without delay, because they did not sin by their own fault.

> Canon LXXIV: A false witness, as perjury is a crime, shall abstain from communion. But if that of which he accused another was not a capital

offense, and he can prove it, he shall abstain for two years. If, however, he can not prove this to the council of the clergy, let him abstain five years.

Canon LXXIX: If any of the faithful shall play at dice for money, he shall abstain from the communion; and if, being reformed, he shall cease to transgress, he may be reconciled after one year. [57]

It is clear from these canons, that the penances mentioned were public acts, and that these acts of penance went on for years if not decades.

Establishing the tone and nature of penance at the time between the councils of Carthage and Nicaea, John McNeill wrote:

Despite urgent efforts on the part of leading Bishops, penance was widely neglected. Where it was maintained, it shows a progressive systemization. In certain areas, during the third and fourth centuries, the so-called 'stations' of penitents were in full vogue. By this arrangement penitents were divided into four classes, and to each was assigned special position at Church meetings. The Council of Nicaea mentions three of these four classes. The one that is omitted is that of the sunklaiontej, or "weepers," who were in the first of lowest stage of penance, and whose station was outside of the door of the church. The other three stations were within the building. The a,krowmenoi "hearers," were placed in the vestibule; they were dismissed after the lesson and sermon and before the Eucharist. The u.popiptontej, or "kneelers," were stationed further forward, yet in the rear of the congregations. When others stood during prayer these were required to kneel. They came to the church in sackcloth and with ashes on their heads. Finally, the sunistame.noi, or "co-standers," were mingled with the congregation although they were not yet permitted to communicate.[58]

At the Council of Nicaea in A.D. 325 similar canons were added to address more penitential needs of the times. Although there are many, one particular example is Canon XII:

If any, being called through the grace of God, have at first manifested their faith by laying aside their military girdle, but afterward have returned to their own vomit, and seek, by offering money and other means, to enter the

[57] The History of the Confessional by John Henry Hopkins. Harper & Brothers Publishers, New York. 1855. 99-100

[58] Medieval Handbooks of Penance. McNeill and Gamer, 7-8.

army again, let them remain ten years among the penitents, after they have remained three years first among the hearers. In all such, however, special attention shall be paid to their disposition, and to the fruits of their penance. For those who show, with all fear, and persevering tears, and good works, that their conversion is not only in words, but in deed and in truth, when their appointed time of hearing is fulfilled, may begin to communicate in the prayers of the Church, and it shall also be lawful for the bishop to think of somewhat more lenient concerning them. But those who treat their fall with indifference, and deem it sufficient that they are allowed to enter the Church, must accomplish the full period appointed.[59]

In this canon we witness the flexibility with which the Church still maintained discretion over penitential matters, despite a canon expressing the need for a time of separation and necessary penance to be performed prior to re-admittance. In the penitential canons of Nicaea it is clear that the penances performed and the various classes of penitence being established that this practice was still quite public and inching more and more toward more codified means of reconciliation, however, there was a demonstrable shift toward the more merciful admittance of those who were deemed to be truly penitent and for whose sins there were mitigating circumstances, such as in sins of idolatry performed during a time of persecution. Here we see a tangible example of leniency towards the lapsed whom, at the previous council, were simply put out of the Church for life.

While the canons of the councils demonstrated a movement toward leniency, the Bishops of the fourth century showed even more. The sacramental distinction of reconciliation or confession was far from being identified, let alone codified at this time, however we can witness in the writings of various saintly bishops the desire to re-admit those to the Church who were of contrite heart and clear conscience, and who publicly admitted their sins. The wealth of citations available to defend this statement are copious, and are best laid out by John Henry Hopkins in his *History of the Confessional* in chapter seven, where he cites the witness of ten fathers of the Church on penance, some of

---

[59] The Decrees of the Ecumenical Councils ed. by Norman P. Tanner S.J.. Georgetown University Press, Washington D.C.. 1990. 11-12.

whom have already been quoted here. Citing Tertullian, Cyprian, Lactanius, Eusebius, Athanasius, Cyril, Hilary, Basil, and the Canons of the Councils already mentioned, Hopkins then concludes:

> These reiterated exhortations of the ancient fathers to disregard the shame of public penitence, in order to obtain the pardon of their sins, afford the strongest proof that the papal system had not yet been invented. For why should a man expose himself to public disgrace who could obtain equal benefit from a private tribunal of strict secrecy? And why should he be told to wait for years without absolution and restoration to the communion, when he could receive them both by the secret authority of a single priest without any delay whatever.[60]

Hopkins' commentary bridges the gap between the beginning of the conciliar movement, and the rise of monasticism, particularly with the citation such witnesses as Basil the Great, demonstrating that a shift in praxis was well underway under the authority of bishops who desired rather to see the repentance of sinners and their return to the Church, than the rigorism of the persecuted Church prior to the fourth century.

The Rise of Monasticism

To conclude our review of the late Patristic Era, we look into the rise and spread of monasticism in the fifth through ninth centuries, and to the effect the codification of monastic living brought to the evolution of spiritual direction. Perhaps the greatest early gifts of monasticism were the various *regula* or rules of the monastic houses which taught their inhabitants how to have stability while living in community. Benedicts Rule, based on earlier stricter rules including the rigid *Regulum of Pachomius,* allowed for groups of men and/or women to live in community by establishing structures of leadership as well as the expectations of the members who belonged to the community, including means of work, study, and common and individual prayer life. It is in this period that we first witness a synthesis and true balance of communal life, and the individual's role and spiritual health within

---

[60] The History of the Confessional, Hopkins, 108.

a community. Where the Old Testament paradigm stressed spiritual life within community, the New Testament maintained this structure while also informing individual spiritual health. We see in the Acts of the Apostles a model of communal life, while we also hear in the words of Paul direction given to communities intended for the healing, repentance, and individual health of their members. It is these latter texts which deeply inform the monastic *regula*. Monastic influences further helped the Church to develop a model in which this could be lived out, and individuals could receive guidance from the elders of the Church in how to maintain spiritual health, and to seek remedies from their pastors or mentors on removing sin.

Several texts from the earlier half of this period demonstrate this trend. Other texts such as *On the Incarnation* and *The Life of St. Antony* by St. Athanasius (ca. A.D. 296-373) provide examples of keen minds within the Church (both St. Antony and Athanasius himself) who wrote to others to guide their thoughts on the practice of their faith—instructions which were both communal and individualized in their application. The *Confessions* of St. Augustine (A.D 354-430), most peculiar for their time, demonstrated the thoughts of a priest and spiritual father who recounted, for all the public to see, a man over a lifetime who openly addressed his own sin, acknowledged his faults, and the torment between the will of his spirit and that of his flesh, and furthermore endowed the world with a record of how he sought to conquer these sins through the aid of spiritual mentors and his own acts of self-deprivation. Such first-hand accounts and autobiographies remain a witness to the spiritual struggles of souls living in a time before any formal process existed to aid in the conquering of sins and temptations.

Authors such as John Cassian (A.D. 360-435), wrote about shaping what he called "the inner man" in a book later titled *Conferences*, which contributed to the development of the spiritual life within the early Church, and would further be a resource cited by those who wrote on the subject in the centuries to follow. In *Conferences*, Cassian describes how he had seen in Egypt the relationship of mentors and students meeting in "conferences" to share with one another their sins and struggles. This relationship was not quite one of a confessor and penitent, but rather a spiritual guide who would help the recognition of sin and the showing of contrition, and then lead the sinner toward an inward change resulting in repentance. Cassian speaks of this guide not as a confessor, but as a teacher. Here are a few passages from the same narrative that show us of the value he placed on subjecting oneself to a mentor:

> If one does not confess a diabolic idea or thought to some soothsayer, to some spiritual person well used to finding in the magic, all-powerful words of scripture an immediate cure for these serpent bites and the means of driving the fatal poison from the heart, there can be no help for the one who is in danger and about to perish. We will most easily come to a precise knowledge of true discernment if we follow the paths of our elders, if we do nothing novel, and if we do not presume to decide anything on the basis of our own private judgment.

> All the skills and disciplines devised by human talent for the benefit of this temporal life can be laid hold of, observed, and understood, but only with the necessary help of some instructor. So then how stupid it is to believe that only this way of life has no need of a teacher. And so the footsteps of our elders must always be followed with the utmost care and every thought in our hearts must be submitted to them, stripped of the cover of false modesty.[61]

It is Cassian who would identify eight principle sins which would become the forerunner to later diagnostic tools we are more familiar with, known as the Seven Deadly Sins. Cassian's list included: gluttony, fornication, avarice, anger, dejection, languor, vainglory, and pride. The later Celtic systems mirrored this list.

Gregory the Great (c. A.D. 540-604) revised Cassian's list, reducing them to seven. Gregory emphasized two in particular: pride and lust, claiming that the former was rooted in sins against God, and the latter, concerning sins of the flesh were a rebellion against the spirit.

---

[61] Conferences by John Cassian, trans. by Colm Luibheid. Paulist Press, New York. 1985. 69-70.

In this he clearly borrowed from the language of Paul at Galatians 5:17. According to Gregory, from pride came vainglory, envy, anger, dejection, avarice, gluttony, and lust. It is this language of Gregory that would persist into the later centuries as a diagnostic tool for determining sin, and applying a remedy accordingly. Gregory's influence was also seen in the widespread publication of his "Book of Pastoral Rule," which not only teaches individual spiritual direction, but also how to administer it to various demographics of people, such as the young and the old, the rich and the poor, the educated and the simple-minded, and so on.

The two-volume text *Councils on the Spiritual Life* by Mark the Monk (d. before 451), although not as popular or widespread as Gregory, Augustine, or Athanasius' texts, was a familiar resource for many who knew of the power it contained in teaching clergy to guide others in their spiritual life. A portion of Mark's text titled *On Repentance* does not go into the means of repentance by any liturgical form, but rather by means of studying the scriptures, holding oneself up to the models to the found therein, to seek to relate to others better, and to continually—even unto the point of death—be seeking the mercy and compassion of God by the repentance of sins, so to achieve reconciliation. He calls repentance "the foundation of the Christian life" and emphasizes repentance even of the small things. Although he does not speak directly about having a confessor, or a spiritual guide, he does emphasize that we cannot do this alone, and are not to be the judges of ourselves, even those who are among the religious. Rather, we obtain mercy by being merciful:

> Doing what is right, for beginners and the advanced and the perfect, means praying and purifying one's thoughts, and patiently enduring whatever comes. Without these, it is not possible to achieve the other virtues that make repentance acceptable. If repentance consists of asking for mercy, the person who has what he needs, needs to take special care not to hear, "You already have everything you need!" [1 Cor. 4:8] If the person who is merciful receives mercy [Matt. 5:7], then it is repentance, I believe, that holds together the whole cosmos. By divine dispensation, the one is helped by the other.[62]

---

[62] <u>Counsels on the Spiritual Life</u> by Mark the Monk, trans. by Tim Tivian and

Each of these Desert Fathers offer us insight into the penitential discipline of the fourth to fifth centuries, which moved from a system of public penances, to a more private system of having spiritual mentors who would assist you in understanding your sins so to master them and find suitable remedies for the sin-sick soul. Even when the people were unable to come to the monasteries, the clergy began to bring some of the monastic practices into the local parishes. Concerning this kind of practice, Kidder writes:

> Since visiting bishops could not bring the entire community of ascetics to the people of their parish, they resolved to introduce some of the ascetics' practices in their parishes during set times of the church year: the practices of sustained prayer, fasting, self-examination, and penance during the weeks before Easter, later known as the season of lent.[63]

Irish Penitentials

Separated from the continental though, the Irish, beginning in fifth century and extending into the eighth and ninth centuries, brought forth various texts on spiritual direction, sometimes known as "Canons," but more popularly known as "The Irish Penitentials." Not all of them were truly Irish, as some originated in Wales, or were more precisely guided by Welsh influences such as St. David of Wales, particularly the writings of Patrick and Finnian. These texts were manuals on hearing confessions and offering spiritual counsel, and the authors were clearly writing in contexts quite different from the continental bishops. John McNeill writes concerning these texts:

> The penitentials, on the other hand, know nothing of a public *exomologesis*, but assume that penance is determined by the confessor in private conference with the penitent; and the penalties they impose, while not uniformly upgraded, bear in general no relation to the classification of penitents presupposed by Basil.[64]

Augustine Casiday. St. Vladimir's Seminary Press, New York. 2009. 161.

[63] Making Confession, Kidder, 19.

[64] Medieval Handbooks of Penance McNeill and Gamer, 8-9.

Some significant examples of these texts are: the *Canons of St. Patrick*, the *Penitential of Finnian*, *The Penitential of Cummean*, the *Canones Hibernenses* ("The Irish Canons"), *The Penitential Canons of Adamnan*, The Old Irish Table of Commutations, *The Bigotian Penitential*, and *The Old Irish Penitential*. Many of these texts would become models for medieval handbooks of penance which most commonly bore the name of "Penitentials" and continued the tradition offering the clergy manuals on confession and spiritual direction. Overall, these texts show us that the Church of the 4th to 8th centuries was aware of the need for individual spiritual direction, and taught their clergy to be better spiritual directors and confessors.

Although the Irish monks did not invent the idea of private confession, some historians claim that the pattern for later private confession seems to come out of the Irish penitential discipline. Concerning this, Kidder writes:

> By the end of the fourth century, monks from Ireland introduced the desert fathers' and mothers' practices to their homeland, among them the practice of private confession, and incorporated them into their monasteries. According to David L. Fleming, private confession "seems to have grown out of the practice of Irish monks who sought spiritual direction for their spiritual development by telling their faults as well as virtues to a spiritual father," so that, "eventually, this monastic practice became common among all church members' in the West." By the fifth century the renewal was ripe to happen, since, "penance, if practiced at all, occurred largely on one's death-bed and penance in time of health was nearly lost."[65]

The application of the penitential system would evolve continually between the 6th and 8th centuries in both Ireland and Wales, and become more widespread outside of the monasteries, to eventually become common in parish churches, where it was accessible to the laity. The widespread use of the various manuals and penitentials allowed for even the simple local clergy to consult higher sources on how to diagnose sin, and prescribe holy remedies. Bridging the gap between the private spiritual direction of the fifth centuries, and the eventual widespread system of private confession on the Continent, Kidder wrote:

---

[65] Making Confession, Kidder, 23.

In the early penitentials, sin is frequently compared to a disease, the sinner to a patient, and the confessor to a physician. Sins are considered, "the wounds, fevers, transgressions, sorrows, sicknesses, and infirmities of the souls," while confessors are "spiritual physicians," who know how "to treat all things unto cleanness, to restore the feeble to the full state of health" (Citing from the penitential of Columban, part B, 251-252). The confessor is viewed as acting as a representative of Christ. Acts of penance were seen as medicinal measures prescribed by the confessor to realign and adjust the Christian's character. Thus they became salvific activities rather than tools for punishment and humiliation.

With the penitentials' popularity and their growing use by ordained priests on the continent, a new system of private penance evolved. This system was eventually regarded as sacramental in nature and came to include a formula for absolution, or the official pronouncement of forgiveness, by the confessor on behalf of the Church and Christ. Since absolution was seen as based on Jesus' handing the keys of the Church to Peter and ceding to him the power to bind and to loose, to absolve sins and retain them (Matt. 16:18-19), the Roman Church reserved the privilege of pronouncing absolution to those only who were Peter's apostolic successors, namely, ordained male clergy. Moreover, Christians could no longer seek out a guide or soul-friend of their own choosing, but were limited to the priest or bishop of their particular parish, regardless of whether there existed a sense of mutual kinship and intimacy, and regardless of the cleric's qualities of pastoral sensitivity, wisdom, and holiness.

This restriction, resulting from confession's sacramental status, introduced an unnatural split whereby spiritual direction and soul guidance was severed from confession—spawning a separation of roles between clerical confessor and lay spiritual director that persists to this day.[66]

While Kidder's conclusions do come across as an indictment against the sacramental system of the "Roman Church," her conclusions appear to be validated by the practice of the Medieval Church, and the many penitential texts of the Medieval period sustain the argument that this transition from monastic discipline and private spiritual direction certainly shifted from the sixth to ninth centuries towards what we now recognize as sacramental confession.

---

[66] Ibid, 34-35.

Before moving into the Medieval Church's witness on confession, it is of note that many of the most popular spiritual directors during this former time were among the monastic religious, many of whom were not priests. As already stated, the sacramental system as we now know it had not been fully defined, and confession and spiritual direction were not yet codified into anything close to what we would identify as "sacramental" practices. Nonetheless, it is safe to say that the administration of confession and penances was a largely sacerdotal function administered by clergy or monastics, or those under their supervision. This comes to be of some importance later in history, as questions would arise over who had the proper authority to absolve sinners of their sin. However, during this time the emphasis was not so much on the means of absolution, which was assumed to come from God alone, than on the process itself. Penitents would seek out a learned individual, tell them of their sins, and seek their guidance in restoring themselves to God, although it was not at all uncommon for this spiritual guide to be someone other than the parish priest or bishop. However, it should also be noted that all of these penitential texts were not really intended for the eyes of the laity, but for those in spiritual authority. In later centuries, some of these texts would become available to the laity, although it was still encouraged that penitents seek out educated spiritual guides who could adequately apply penitential discipline with authority.

CHAPTER FOUR
Medieval Application of Confession

The term "penitent" first appeared in the language of the councils at the Council of Toledo in the fifth century. "And by this word Penitent, we mean him who, after baptism having performed public penitence in sackcloth, either for homicide or for various other grievous crimes shall have been reconciled to the divine altar."[67] Already, we see a vast distinction from the rigor prior to the fourth century. However, this distinction would change even more over the course of the next four centuries leading up to the early Medieval period. The Council of Chalons-sur-Saone in A.D. 813 reports, "The exercise of penitence, according to the ancient constitution of the Canons, has fallen into disuse in most places, and neither in excommunicating nor in reconciling is the order of the old practice preserved."[68] *Ancrene Wisse: A Guide for Anchoresses,* probably written sometime between the late Patristic and the early Medieval period, speaks of the practice of confession, yet does not refer to it as a sacrament. Although all of the elements are there, this text does not mention the restriction of confession to a local priest, which would have been the case after the Fourth Lateran Council. Quite unique in its approach, "Part Five" of this text defines a sixteen-point approach to making a confession, yet concludes: "The priest need not lay on you for any fault, unless it be great enough, other penance than the life that you lead in accordance with this rule."[69] Here we see that confession is a common practice, yet not as yet defined as a sacrament, although it appears that these anchoresses had their own customary for

---

[67] History of the Confessional, Hopkins, 169.

[68] Ibid, 170.

[69] Ancrene Wisse: A Guide for Anchoresses trans. by. Hugh White. Penguin Books, London, 1993. 159.

the priest hearing their confessions, and their own local custom.

Leading into the eve of the Medieval period, St. Dunstan, the Archbishop of Canterbury, drew up the *Ecclesiastical Laws of King Edward* including canons on confession that illustrate, to some degree, the usage of this practice around the time of A.D. 967.

> *On Confession:* When anyone desires to make confession of his sins, let him act the man, and not blush to acknowledge his crimes and wickedness by accusing himself; because hence comes pardon, and because there is no forgiveness without confession.[70]

Here we see the understanding was that forgiveness was not available without making a confession in the Church. Then followed in the Laws a prescribed ritual of making the confession, accompanied by instructions for the confessor, including a "mode of imposing penance," which resembles to some degree the old penitential canons, except that in place of being in the "roll of penitents," the penitents are to fast for a prescribed number of years according to the sin committed. For example:

> Canon VIII: If a layman shall have killed another unwillingly, let him fast three years: one on bread and water, and two of them as his confessor shall appoint, and let him lament his transgression always. [71]

This then brings us to the *satisfaction* of the sin, which is a new contribution to the confessional process. Here, for the first time we witness mention of a form of payment for sins that was not a ritual sacrifice.

> Canon XIII: The compounding of sins with God is made in various manners, and alms-giving conduces chiefly to their payment.

> Canon XIV: Let him who is rich enough build churches to the praise of God; and if he is able to do more, let him add manors, and bring in young men who may perform the holy service for him, and daily celebrate unto God the holy mysteries.[72]

Hopkins, commenting on these Canons wrote:

---

[70] History of the Confessional, Hopkins, 173-174.

[71] Ibid, 176.

[72] Ibid, 177.

There is not a trace of all this to be found in the ancient canons, nor in the primitive fathers. That a wealthy sinner could compound his penitence for sin by building churches, endowing monasteries, making roads and bridges, and etc., as a proof of repentance, was a new idea; but yet it became speedily prevalent, since, however delusive it might be to the sinner, it was profitable to the Church and the priesthood, and formed the principal fund of their wealth for centuries together.[73]

These canons continue by demonstrating other forms of payment, by prayer, fasting, and by alms. Although the prayer requirements were worse than the fasting, the alms-giving was by comparison easier than either: "Canon XVIII: Anyone may redeem a fast of one day by one penny."[74] Although this code seemed to ease the burden of penance by offering payment, it also called for greater rigor based on the status of the sinner. To this, Hopkins comments:

And at the close of this code we have the following accommodating plan for men of rank and consequence, notwithstanding it is so strongly declared that the greater and more powerful anyone might be, in the same proportion must his sins be punished before God and man.[75]

This was to accommodate the fact that wealthy men could employ others to do their penance for them; and, as such, their penances had to be greater since their actual labor was lessened.

Overall, we see during this time of transition that the ancient Canons were of little use in the Church, and local customs were being devised to meet the needs of the Church, rather than the needs of the penitent. It would not take long for this to catch on, and for it to become a necessary point of discussion for the Church meeting in council. Kidder asserts that this new mode of payment for sins was in fact fairly natural given the nature of society at the time.

The belief in shared merit was a longstanding tradition in medieval society. From the religious perspective there existed and understanding

---

[73] Ibid, 177-178.

[74] Ibid, 178.

[75] Ibid, 178-179.

of the communion of the saints in heaven and on earth with whom one was invariably connected in spirit and through prayer and with whom one shared both joys and sorrows. From a secular perspective, the solidarity of the tribe, clan, or extended family superseded individual rights and obligations, so that relatives of the evildoer could make vicarious restitution for them in the hope of restoring the group's good name and honor. The growth of indulgences was especially apparent in the Germanic nations, where the payment of money in place of punishment in criminal cases was common, so that the practice of paying fines instead of doing acts of penance was a natural development. In addition, substitutions or indulgences for penitential obligations could be performed not only by the prayers and good works of other Church members, but also by the unused merits of the saints to whom one made devotion, or by making a pilgrimage to the Holy Land or Rome.[76]

She goes on to explain that the indulgence became official in 1095 when Pope Urban II proclaimed the first "plenary indulgence" at the beginning of the First Crusade.

Another indication of the shift in the teaching of the Church on hearing confessions arrives in the Canons of the First Lateran Council in Rome in 1123. While the practice of hearing confessions privately likely originated in the monasteries in the late Patristic period, by the Medieval period this act was not only discouraged, but forbidden. Canon XV of the First Lateran Council reads:

> Following in the footsteps of the holy fathers, we order by general decree that monks be subject to their own bishops with all humility, as if to masters and shepherds of the Church of God. They [the monks] may not celebrate masses in public anywhere. Moreover, let them completely abstain from public visitations of the sick, from anointings and even from hearing confessions, for these things in no way pertain to their calling.[77]

Fourth Lateran Council

From the time indulgences first appeared the abuses of taking money in exchange for absolution became equally widespread. Just

---

[76] Making Confession, Kidder, 53.

[77] Decrees, Tanner, 193.

barely over one hundred years after Pope Urban had issued the first plenary indulgence, a council was called in the Lateran Palace at Rome in 1215 by Pope Innocent III, supposedly to address various heresies, but in which the abuses of the confessional were also addressed. This vast gathering of bishops, abbots, and even lay delegates and royal legates brought together the authorities of the world to address with great authority the abuses of the Church. Canon XXI required all people to confess to their parish priest no less than once a year, otherwise they were to be denied access to communion, and if they died, also denied a Christian burial. Provision was also made for the penitent to make a confession to another priest, provided that they received a license from their own priest to do so. This Canon also concluded with a warning to the clergy to maintain the secrecy of the confessions, or otherwise be cast into a monastery for life to "perform perpetual penance."[78]

Canon XL addressed the concern of extorting money from those who could not afford to pay for the penalty of their sin, particularly when the priests were excommunicating members who could not pay, and apparently in some cases, even those who had already been absolved: "We forbid this especially in regions where by custom an excommunicated person is punished by a money penalty when he is absolved."[79] Of course, it should be understood that at this time that, people were absolved in the confessional prior to the performance of penances as it was expected that payment would come immediately after the confession. Canon LXII addressed the sale of relics, which was also a common penance at the time, due to the popular devotion to the saints, and in hopes of gaining their merit. These canons also forbid the practice of "alms-collectors" who were not only out trying to collect monies owed the Church, but who were also leading people to believe they could buy them in advance. "We also forbid the recognition of alms-collectors, some of whom deceive other people by proposing various errors in their preaching, unless they show authentic letters

---

[78] <u>Decrees</u>, Tanner, 245.

[79] Ibid, 257.

from the Apostolic See or from the diocesan Bishop."[80] This is further proof that there were in fact licensed alms-collectors sent out by the Holy See to collect owed funds. Finally, Canons LXV and LXVI forbid the clergy from charging a fee for things that were rightly a part of their normal duties:

> Canon LXVI: It has frequently been reported to the apostolic see that certain clerics demand and extort payments for funeral rites for the dead, and blessing of those marrying, and the like; and if it happens that their greed is not satisfied, they deceitfully set up false impediments. On the other hand some lay people, stirred by a ferment of heretical wickedness, strive to infringe a praiseworthy custom of holy church, introduced by pious devotion of the faithful, under the pretext of canonical scruples. We therefore both forbid wicked exactions to be made in these matters and order pious customs to be observed, ordaining that the church's sacraments are to be given freely but also that those who maliciously try to change a praiseworthy custom are to be restrained, when the truth is known, by the Bishop of the place.[81]

It is clear that the practice of selling what would come to be called indulgences was not only being abused by some of the clergy who sought to be paid for every sacerdotal act, but also that some of the lay people sought to buy their way out of anything. Kidder asserts that with the close of the Fourth Lateran Council, confession was finally given the status of "the sacrament of penance," and was required of every Christian at least once a year. Although it was required, as we have already demonstrated, nowhere in the Canons of the Fourth Lateran Council is penance or confession referred to as a sacrament. It is not until after the writing of Thomas Aquinas, which we shall next examine, that the sacrament of penance is identified specifically as a sacrament.

Thomas Aquinas

Thomas Aquinas was born in 1224, within a decade after the Fourth Lateran Council had concluded, and died at age fifty in 1274.

---

[80] Ibid, 263.

[81] Ibid, 265.

For Thomas, the decrees of the Fourth Lateran Council were a recent foundation upon which he wrote about the sacraments of the Church, and particularly about the absolution to be given by the priest. Prior to this time, most of the sacramentaries or rituals for confession involved the priest bidding, in the presence of the penitent, the absolution of God for the forgiveness of their sins. However, Thomas argues in favor of the priest claiming authority over the absolution of the penitent. Hopkins cites a passage from the Benedictine scholar Hugo Menard's notes on the Sacramentary of Gregory the Great, in which he mentions this change, and indicates that it had only appeared in the last thirty years:

> There was formerly a controversy between St. Thomas and a certain Doctor concerning the form of absolution; the doctor asserting that it was precatory, and that scarcely thirty years had elapsed since all used this form only: May the omnipotent God grant to thee absolution and remission. While the other [Thomas] contended that the form of absolution was enunciatory or indicative, in these words: I absolve thee, & etc., which indicates the juridical power of the Priest.[82]

As for the sacramental distinction of penance, Thomas asks in question eighty-one of the Third Part of the Summa concerning Sacraments, "Whether Penitence is a Sacrament?" If this were a given truth according to the Canons of the Fourth Lateran Council, which he assumes it is, he could have simply appealed to the Canons of the Council to make his argument. Instead, he appeals to Scripture. "As baptism is employed for the purifying from sin, so also is penitence. But baptism is a sacrament, as has been shown. Therefore, by equal reason, penitence is so likewise."[83] He also goes on to assert in his conclusion:

> I answer that, as Gregory says "a sacrament consists in a solemn act, whereby something is so done that we understand it to signify the holiness which it confers." Now it is evident that in Penance something is done so that something holy is signified both on the part of the penitent sinner, and

---

[82] History of the Confessional, Hopkins, 184.

[83] Summa Theologica, by Thomas Aquinas. Benzinger Brothers. New York, 1952. Third Part, Question 81.

on the part of the priest absolving, because the penitent sinner, by deed and word, shows his heart to have renounced sin, and in like manner the priest, by his deed and word with regard to the penitent, signifies the work of God Who forgives his sins. Therefore it is evident that Penance, as practiced in the Church, is a sacrament.[84]

Other Primary Medieval Authors

Further evidence of confessional practice in the Medieval period can be seen in the primary writing of the most influential Medieval texts: *Ancrene Wisse, The Cloud of Unknowing, The Book of Margery Kempe,* Richard Rolle's: *The Form of Living,* the *Showings* or *Revelations of Divine Love* of Julian of Norwich, and Walter Hilton's *Scale (or Ladder) of Perfection.* Furthermore, we have many examples of Medieval penitentials, borrowing from the language of the Irish Penitentials, but adding in indulgences and the confessional practice of their time. These demonstrate the common practice of confessions made to the local priest. Each of these texts demonstrate not only the perspective of the authors on confessing sins but, particularly in *The Book of Margery Kempe,* we hear from her strange autobiography concerning her acts of regular confession as well as the penances she performed, which included the prescribed pilgrimages she made to Rome, Assisi, the Holy Land, and to Compostela, Spain.

In *The Cloud of Unknowing,* written in the late fourteenth century, the anonymous author suggests as a primary step toward contemplation a prerequisite confession according to the law of the Church: "If you ask me when a person should begin contemplative work I would answer: not until he has first purified his conscience of all particular sins in the Sacrament of Penance as the church prescribes."[85] Here it is obvious that the author presumes Penance is a sacrament and that the Church has laws governing how it is to be administered.

---

[84] Ibid.

[85] The Cloud of Unknowing ed. by. William Johnson. Doubleday/Image Books, New York, 1973. 85.

Richard Rolle (1230-1349), in The Form of Living prescribes not only a presumption for the sacrament of penance, but furthermore an articulated pattern for making a valid confession. This goes beyond simply the nature of sacramental confession, into theory and even doctrine of what makes the confession true and the penitent truly absolved. For Rolle, the pattern was three-fold, although he is fond of making sub-points to all of his points in his writing. In chapter six of this text he defined that the necessary elements for purification were contrition, confession, and satisfaction. Under the second point, Rolle states:

> The second is confession, to counteract the sins of speech, and this must prompt without delay, frank without any excuses, complete without any separating, such as telling one sin to one priest, and another to another: say everything you are conscious of to one, or the whole confession will be useless."[86]

Probably the most widely printed and circulated spiritual text of the Medieval period, a text which influenced the writing of Julian of Norwich, is Walter Hilton's (d. 1396) The Scale (or Ladder) of Perfection. In chapter five of the second book Hilton expounds the need for the "Sacrament of Penance," although it appears he rebelled somewhat from the practice of penances, arguing in favor for a "loathing of sin, and a forsaking of the will for the love of Him."[87] Hilton takes a different approach, speaking of repentance in the light of being made in the image of God, although through his writing we see the diagnostic tools for sin in his day being worked out in his instruction:

> Moreover, Christian men or women that have lost the likeness of God though a deadly sin in breaking God's commandments, if he through the touching of grace in his heart doth truly forsake his sin, with sorrow and contrition of heart, and be in full purpose to amend and turn to a good life; and in this foresaid purpose and will receiveth the Sacrament of Penance,

---

[86] Richard Rolle: The English Writings trans. and ed. by Rosamund Allen. Paulist Press, New York, 1988. 166.

[87] The Scale (or Ladder) of Perfection by Walter Hilton. Art and Book Company, Westminster, 1901. 145.

if he may come by it, or if he cannot have a will and desire to come by it, surely, I say this man or woman's soul, that was before misshapen to the likeness of the devil through deadly sin, is now by the sacrament of penance restored and shapen again to the image of our Lord God.[88]

Hilton goes on to explain the necessity of confession to a priest, not as a means of contrition, but rather as a token of humility. "It is not enough for him," he says, "to have forgiveness of God only by contrition between God and him, unless he have a charter also made by holy Church, and this is the Sacrament of Penance, which is his charter and token of forgiveness."[89] It is clear that by the time of the writing of *The Scale of Perfection*—Hilton's environment was one that presumed confession was not only a sacrament—but a necessary token of forgiveness beyond mere contrition. For Hilton it is not enough to merely seek forgiveness of God, but also of the Church, which is to say by a priest, unless hindered by availability from doing so. Hilton argues later in the chapter that it is not often that a penitent will come to true contrition without the sacramental guidance of the priest in the confession, and this is further evidence for the need of a confessor in the process.

Julian of Norwich (ca. 1342-1416), a Benedictine anchoress in Norwich, England, wrote of various visions she had of God, heaven, and of His perspectives towards our lives. In Chapter seventeen of her *Revelations* Julian speaks directly of sin, and indicates by her indictment against sin that one is to confess according to the rules of the Church:

> Sin is the sharpest scourge with which any chosen soul can be beaten, and this scourge belabors and breaks men and women, and they become so despicable in their own sight that is seems to them that they are fit for nothing but as it were to sink into hell; but when the inspiration of the Holy Spirit contrition seizes them, then the Spirit turns bitterness into hope of God's mercy. And then the wounds begin to heal and the soul to revive, restored to the life of Holy Church. The Holy Spirit leads him to confession willing to reveal his sins, nakedly and truthfully, with great sorrow and

---

[88] Ibid.

[89] Ibid, 146.

great shame that he has so befouled God's fair image. Then he accepts the penance for every sin imposed by his confessor, for this is established in Holy Church by the teaching of the Holy Spirit. Every sinful soul must be healed by this medicine, especially of the sins which are mortal to him. Though he be healed, his wounds are not seen by God as wounds, but as honors.[90]

It would seem here that Julian's writings are not only inspired by her visions, but by the practice of the local Church in England at the time of her writing, and also possibly by the influence of the writing of Walter Hilton as she also speaks of marring God's image.

In sum, the writing of the Medieval authors illustrate a shift in penance from a private monastic practice, to the more formally codified system of the sacrament of penance, along with a number of regular means of diagnosing sin, and putting it away though confession to a priest, particularly to their own priest according to Lateran IV, as opposed to another spiritual director or monk. The medieval period also witnesses to the beginnings of a trend that will be part of the cause of the Reformation in the repudiation of penances for the forgiveness of sin, in particular the selling of indulgences and tapping into the treasury of the merit of the saints.

---

[90] Showings by Julian of Norwich, trans. by Edmund College and James Walsh. Paulist Press, New York, 1978. 154-155.

Dogmatic Theology

CHAPTER FIVE
Reformation

The Reformation, as the title suggests, brought about reform of the Church, but also raised many questions as to the nature of the sacrament of reconciliation, the effects of which ultimately divided the Church over matters of understanding justification, confessional practice, and requirements for forgiveness. We will begin by examining the writings of Martin Luther, then his English adversary King Henry VIII, who would be given the title "Defender of the Faith" for his arguments against Luther. We will then examine the writings of John Calvin on this subject, and witness the declarations of the "Catholic Church" in the decrees of the Council of Trent.

Luther Against Abuses of Penance

By 1517 the acts of commuting penances for money had been well established for a few hundred years. With these "indulgences" came many abuses. The practice was so widespread by the time of Martin Luther that he most vehemently, and bravely, considering his position as a priest of the Church, spoke out against the practice by posting a text titled: *Disputation on the Power and Efficacy of Indulgences,* which became known simply as his *Ninety-Five Theses,* on the castle church door of Wittenberg on either October 31st or November 1st of 1517. These Theses almost entirely addressed the single subject: the administration of the Sacrament of Penance. However he more specifically addressed the practice of accepting indulgences and what they were said to commute or alleviate, which in his view went well beyond the normal or appropriate bounds for penances. Furthermore, he questioned the authority of the clergy, particularly the Pope, of permitting and even promulgating these acts. While a student of this subject could easily read all ninety five in a few minutes, we will just highlight a few of Luther's points here to establish the tone of his document:

1. When our Lord and Master, Jesus Christ, said "Repent," he called for the entire life of believers to be one of penitence.

2. The word cannot be properly understood as referring to the sacrament of penance, i.e., confession and satisfaction, as administered by the clergy.

6. The Pope himself cannot remit guilt, but only declare and confirm that it has been remitted by God; or, at most, he can remit it in cases reserved to his discretion. Except for these cases, the guilt remains untouched.

10. it is a wrongful act, due to ignorance, when priests retain the canonical penalties on the dead in Purgatory.

21. Hence, those who preach indulgences are in error when they say that a man is absolved and saved from every penalty by the Pope's indulgences.

27. There is no divine authority for preaching that the soul flies out of purgatory immediately when the money clinks in the bottom of the chest.

32. All those who believe themselves certain of their own salvation by means of letters of indulgence, will be eternally damned, together with their teachers.

35. It is not in accordance with Christian doctrine to preach and teach that those who buy off souls, or purchase confessional licenses, have no need to repent of their sins.

81. This unbridled preaching of indulgences makes it difficult for learned men to guard the respect due to the Pope against false accusations, or at least from keen criticisms of the laity;

82. They ask, "Why does not the Pope liberate everyone from purgatory for the sake of love (a most holy thing) and because of the supreme necessity

of their souls?" This would be morally the best of all reasons. Meanwhile he redeems innumerable souls for money, a most perishable thing, with which to build St. Peter's church, a minor purpose.

94. Christians should be exhorted to be zealous to follow Christ, their head, through penalties, deaths and hells;

95. And let them thus be more confident of entering heaven through many tribulations rather than through a false assurance of peace. [91]

Here we can see a clear outline of Luther's main points, namely that indulgences are of no effect, and those that teach them are doing more harm than good to the souls they convince to buy the indulgences. He also attacks the idea of purgatory, which was apparently a large motivator for the sales of indulgences at the time of Luther.

Three years later in 1520, Luther wrote a text called *The Babylonian Captivity of the Church,* in which he makes two arguments to contend with the greater Church about the abuses of the confessional practice. He begins under the context of discussing Baptism:

In this way, you will see how rich a Christian is, i.e., one who has been baptized. Even if he wished, he could not lose his salvation however often he sinned, save only if he refused to believe. No sins have it in their power to damn him, but only unbelief... But "contrition" and "confession of sin" followed by "satisfaction," and all of the other devices thought out by men, will desert you suddenly and leave you in distress, if you forget this divine truth and batten upon those things. Whatever is done apart from faith in the truth of God, is vanity of vanities and vexation of spirit. [92]

From this brief text, we see a perspective of Martin Luther's thought which held that after baptism, no sins could damn a person except their unbelief. This was the cornerstone of his belief against indulgences, purgatory, and the entire confessional requirement of the Church. This was also the foundation of his core theology which focused primarily on justification being achieved through the faith

---

[91] Martin Luther: Selections from His Writings ed. by John Dillenberger, Anchor Books Doubleday, New York, 1961. 489-500.

[92] Martin Luther, Dillenberger, 295.

of the believer. He continues his indictment under the heading *The Sacrament of Penance* in which the following select quotes illuminate his perspective on the practice of private confession and the abuses of the clergy and popes:

> In the present instance, and for the sake of unveiling the tyranny which is as aggressive here as in the case of the sacrament of the bread, I must briefly repeat on what I have said. On account of the many opportunities afforded by these two sacraments for money-making and self-seeking, the greed of the shepherds has raged with unbelievable activity against Christ's sheep.

> They have adapted the words of promise in which Christ said, in Matthew 16:19, "Whatever thou shalt bind," etc. and in John 20:23, "Whosoever sins ye remit, they are remitted unto them," etc. These words evoke the faith of the penitents, and make them fit to receive forgiveness of sins.

> At length, some have begun to command angels in heaven; they give themselves airs, in their incredibly rampant impiety, as if they had received in these words the right of ruling heaven and earth, and possessing the power of "binding" even in heaven. They say nothing about the saving faith required of the people, but are garrulous about the absolute power of the popes.

> The only thing instituted was the service rendered by those who perform the act of baptizing. Similarly, in the place where it says, "Whatsoever thou shalt bind," etc., Christ is calling out the faith of the penitent, by giving a certitude on the words of the promise, that, if he be forgiven as a believer here below, his forgiveness holds good in heaven. This passage makes no mention at all of the conferring of power, but only deals with the service performed by the administrator promising the words of forgiveness.[93]

Here, Luther contests not only the abuses, but the citations from Matthew and John which had long been held as the scriptural warrants for clerical authority in hearing confessions and granting absolution. He then continues his attack on the method of confession in the greater Church, breaking it down by contrition, confession, and satisfaction, but beginning by once again uplifting faith as a key element to forgiveness, corresponding to contrition:

---

[93] Martin Luther, Dillinberger, 314-316.1

Wherever faith is found, the certainty of punishment causes contrition, and the trustworthiness of the promises in the means of consolation; and through this faith a man merits forgiveness of sin.

This is far better than to meditate on one's seething sins, which, if considered before taking God's truth into account, will rather refresh and increase the desire for sin, than produce contrition.

Confession and satisfaction, on the other hand, have been made into an egregious factory of money and power.[94]

Secondly, against confession, Luther summarizes:

Without doubt, confession is necessary, and in accordance with the divine commandments...as for secret confession as practices today, though it cannot be proved from scripture, yet it seems a highly satisfactory practice to me; it is useful and even necessary. I would not wish it to cease; rather I rejoice that it exists in the Church of Christ, for it is a singular medicine for afflicted consciences...what I reject is solely that this kind of confession should be transformed into a means of oppression and extortion on the part of the pontiffs. The impious despots reserve to themselves those trespasses which are mostly of little moment, while the greater, sure enough, they leave everywhere to the common rule of priests...they even teach and approve things which are adverse to the worship of God, to the faith, and to the chief commandments. One might specify such things such as running about on pilgrimages, the perverse worship of saints, the mendacious legends of saints, various beliefs in works and in the practice of ceremonies [so to gain indulgences]; by all of which faith in God is lessened, while idolatry is fostered, as is the case nowadays. [95]

Here we see that Luther was not opposed to confession, but rather to how it was practiced by his contemporaries. He then continues in this passage to support the practice of confessing to a neighbor or a brother privately:

There is no doubt in my mind that a man's secret sins are forgiven him when he makes a voluntary confession before a brother in private, and on reproof, he asks for pardon and mends his ways. No matter how much any pope may rage against these contentions, the fact is that Christ manifestly gave

---

[94] Dillinberger, 317-319.
[95] Ibid, 319-320.

the power of pronouncing forgiveness to anyone who had faith in Him... therefore I would admonish those "princes in Babylon" to refrain from making reserved cases of any kind; and secondly, to give free permission for any brother or sister to hear confessions of secret sins.[96]

Finally, Luther concludes with admonishing the practices related to "satisfaction" in the final step of the confessional practice of his day, while also condemning the practice of sending penitents on long excursions or to put them through other practices so to achieve forgiveness claiming that this practice went well beyond the boundaries of the confessional:

> In regard to "satisfaction," how unworthily the Romanists have dealt with it! I have discussed it in detail in dealing with indulgences. They have abused it to an extraordinary extent, to the ruin of Christians in body and soul. In the first place, they have expounded it in such a matter that the people in general have not the slightest understanding of the true satisfaction, although it means the renovation of life... they leave no room for faith in Christ. With consciences pitilessly tortured by scruples on this point, on person runs to Rome, another here, another there... one flays himself with rods, while another is mortifying his body with vigils and fasting... by these enormities, thou hast brought the world into such disorder that men think they can propitiate God for sins by the means of their works, whereas he is propitiated only by faith in the contrite heart. [97]

With these final words from Luther in this section, we can interpret that there was much confusion over the practice of satisfaction, and that people were prescribed a grand variety of penances so to achieve forgiveness, including paying money for indulgences, going on pilgrimages, and even performing self-flagellations or extreme fasts— all of which Luther saw as not only confusing, but contrary to the spirit of true contrition and satisfaction through a lively faith in Jesus.

---

[96] Ibid, 321.

[97] Ibid, 323.

Henry vs. Luther

Henry VIII (probably aided by Thomas Cranmer), writing directly in contrast to Luther's *The Sacrament of Penance*, fully supported the practice of those whom Luther called the "Romanists" in his extended treatise *Assertio Septem Sacramentorum* or *Defense of the Seven Sacraments,* in which the king defends the Church in the same pattern in which Luther criticized the practices. Henry begins by pointing the finger at Luther's arguments and calling them: "absurd, impious, and contradictory." Henry's primary defense is that this practice had such ancient antiquity: "Let Luther then propose that no more for a thing so new, and strange to us, which everybody already knows. Let him no longer complain, that this is out of use, than which nothing is more usual."[98]

Defending contrition, Henry writes:

He (Luther) teaches Contrition to be a great thing, not easily had. He commands all men to be certain that they have it; and to believe undoubtedly, that, through the words of the promise, all their sins are forgiven them; and that after they are loosed by the Word of Man here on earth, they are absolved by God in heaven. In which thing, his own assertion will either fall back upon what he has already reprehended, or else will appear more absurd ... if he has promised forgiveness only to those who are as contrite as the greatness of their crimes requires, then cannot Luther himself (as he commands all others to be) be assured, and out of doubt, that his sins are forgiven him. For how will he be certain of obtaining the promise, when he can in no wise know that he is sufficiently contrite for his sins? For no mortal man has ever yet known how great contrition is required for mortal sin ... wherefore he admits but only contrition, that is, a sufficient grief, then can no body be assured that he is absolved; and Luther's certain and undoubted confidence of absolution, will perish, or be false and erroneous. [99]

---

[98] <u>Defense of the Seven Sacraments</u> by Henry VIII, re-ed. by Rev. Louis O'Donovan. Benziger Brothers, New York, 1908. 181.

[99] Ibid, 183.

Henry's argument here seems to be that Luther is flawed in claiming that no man can forgive sins, yet he believes Luther also claims we can confess to each other, which becomes self-defeating in Luther's theology in that no man can forgive sins. He also seems to argue in favor of contrition, yet in the same vein argues that no man can know the adequacy of contrition for a penitent. This argument is itself somewhat self-defeating.

Henry also elaborates on an argument Luther only briefly makes, concerning the difference between contrition and attrition as adequate foundations for sufficient sorrow for sin prior to a confession:

> What is this different from the opinion of those whom he reproves, who say, that attrition, by means of the sacrament of penance, is made contrition? For what is wanting to men is supplied by the sacrament; or else Luther's position that man must be certain of absolution, is false. [100]

Concerning confession, Henry seems to be somewhat confused as to Luther's stance.

> He so treats confession as to hold, "That in public crimes, where the sin is known to all people, without confession, there (where it is less matter), confession is to be made." But, in the confession of secret sins, he has so uncertain turnings, that, though he seem not altogether to reject it, yet can it not be known by him whether he admits it as a thing commanded, or no: for he denies it to be proved by Scripture; and yet says, "That is pleases him well, and that it is profitable and necessary;" yet he does not say it to be necessity to all; but, as I suppose, only to pacify troubled consciences. [101]

Henry admits from his own text that he is somewhat "supposing" Luther's desired ends rather than addressing the actual abuses of the practice that Luther was addressing. Henry then goes on for several paragraphs to speak to the necessity of confession, and extracting from various texts proof-texts to demonstrate that the system of contrition, confession, and satisfaction was ancient and hallowed. He cites Ecclesiastes, John Chrysostom, Numbers, St. James, St. Ambrose, Isaiah, and St. Augustine, only making the point that confession is

[100] Ibid, 184.
[101] Ibid, 185.

necessary and seems to have a defined pattern of effectiveness, which is a point Luther was not contesting.

Henry does eventually come to the points which Luther was contesting, specifically, the reservation of certain sins to the judgment of bishops or popes, and confession in general to be made to a priest. Henry's appeal to the first point is general in nature, addressing simply that many clergy are without the education necessary to judge sin properly, so why shouldn't the bishops reserve to themselves the judgments of certain sins.

> What wonder then, if the Bishop reserves some things to himself, whose care is greater than what might be committed to every person, though not the least learned, when it has been for so many ages observed; fearing lest the people should fall more pronely into sin, when the power of remission should be proposed to them in so easy a manner.[102]

This point is also made in the medieval penitentials and customaries of certain dioceses which also addressed the ignorance of some clergy. To the second point Henry appeals again to scripture and antiquity: Leo the Great, Bede, St. Ambrose, and St. Augustine, which all affirm Henry's point that confessions should be made to the priest, just, as Henry argues, the people under the Old Law presented themselves to the priests for judgments on their ritual purity after atonement was made. He specifically refutes Luther's claim that the command of Jesus to "bind and loose sins" was intended for the laity, rather than the apostolic priesthood.

> Likewise, St. Augustine in another place writes most plainly saying, "He that doth penance, without the appointment of the Priest, frustrates the keys of the church." Now let anyone judge the truth of Luther's opinion, who, contrary to sentiments of all the holy fathers, draws the keys of the church to the laity, and to women; and says that these words of Christ, Whatsoever you bind, &c. are spoken not to Priests, but also to the faithful.[103]

Concerning satisfaction, which really is Luther's most vehement point, Henry doesn't really even speak to the matter of indulgences,

---

[102] Ibid, 187.
[103] Ibid, 188.

but notes philosophically that penances should be made. "For to do penance, is to bewail our sins formerly committed, and resolve not to do anything hereafter that we should have cause to sorrow for."[104] Henry focuses instead on Luther's argument of the necessity of faith, which he outright and easily dismisses:

> Finally, when he says, "That we cannot satisfy God by works, but by faith alone;" if he means, that by works alone, without faith, we cannot do it; he shows but his folly, by railing against the See of Rome; in which was ever yet so foolish, as to say, that works, without faith, can satisfy; being not ignorant that of St. Paul, "What is not of faith is sin." But if he thinks that works are superfluous, and that faith alone is sufficient, whatever the works be; then he says something, and dissents truly from the Roman Church; which, with St. James believes, "That faith, without works, is dead."[105]

Henry comes closest to addressing the abuses Luther spoke of only in citing Augustine in support of penances that included fasting and "alms deeds":

> Let us hear what St. Augustine has writ on this subject: "It is not sufficient (says he) to change our manners to better, and forsake our former wickedness; unless we do also satisfy our Lord for the sins committed, by the sorrows of penance, by the sobs of humility, by the sacrifice of the contrite heart, and with co-operation of alms-deeds, and fasts."[106]

One might wonder if this were the actual case at the time of Luther and Henry, and whether Luther would have argued this point. Luther did not argue against penances as a whole, but rather the superfluous penances such as pilgrimages and indulgences, which in his eyes were not really giving alms-offerings for the poor but graft benefitting the clergy and the pope. Luther also argued about the inconsistency of the practices thereof. Henry simply dismisses his concerns as naïveté concerning what he claimed were "ancient" practices.

Finally, Henry concludes by pointing out what he defines as Luther's "absurdity" in denying that these practices are ancient, and that Penance was a sacrament.

---

[104] Ibid, 191.

[105] Ibid, 192.

[106] Ibid, 193.

I hope I have plainly made appear how absurd he is against the holy Fathers; against the Scriptures; against the public faith of the Church; against the consent of so many ages and people; even against common sense itself; with all which, he is not yet content; but after having held a long time that Penance is a sacrament, he began, in the end of his book, to repent himself, that it should contain anything of the truth at all; and therefore, as his custom is, changes his opinion into a worse, and wholly denies penance to be a sacrament.[107]

Henry's overall defense of this subject seems to be somewhat absent-minded of attending to the abuses Luther was actually addressing, although he does make valid arguments from the Fathers, from Scripture, and from the common practice of the Church that the penitential system was of antiquity, and that the clergy played a specific role in administering the "sacrament."

John Calvin

John Calvin (1509-1564) wrote well after the Fourth Lateran Council, just prior to the Council of Trent, and a generation after Luther. Although agreeing somewhat with Luther, Calvin was not in favor of calling Penance a sacrament. He firmly believed Baptism to be the Sacrament of Repentance. Calvin argued against what Luther called the "Romanist view" of confession, which Calvin calls the "Scholastic Sophist" position, from a theological standpoint. He does not spend any time in his Institutes of Christian Religion (1536) engaging the problems of the penances, indulgences, and pilgrimages beyond stating the absurdity of trying to measure out acceptable satisfaction for sins. Rather, Calvin approached the argument more academically, and by various proofs he dismisses the whole process as something imagined by men. This is not to say that Calvin did not uphold the value of repentance—far from it. Rather, Calvin asserted that the Romanists never understood what repentance truly meant. In Chapter IV of his Institutes, Calvin begins by stating clearly his intent in discussing penitence:

---

[107] Ibid, 193.

I come now to an examination of what the scholastic sophists teach concerning repentance. This I will do as briefly as possible; for I have no intention of taking up every point, lest this work, which I am desirous to frame as a compendium of doctrine, should exceed all bounds. They have managed to envelop a matter, otherwise not much involved, in so many perplexities, that it will be difficult to find an outlet if once you get plunged in but a little way into their mire. And, first, in giving a definition, they plainly show they never understood what repentance means. For they fasten on some expressions of the Fathers which are very far from expressing the nature of repentance. For instance, that to repent is to deplore past sins and not commit what is to be deplored. Again, that it is to bewail past evils, and not again to do what was bewailed…again it is sorrow of heart and bitterness of soul for the sins which the individual has committed, or to which he has consented. Supposing we grant that these things were well said by the Fathers, they were not, however, said with the view of describing repentance, but only of exhorting penitents not again to fall into the same faults from which they had been delivered.[108]

Calvin's argument, slightly similar in this respect to Luther's argument, is that the Scholastic Sophists misinterpreted what the fathers meant for the benefit of their arguments in favor of the sacramental system. Calvin argued in favor of repentance in the simple terms of stopping the behavior, lamenting it, and then turning away from repeating the same sins in the future. This, he says, is what the fathers meant when they spoke of repentance. He also points out that there is a "strange silence" when referring to the amendment of life to follow confession, as he believed that the doctrines created by these Scholastic Sophists went well beyond even their own definitions of repentance:

Moreover, the doctrine which they afterwards deliver is somewhat worse than their definition. For they are so keenly bent on external exercises, that all you can gather from immense volumes is, that repentance is a discipline, and austerity, which serves partly to subdue the flesh, partly to chasten and punish sins: if internal renovation of mind, bringing with it true amendment of life, there is a strange silence. No doubt, they talk much of

---

[108] Institutes of Christian Religion by John Calvin, trans. by. Henry Beveridge. Eerdmans, Michigan, 1972. Book I, 533-534. (Emphasis original to the text)

contrition and attrition, torment of the soul and many scruples, and involve it in great trouble and anxiety; but when they seem to have deeply wounded the heart, they cure all its bitterness by a slight sprinkling of ceremonies. Repentance thus shrewdly defined, thy divide into contrition of heart, confession of the mouth, and satisfaction of works. This is not more logical than the definition, though they would be thought to have spent their whole lives in framing syllogisms.[109]

It is clear from this statement that Calvin's argument is firmly against the ceremonies required for absolution to be granted, and furthermore against the abuses of mind and wallet that went along with them at the time.

Beyond these statements, much of Calvin's arguments mirror Luther's complaints, such as: "Repentance can exist without confession,"[110] and that this formal process of contrition, confession, and satisfaction, is not necessary for the forgiveness of sins, which was contrary to the Scholastic Sophists position. Rather, in place of contrition, he argued that: "the soul look not to its own compunction or its own tears, but fixed both eyes in the mercy of God alone."[111] Against confession, Calvin focused more on the fact that, in his view, it was not a "divine commandment." Calvin argues fully against any sense that the priesthood, either Levitical, or as descendants of the apostles via Jesus, have any power to "bind or to loose" sins. This forgiveness, he believed, came from God alone. Here, he returns to his argument that Baptism is the sacrament of forgiveness:

They now come to closer quarters, while they support their view by passages of Scripture which they think clearly in their favor. Those who came to John's baptism confessed their sins, and James bids us confess our sins to one another. It is not strange that those who wished to be baptized confessed their sins. It has already been mentioned, that John preached the baptism of repentance, baptized with water into repentance. Whom then could he baptize, but those who confessed that they were sinners? Baptism is a symbol of the forgiveness of sins; and who could be admitted to receive the symbol but sinners acknowledging themselves as such.[112]

---

109 Ibid, 534.

110 Ibid, 535.

111 Ibid, 536.

112 Ibid, 539.

This argument, although treated as somewhat obvious, does not do much to negate the commission against which he is preaching, which is post-baptismal sin. He continues with his argument against the use of the verses in James:

> Now without good reason does James enjoin us to confess our sins one to another. But if they would attend to what immediately follows, they would perceive that this gives them little support. The words are, "Confess your sins to one another, and pray for one another." He joins together mutual confession and mutual prayer. If, then, we are to confess to priests only, we are also to pray for them only. What? It would even follow from the words of James that priests alone can confess. In saying that we are to confess mutually, he must be addressing those only who can hear the confession of others. But those only can confess reciprocally who are fit to hear confession. This being a privilege which they bestow on priests only, we also leave them the office of confessing to each other. Have done then with such frivolous absurdities, and let us receive the true meaning of the Apostle, which is plain and simple: first, that we are to deposit our infirmities in the breasts of each other, with the view of receiving mutual counsel, sympathy, and comfort; and secondly, that mutually conscious of the infirmities of the brethren, we are to pray to the Lord for them.[113]

Here, we find a similar argument made by Luther, although with slightly more accountability, that we are to confess to one another for mutual support and prayer rather than to priests only.

Beyond this, Calvin continues his argument against the antiquity of the practice, against the pronouncements of the Canons of the Fourth Lateran Council, and hearkens back to the practices of the Patristic period, citing the days of Nectarius and St. John Chrysostom when auricular confession was abolished. He argues that if confession in this manner was at one time abolished, then it could not be a divine command. Calvin's argument is fairly clear—it is God alone who cures us of sins. As such, Calvin was very much in favor of the general confession in the Church, and yearned for an earlier time when the community of the Church lifted up the public admission of sins, and a process for restoring repentant sinners to the fold. It is is curious that

---

[113] Ibid, 539-540.

although he is against the "ceremonies" prescribed by the Scholastic Sophists, he acknowledges the patterns of the early Church and the patristic fathers prior to the fifth century, in the laying on of hands after a process of reconciling the excommunicated members over time, and says that he longs for a return of their practices:

> Although Cyprian somewhere says that not the Bishop only laid hands, but also the whole clergy. For he this speaks, "They do penitence for a proper time; next they come to communion, and receive the right of communion by the laying on of the hands of the Bishop and the clergy." Afterwards, in process of time, the matter came to this, that they used the ceremony in private absolutions also without public penitence. Hence the distinction of Gratian between public and private reconciliation. I consider that ancient observance of which Cyprian speaks to have been holy and salutary to the Church, and I wish it could be restored in the present day. The more modern form, though I dare not disapprove, or at least strongly condemn, I deem to be less necessary.[114]

In this citation, from the second volume of his *Institutes*, Calvin is careful to disagree with the practice of the Church, although he recognizes an issue which was also presented by Luther, that the inconsistency of the practice leaves many wondering exactly what makes Penance a sacrament:

> The Romanists and Schoolmen, whose wont it is to corrupt all things by erroneous interpretation, anxiously labor to find a sacrament here, and it cannot seem wonderful, for they seek a thing where it is not. At best they leave the matter involved, undecided, uncertain, confused, and confounded by the variety of opinions.[115]

Instead, Calvin argued, as he had in previous discourses on Baptism, that Baptism is the sacrament of repentance. To this end, he makes the following conclusion:

> Lest they become elated, however, whatever be the part in which they place the sacrament, I deny that it can justly be regarded as a sacrament; first, because there exists not to this effect and special promise of God, which is

---

[114] Institutes, John Calvin, Book II, 633.
[115] Ibid.

the only ground for a sacrament; and secondly, because whatever ceremony is here used is a mere invention of man; whereas, as has already been shown, there ceremonies of the sacraments can only be appointed by God.

What Jerome said harshly and improperly—vis. That baptism, which is fall from those who deserve to be excommunicated from the Church, is repaired by penitence, there worth expositors wrest to their own impiety. You will speak most correctly, therefore, if you call baptism the sacrament of penitence, seeing it as given to those who aim at repentance to confirm their faith and seal their confidence.[116]

As the Protestant wing of the Western Church has largely looked to Calvin for their theology, there is little wonder at the perspective held there concerning repentance, and methods of restoring to the Church those who fall away after receiving Baptism. Calvin himself yearned for a return to the practices of the early Church, although they have not yet returned. Some conjecture might be in order here as to how those who pursue Calvin's line of reasoning reconcile sins without tending to become Anabaptists—those who offer baptism more than once for the repentance of sins. Calvin left unsettled the concern of how to handle post-baptismal sin.

Ignatius of Loyola

Another significant player in the influence of confession during the Reformation, and for generations to follow was Ignatius of Loyola (1491-1556). Ignatius, after his conversion from a somewhat decadent adolescence, set out with a goal to outdo all of the saints in the way of penance. The means of conquering sin, for Ignatius, was in a tedious and somewhat scrupulous self-examination of one's sin repeated over a series of weeks if not months of continual purging of sin through self-examination, meditation, and intense repeated confession. His text, now called *The Spiritual Exercises of St. Ignatius,* was based on a series of exercises he had performed for some time but began to record beginning in 152. The exercises were probably finalized in 1522, and

---

[116] Ibid, 635.

followed a four-fold pattern of meditation, which was also strictly followed by all of those in his charge. Following a nearly fatal sickness and a failed attempt at a pilgrimage to Jerusalem, followed by many troubled and tortuous years of harassment, temptations, and studies in many educational institutions from Spain to France, Ignatius eventually attracted a sizable group of followers who were devoted to each other under his headship and guidance, although not bound by any authority of the Church. That was, until 1537, when the whole group submitted themselves to the Pope Paul III, who commissioned them by Papal Bull as the *Societas Jesu*, or the Society of Jesus. Their specific rule and role within the Church would begin to be put to paper by November of 1538. The role of this new society was gradually revised and amended until 1541, when Ignatius was charged by the Pope to draw up the constitution of the group, which he did not be begin until 1547, and finally completed in 1550. After many years of reform and definition, under the authority and guidance of the pope, this company of priest companions would eventually be charged primarily with the furtherance of education in the Catholic Church.

These Jesuits, as they would come to be known (although it was initially considered a derogatory term), would be responsible for promulgating much of the teaching of the Church, particularly the faith outlined at the Council of Trent. The Ignatian exercises would come to eventually be an annual requirement of all priests belonging to the Society, while also attracting many people who sought to pray and meditate in the way of the Jesuits. These "Ignatian Retreats" can be four weeks, or even four months long. The four-fold pattern begins with repeated and continually purging confession, asking questions that make the confession deeper, more specific, and examining the frequency as well as the mitigating factors that might make a sin graver by all kinds of factors. Once all sin has been purged, the participant then meditates on specific verses of scripture which outline the life of Jesus, the death of Jesus, and finally the resurrection appearances of Jesus. The influences of the Society of Jesus, and this program originating from

St. Ignatius' early days at Montserrat, and the influence of the Jesuit practices throughout the Reformation, would become widespread and continue to this day in the education of youth, and in the guiding of souls closer to God through guided retreats. The more fully developed codification of Roman doctrine came with the Council of Trent, which was convening contemporaneously with the development of this order, would lead to a widespread influence of the Society of Jesus on the promulgation of confession as the principle means of atonement for the world's largest catholic body of Christians for centuries to follow.

Council of Trent

While Lateran IV does not directly call penance or confession a "sacrament"—although it certainly treated it as such—the Council of Trent, which began in 1551, covered this gap by not only calling it a sacrament, but by further defining and pronouncing the elements that made it a valid sacrament.

> SESSION XIV; CHAPTER III: This holy council teaches that the form of the sacrament of penance, in which its power chiefly resides, is placed in these words of the minister, I absolve thee, &c. To which, indeed, by the custom of the holy Church, certain prayers are laudably added, although they do not affect the essence of the form itself, nor are they necessary to the administration of the sacrament. And the acts of the penitent himself, namely, contrition, confession, and satisfaction, are, as it were, the elements of this sacrament, which acts, forasmuch as they are required in the penitent by the institution of God, to the integrity of the sacrament, to the full and perfect remission of sins, for this reason are called the parts of penitence. And truly the substance and effect of this sacrament, so far as concerns its virtue and efficacy, is reconciled with God.[117]

This council further spoke not only in favor of the sacrament being performed by a priest, but furthermore prescribed the priestly office as a necessity for absolution:

---

[117] Decrees, Tanner, 704.

CHAPTER V. *Of Confession:* From the institution of the Sacrament of Penance, already explained, the universal Church has always understood, that the entire confession of sins was instituted by the Lord himself, and made necessary by the divine law for all who sin after baptism; because our Lord Jesus Christ, being about to ascend from the earth to heaven, left his priests, the vicars of himself, as presidents and judges, to whom all mortal crimes might be brought into which the faithful of Christ might fall; to the end that by the power of the keys they should pronounce the sentence of remission or retention of sins. For it is evident that the priests cannot exercise this judgment without knowing cause; nor can they observe equity in the imposing of penance, if they declare their sins in kind only, and not rather in species, and in special detail. From which it is rightly inferred that penitents must enumerate in confession all the mortal sins of which, after diligent self-examination, they are conscious, even the most hidden, including those which are only committed against the last two precepts of the Decalogue; which sometimes wound the soul more seriously, and are more dangerous than those which are manifested openly.[118]

Here we see a firm foundation that not only were sins to be confessed to a priest, but also in great detail, not omitting the particulars by simply stating the categories in which they sinned, but by offering details that would assist the priest to lead them to a full confession.

While Luther and Calvin had argued against confession being a sacrament, let alone a sacrament instituted by Christ himself, the council took the opposing position, claiming not only the authority of the Church to offer sacramental confession, but also the antiquity of the practice. The interpretation of the Bible verses contended by Luther and Calvin concerning the authority of the clergy or the commissioning of them by Christ to "bind and loose" is here defined clearly. The priests are called "vicars of himself, presidents and judges, to whom all mortal crimes might be brought...that by the power of the keys, they should pronounce the sentence of remission or retention of sins."[119]

It should be of note that it is this language of the Council of Trent which has made its way into the Catechism of the Catholic Church, and

---

[118] Decrees, Tanner, 705-706.

[119] Ibid.

has been the standard interpretation of the Roman Catholic Church on these matters from the Council of Trent until today. The Catechism, which began to be assembled in 1564, was expanded greatly over several centuries and ultimately published in English in 1995. However, even the current edition retains much of the exact same material as the Council of Trent, expounding the practice over some twenty one pages. The summary of the Catechism, offered below, offers us a brief outline of the teaching, and demonstrates the position the Catholic Church has retained over five hundred years later:

IN BRIEF

1485 "On the evening of that day, the first day of the week," Jesus showed himself to his apostles. "He breathed on them, and said to them: 'Receive the Holy Spirit. If you forgive the sins of any, they are forgiven, if you retain the sins of any, they are retained." (John 20:19, 22-23).

1486 The forgiveness of sins committed after baptism is conferred by a particular sacrament called the sacrament of conversion, confession, penance, or reconciliation.

1487 The sinner wounds God's honor and love, his own human dignity as a man called to be a son of God, the spiritual well-being of the Church, of which each Christian ought to be a living stone.

1488 To the eyes of faith no evil is greater than sin and nothing has worse consequences for sinners themselves, for the Church, and for the whole world.

1489 To return to communion with God after having lost it through sin is a process born of the grace of God which is rich in mercy and solicitous for the salvation of men. One must ask for this precious gift for oneself, and for others.

1490 The movement of return to God, called conversion and repentance, entails sorrow for and abhorrence of sins committed, and the firm purpose of sinning no more in the future. Conversion touches the past and the future and is nourished by hope in God's mercy.

1491 The sacrament of Penance is whole consisting in three actions of the penitent and the priest's absolution. The penitents acts are repentance, confession or disclosure of sins to the priest, and the intention to make reparation and do works of reparation.

1492 Repentance (also called contrition) must be inspired by motives that arise from faith. If repentance arises from love of charity for God, it is called "perfect" contrition; if it is founded on other motives, it is called "imperfect."

1493 One who desires to obtain reconciliation with God and with the Church, must confess to a priest all the un-confessed grave sins he remembers after having carefully examined his conscience. The confession of venial faults, without being necessary in itself, is nevertheless strongly recommended by the Church.

1494 The confessor proposes the performance of certain acts of "satisfaction" or "penance" to be performed by the penitent in order to repair the harm caused by sin and to re-establish habits befitting a disciple of Christ.

1495 Only priests who have received the faculty of absolving from the authority of the Church can forgive sins in the name of Christ.

1496 The spiritual effects of the sacrament of Penance are:
—reconciliation with God by which the penitent recovers grace;
—reconciliation with the Church;
—remission of the eternal punishment incurred by mortal sins;
—remission, at least in part, of temporal punishments resulting from sin;
—peace and serenity of conscience, and spiritual consolation;
—an increase of spiritual strength for the Christian battle.

1497 Individual and integral confession of grave sins followed by absolution remains the only ordinary means of reconciliation with God and with the Church.

1498 Through indulgences the faithful can obtain the remission of temporal punishment resulting from sin for themselves and also for the souls in Purgatory. [120]

---

[120] Catechism of the Catholic Church Doubleday, New York. 1995. 415-417.

Here, centuries later, we can see that the Catechism retains much of the exact same language as the Council of Trent, although expounded theologically over many pages in an apologetic style. The content contains little variance, and little influence from the continental reformers, other than cementing the position of the Roman Catholic Church, and perhaps some elaboration on the "elements" of the sacrament for the sake of argument against the reformers. Otherwise, the language of Trent remains, for the most part, intact in the pages of the Roman Catechism.

CHAPTER SIX
Confession in Anglicanism from
The Reformation to Now

Anglicanism, which finds its root in what Luther called the *Romanist Church* of the sixteenth century, undoubtedly retains much of the character of its mother church. From theology to liturgy, we, as Anglicans, have a western and distinctively Roman heritage. However, in theology and practice, we have not remained so over the last five hundred years. Anglicanism today is divided within itself, containing simultaneously extreme Catholic and Protestant veins. This chapter will endeavor to point out the highlights in Anglican theology, as well as in liturgy, beginning after the writing of King Henry VIII, already discussed, until now.

Theology

Defining "Anglican Theology" can be tricky for many, as most Anglicans are not well versed in the writings of Anglican theologians. This is not really all that surprising, considering that there are so few well-known Anglican theologians, and few among them are of harmonious thought in doctrine or praxis. Truly, how does one define an "Anglican Theologian?" The Church of England witnessed so many violent transitions from Catholicism to Puritanism and back, to somewhere in between, in the course of only a few generations. The effects of these transitions have left their mark, and it is most difficult to settle on any purely defined "Anglican" faith beyond a general sense of what the Church expressed in the creeds of the conciliar period. For the sake of this study, we shall attempt to define the parameters by examining the writing among those who wrote in and of the Church in England, between 1500 and 1900, particularly at the end of the sixteenth century, and as affected by the doctrinal development defined by the Council of Trent. Among the so-called "Anglican Divines" of this period, the first two names that come forward are John Jewel (1522-1571), and Richard Hooker (1554-1600). We will then highlight a few citations from less well-known Anglican theologians on this subject. The writings of Thomas Cranmer will be reserved to the following section on liturgy.

John Jewell

John Jewell's career spanned a tumultuous time in the Church of England. His career witnessed the brief reign of Edward VI, the nine-day reign of Jane Grey, the bloody reign of Mary with the return of Catholicism, and the transition from that most bloody time to Elizabethan spirituality. Throughout Jewell's lifetime the hostilities within the Church over these matters of confession and Roman authority burned hotly. Reluctantly chosen as Bishop of Salisbury in 1559, Jewel set about to prepare the Church of England for the Elizabethan settlement, which included the *Statutes of Supremacy and Authority* recently adopted, and to engage anyone that was willing to confront him in an open debate concerning what he saw as the abuses of the Catholic Church concerning the antiquity of the practices promulgated by Rome, including: private Mass, communion in one kind, prayers in a foreign tongue, the Pope as the head of the Church, Christ as substantially present in the Eucharist, transubstantiation, the use of images in worship, and so on. In short, Jewell challenged the so-called "antiquity" or "Biblical grounding" for the many revisions made by the Roman church during the Council of Trent and in the years leading up to it, which revisions had found wide-spread use in many English churches during the reign of Mary.

In short, at the time Jewell was contending for the faith of the Church of England, the spirituality, discipline, and theology of the

Churches in England was far from contiguous. In an attempt to publically address some of these issues, Jewell was enticed to write an anonymous letter to promulgate his thoughts, titled: *The letter of a certain Englishman, in which is asserted the consensus of true religion, doctrine, and ceremonies in England, against the empty scoffing of some who try to impugn the truth in their sermons to the simple people.* In this text he describes the clergy of the Church of England, saying that:

> They are split into factions and sects by partialities and arguments; that among us nothing is certain; that there is agreement neither of bishops among themselves, nor preachers, nor ministers of the church, nor individual men, either about doctrine or about ceremonies; that everyone makes his own church for himself according to his whim.[121]

It is clear, even at the time of Jewell, things were much then as they are now: there was no uniformity of doctrine, teaching, preaching, liturgy, or any practices universally known to the Church among all of the clergy and parishes. Each local clergyman interpreted things as they saw fit, and divergent practices kept people from uniting on theological or practical grounds.

His *Apology* was long in the making, and postponed a few times due to political climate and a continuous need to address more and more issues of contention within the Church. Jewell's text was an attempt to explain, in a clear and uniform way, the polity of the Church of England at a time when there was much need for clarity on where the country stood as a whole in the light of Trent, and in an ever unbalanced state of Roman and Protestant tensions. Now, concerning "auricular confession," as he briefly called it in this text, Jewel had much to say. The context of his teaching on confession is seated in an argument refuting the power of the Pope to be the sole mediator of certain issues of sin, which was a popular teaching of the Roman Church reaching back into the medieval period. In this context, Jewell expounded, as he saw it,

---

[121] An Apology of the Church of England by John Jewell, ed. by J.E. Booty. Cornell University Press, Ithica, New York, 1963. 19.

the Church of England's teaching on the clergy's role in hearing and guiding confessions:

> Moreover, we say that Christ hath given to His ministers power to bind, to loose, to open, to shut. And that the office of loosing consisteth in this point: that the minister should either offer by the preaching of the Gospel the merits of Christ and full pardon, to such as have lowly and contrite hearts, and do unfeignedly repent themselves, pronouncing unto the same a sure and undoubted forgiveness of their sins, and hope of everlasting salvation: or else that the same minister, when any have offended their brothers' minds with a great offence, with a notable and open fault, whereby they have, as it were, banished and made themselves strangers from the common fellowship, and from the body of Christ; then after perfect amendment of such persons, doth reconcile them, and bring them home again, and restore them to the company and unity of the faithful. We say also, that the minister doth execute the authority of binding and shutting, as often as he shutteth up the gate of the kingdom of heaven against the unbelieving and stubborn persons, denouncing unto them God's vengeance, and everlasting punishment: or else, when he doth quite shut them out from the bosom of the Church by open excommunication. Out of doubt, what sentence soever the minister of God shall give in this sort, God Himself doth so well allow of it, that whatsoever here in earth by their means is loosed and bound, God Himself will loose and bind, and confirm the same in heaven.

> Moreover, that Christ's disciples did receive this authority, not that they should hear the private confessions of the people and listen to their whisperings, as the common massing-priests do everywhere nowadays, and do it so, as though in that one point lay all the virtue and use of the keys: but to the end they should go, they should teach, they should publish abroad the Gospel, and be unto the believing a sweet savour of life unto life, and unto the unbelieving and unfaithful a savour of death unto death; and that the minds of godly persons being brought low by the remorse of their former life and errors, after they once began to look up unto the light of the Gospel, and believe in Christ, might be opened with the Word of God, even as a door is opened with a key. Contrariwise, that the wicked and willful folk, and such as would not believe, nor return into the right way, should be left still as fast locked, and shut up, and, as St. Paul saith, "wax worse and worse." This take we to be the meaning of the keys.[122]

---

[122] Ibid, 26-28. (emphasis added)

Clearly, Jewell's understanding of confession in the Church of England was one in which the priest was a spiritual guide, possessing the power, "according to the keys" of binding and loosing, of offering absolution for sins "to such as have lowly and contrite hearts, and do unfeignedly repent themselves, pronouncing unto the same a sure and undoubted forgiveness of their sins, and hope of everlasting salvation." It seems Jewell was not in favor of private auricular confession as it was taught by the Romanists, the manner of which he does not here expound upon, but that he was in favor of confession, and that the clergy did in fact have the power to offer absolution to their people. Jewell's portrayal of confession seems in every sense to be public; and he seems, as Calvin did, to long for the confession of the Early Church, in which people were excommunicated for a time, and restored over time through public repentance. One might say that Jewell believed in the power of the clergy to forgive sins on behalf of the Church, and to be commissioned as such to do so. However, he does not limit repentance of sins to this process, per se, as the Fourth Lateran council had, and which Trent continued to uphold. Here, he outlines the process, but does not limit it to a context within the Church. Interestingly enough, he also emphasizes the power of the clergy to bind those who are stubborn in clinging to their sins. This, Jewell taught, was in opposition to the point that the Pope claimed authority to retain absolution in certain cases unto his own discretion. Jewell does not appear to be opposed to the confessional process itself, so much as the reservation of the power to those who have, according to him, given themselves this power to reserve certain sins to the pontiff. In no place does Jewell address, denounce, or refute the indulgences, pilgrimages, or other things which accompanied the "satisfaction" realm of the Roman confession. However he does affirm the genuineness of absolution of the contrite heart, and the power of the clergy to pronounce this absolution. Jewell's confessional is an interesting hybrid, as one would expect of Anglicanism, of Protestant ideals with the authority of the clergy to absolve sinners provided they are contrite. In Book III of his apology, Jewell addresses "auricular confession" only briefly, and in doing so, only to state that even among the Romanists, there was dissention on the matter:

> Why say the canonists, that auricular confession is appointed by the positive law of man: and the schoolmen contrariwise, that it is appointed by the law of God? Why doth Albertus Pighius dissent from Cajetanus? Why doth Thomas dissent from Lombardus, Scotus from Thomas, Occamus from Scotus, Alliacensis from Occamus?[123]

Jewell considered it sufficient to state that even among the Romans, there was dissention over whether it was a law of man, or of God. He does not expound, as Hooker will, on the distinction.

Richard Hooker

Richard Hooker (1554-1600) wrote exhaustively on this subject, as it is the primary topic of Book VI of *On the Laws of Ecclesiastical Polity*. The contexts of Hooker's discourse on the subject of penance is, as it is on other subjects, nestled in what he viewed as the natural laws infused by God into his creation. He argues in favor of penance as a practice natural to the need of all men to be reconciled to God, yet he does not believe that the Romanist view of penance as a sacrament holds up to the measure of natural law. In this text, Hooker finds himself arguing against two contrary systems, as is the natural Anglican way. He refutes the overly doctrinal arguments of Lateran IV and Trent, but he also refutes the practices that arose in Geneva under the influence of John Calvin. By this time the Church system established by Calvin, which was composed of a leadership which was two-thirds lay-led and one-third clergy led, had been well-established and apparently allowed for some lay-leaders to bear the judgment of penances instead of the clergy. Hooker argued in favor of the natural order for clergy to bear this responsibility, yet he also argued against the Roman system which held that only the local clergyman was permitted to "bind or loose" penitents from their sins, and that certain sins were retained to the bishop or

---

[123] Ibid, 45-46

pope. What follows are a few citations which outline Hooker's belief and teaching on this practice.

Concerning the ecclesiastical governance as set forth in Geneva, Hooker writes:

> Notwithstanding whether they [the Calvinists] saw it necessary for them so to persuade the people, without whose help they can do nothing; or else, the affection which they bare towards this new form of government made them to imagine it God's own ordinance, their doctrine is, "that by the law of God, there must be forever in all congregations certain lay-elders, ministers of ecclesiastical jurisdiction," inasmuch as our Lord and Savior by testimony (for so they presume) hath left all ministers or pastors in the Church executors equally to the whole power of spiritual jurisdiction, and with them hath joined the people as colleagues.[124]

Hooker explains that this system seems to have two advantages: the people seem to like it, and if someone contradicts the leadership, this system defends them under the premise of "divine authority." However, he argues that majority rule has not always worked out so well in the past:

> Now, on the contrary side, if this their surmise prove false; if such, as in justification whereof no evidence sufficient hath been or can be alleged, let them consider whether the words of Corah, Dathan, and Abiram against Moses and Aaron, "It is too much that ye take upon you, seeing that the congregation is holy," be not the very true abstract and abridgement of all their published Admonitions, Demonstrations, Supplications, and Treatises whatsoever, whereby they have labored to void the rooms of their superiors before authorized, and to advance the new fancied scepter by lay prebyterial power... by this therefore, we see a manifest difference acknowledged between the power of Ecclesiastical order, and the power of Jurisdiction ecclesiastical.[125]

Contrary to this consideration, Hooker defends the premise that the Church was established by God, and as such, these lay-people do not have the power to institute something which Christ did not institute.

---

[124] Of the Laws of Ecclesiastical Polity by Richard Hooker, ed. by P.G. Stanwood. Harvard University Press, Cambridge, Massachusetts. 1981. Book VI, 2-3.

[125] Ibid, 3-4.

The spiritual power of the Church being such as neither can be challenged by right of nature, nor could by human authority be instituted, because the forces and effects thereof are supernatural and divine; we are to make no doubt or question, but that from him which is the Head it hath descended to us that are the body now invested therewith. He gave it for the benefit and good of souls, as a means to keep them within the path which leadeth unto endless felicity, a bridle to hold them within their due and convenient bounds, and if they go astray, a forcible help to reclaim them. Now although there be no kind of spiritual power, for which our Lord Jesus Christ did not give both commission to exercise, and direction how to use the same, although his laws in that behalf recorded by the holy evangelists be the only ground and foundation, whereupon the practice of the Church must sustain itself: yet, as all multitudes, once grown to form societies, are even thereby naturally warranted to enforce upon their own subjects particularly those things which public wisdom shall judge expedient for the common good: so it were absurd to imagine the Church itself, the most glorious amongst them, abridged this liberty...in sum, often to vary, alter, and change customs incident to the manner of exercising that power which doth itself continue always one and the same. I therefore conclude that spiritual authority is a power which Christ hath given to be used over them which are subject unto it for the eternal good of their souls, according to his own most sacred laws and wholesome positive constitutions of his Church.[126]

Here we see Hooker defending the divine authority of the Church over institutions or societies created by men, although acknowledging that the church, being such a large institution, has a natural tendency to create things that help us govern our people expediently, and thereby to stretch the bounds of scriptural warrants toward that which seems necessary to this end.

Now, as to what Hooker sees at the ideal divine command of Jesus on this subject, Hooker explains:

Seeing then that the chiefest cause of spiritual direction is to provide for the health and safety of men's souls, by bringing them to see and repent their grievous offenses committed against God, as also to reform all injuries offered with the breach of Christian love and charity, towards their brethren, in matters of ecclesiastical cognizance; the use of this power shall by so much the plainer appear, if first the nature of repentance itself be known.

---

[126] Ibid, 4-5.

We are by repentance to appease him whom we have offended by sin. For which cause, whereas all sins deprive us of our favor of Almighty God, our way of reconciliation with him is the inward secret repentance of the heart; which inward repentance alone sufficeth, unless some special thing, in the quality of sin committed, or in the party who hath done amiss, require more. For besides our submission in God's sight, repentance must not only proceed to the private contestation of men, if the sin be a crime injurious; but also further, where the wholesome discipline of God's Church exacteth a more exemplary and open satisfaction...repentance being therefore either in the sight of God alone, or else with the notice also of men: without the one, sometimes thoroughly performed, by practiced more or less, in our daily devotions and prayers, we have no remedy for any fault. The virtue of repentance in the heart of man is God's handiwork, a fruit of divine grace.[127]

Hooker gets to the heart of the most common question offered by parties on both sides of this confessional argument: "Is confession to God alone, in the heart sufficient for forgiveness?" Hooker's answer is, sometimes *yes*, and sometimes *no*. It depends on the nature of the sin, and who was offended. Sometimes people can confess to God the sins they have committed against Him and their own souls, while criminal endeavors or those which have been committed against the community often require discipline, accountability, and a process of restoring the sinner to the community or the Church through the penitential discipline of those commissioned by God to perform them on behalf of God and the Church.

While Hooker was in favor of genuine confession, and he believed the power of "the keys" when it comes to the divine authority of the priesthood, he was not in favor of the Roman system of confession, particularly as defined by the Fourth Lateran Council, or by the Council of Trent. First, to define what he supported in the natural order and "power of the keys," Hooker explains:

Our Lord and Saviour in the sixteenth chapter of St. Matthew's Gospel giveth to the Apostles regiment in general over God's Church. For they that have the keys of the kingdom of heaven are thereby signified to be stewards of the house of God, under whom they guide, command, judge, and correct

---

his family. The souls of men are God's treasure, committed to the trust and fidelity of such as must render a strict account for the very least which is under their custody. God hath not invested them with the power to make a revenue thereof, but to use it for the good of them whom Jesus Christ hath most dearly bought.[128]

Hooker gives a not-so-subtle defense against indulgences or any financial gain for the Church beyond the readmission of a soul once lost to sin, saying above, "He hath not invested them (the Clergy) with power to make a revenue thereof." He goes on to explain that with the power of the keys also come the powers of ecclesiastical discipline, which sometimes result in the excommunication of rebellious persons which refuse to obey. He then goes on to demonstrate how this power did not stop with the Apostles, but is handed down through the Apostolic Succession:

> Furthermore, lest their acts should be slenderly accounted of, or had in contempt, whether they admit to the fellowship of saints or seclude from it, whether they bind offenders or set them again at liberty, whether they remit or retain sins, whatsoever is done by way of orderly and lawful proceeding, the Lord himself hath promised to ratify. This is that grand original warrant, by force whereof the guides and prelates in God's Church, first his Apostles, and afterwards others following them successively, did both use and uphold that discipline, the end whereof is to heal men's consciences, to cure their sins, to reclaim offenders from iniquity, and to make them by repentance just.[129]

Hooker is surprisingly in concert with Calvin on one point, in that both were in favor of a confessional process, although Calvin extended this authority to the lay-elders also. Yet both of them hearkened to, and yearned for a return of the penitential discipline of the Patristic period, with the practices of public confession, and a public re-admission of sinners after a time of public penance, followed by a restoration of the excommunicated penitent to the Church in a public laying on of hands. Concerning this, Hooker briefly states:

---

[128] Ibid, 12-13.

[129] Ibid, 12-13.

The course of discipline in former ages reformed open transgressions by putting them into offices of open repentance; especially confession, whereby they declared their own crimes in the hearing of the whole Church, and were not from the first time of their first convention capable of the holy mysteries of Christ, until they had solemnly discharged this duty.[130]

Both Hooker and Calvin were also in concert against the practices of the Roman Church of requiring certain aspects of satisfaction for the forgiveness of sins, and in the three-fold requirement of: contrition, confession, and satisfaction. Here, their theologies find much common ground. Both define the trend leading toward the private confession of sins that took place between the patristic period, and the Fourth Lateran Council, with Lateran beginning the usurping of practice in the Latin Church, and the formulation of the requirements for regular private confession to one's own priest, as has already been defined in depth. Concerning this transition, and the definition to follow at the Council of Trent, Hooker expounds:

Instead whereof, when once private and secret confession had taken place with the Latins, it continued as a profitable ordinance, till the Lateran Council had decreed, that all men once in a year at the least should confess themselves to the priest. So that being made a just thing both general and necessary, the next degree of estimation whereunto it grew, was to be honored and lifted up to the nature of a sacrament, that as Christ did institute Baptism to give life, and the Eucharist to nourish life, so Penitency might be thought a sacrament ordained to recover life, and confession a part of the sacrament...Now, although they have only external repentance for a sacrament, internal for a virtue, yet they make sacramental repentance nevertheless to be composed of three parts: contrition, confession, and satisfaction: which is absurd; because contrition, being an outward thing, belongeth to the virtue and not the sacrament of repentance, which must consist of external parts, of the nature thereof be external. Besides, which is more absurd, they leave out absolution; whereas some of their school divines, handling penance in the nature of a sacrament, and being not able to espy the least resemblance of a sacrament save only in the absolution (for a sacrament by their doctrine must both signify and also confer or bestow some special divine grace), resolved themselves, that the duties of

---

[130] Ibid, 13-14.

the penitent could be but merely preparations to the sacrament, and that the sacrament itself was wholly in absolution. [131]

Hooker's argument against this process being a sacrament as defined above, emphasized that the absolution, which is the end of this sacrament, is not defined by the Romans who sought to define it as such, but rather that they omitted it. It was left to the later School-men or apologists to explain that the three-fold order of confession were the steps leading to the true sacrament, which was the absolution of the sin.

In summary, Hooker's position is somewhat of a hybrid of Reformed theology, in that he upholds the authority of "the keys" of the Apostolic priesthood to absolve sinners, and to retain sins of those who refute the authority or discipline of the Church, yet he contends against the nature of this process as a sacrament, arguing that most of the factors required for the sacrament are external, while in confession the elements are largely internal and, therefore, difficult to define purely as a sacrament. Hooker upholds the need for a communal discipline within the Church, with the public confession of sins as a natural or divine law of God expressed in nature and in the Church. Like Calvin, he is in favor of restoring the practices of the Church to those of antiquity, and of the abolition of the process of confession and absolution under which the retentions of sins led to the abuses that came with the confessional requirements of Lateran IV and Trent. Hooker states, summarily,

> They are of the two happier therefore that can content and satisfy themselves by judging discreetly what they perform, and soundly what God doth require of them ... that to frustrate men's confessions and considerations of men, is a merciless extremity, and to shut up the doors of mercy against penitents which come short thereof in the devotion of their prayers, in the continuance of their fasts, in the largeness and bounty of their alms, or in the course of and other like duties, is more than God himself thought meet, and consequently more than mortal men should presume to do. That which God doth chiefly respect in men's penitency, is their hearts. The heart is it which maketh repentance sincere, sincerity that which findeth favour in God's sight, and the favour with which supplieth by gracious acceptation

---

[131] Ibid, 15-16.

whatsoever may seem defective in the faithful, hearty, and true offices of his servants.[132]

Other Anglican Citations

Anglican authors writing since the time of Jewell and Hooker take several positions on auricular confession. The following are a few survey quotations from various Anglican authors on the subject beginning in the seventeenth century and carrying on to the nineteenth century.

Jeremy Taylor (1613-1667) wrote several influential pieces on confession, faith, and repentance within the context of his works, most notably: *Unum Necessarium*, containing an article called *Of Ecclesiastical Penance and Confession*, and one of his most famous texts: *Holy Living and Holy Dying*. Taylor's interpretation of James on confession is yet another amalgamation of varying thoughts. While some, like Luther and Calvin, contended that it meant that Christians should confess to other Christians, and others such as Hooker and Jewell contended for confession to the clergy (albeit outside of the Roman-prescribed process), Taylor asserts both in the same paragraph. In *Unum Necessarium* Taylor writes:

> Confession of sins is so necessary a duty that in all scriptures it is the immediate preface to pardon: that in all ages of the Gospel it hath been taught and practiced; that it is by all churches esteemed a duty necessary to be done in cases of a troubled conscience; that St. James gives an express precept that we Christians should confess our sins to each other, that is, Christian to Christian, brother to brother, and the people to their minister: and that the ministers of the gospel are the ministers of reconciliation and are commanded to restore such persons as are overtaken in a fault, if they make cognizance of the fault.

> The Spiritual man is appointed to restore us and to pray for us and to receive our confessions and to inquire into or wounds, and to infuse holy oil and remedy and to pronounce pardon: if we be cut off from the communion of the faithful by our own demerits, their holy hands must reconcile us and give us peace; they are our appointed comforters, our instructors, our ordinary judges. [133]

---

[132] Ibid, 106.

[133] Jeremy Taylor: Selected Works ed. by Thomas K. Carroll. Paulist Press, New York. 1990. 274-275.

In one sense, Taylor "splits the difference" and appeals to both sides of the argument, allowing for public confession, while also commending private confession to a priest.

The anonymously submitted text *The Whole Duty of Man,* published in London in 1684, speaks of confession in the context of things to be done before receiving Holy Communion. This text argues in favor of going to a priest for confession, based on the grounds that we are likely to be loose judges of ourselves. To this, the author suggests,

> I would, as I said before, exhort him not to trust his own judgment, but to make known his case to some discreet and godly Minister, and rather be guided by his [judgment], who will probably be better to judge of him than he of himself. This is the counsel the church gives in the Exhortation before the Communion, where it is advised that if any by other means there forementioned "cannot quiet his own conscience, but require further counsel and comfort, let him go to some discreet and learned Minister of God's Word and open his grief, that he may receive such ghostly counsel, advice, and comfort that his conscience may be relieved, etc." This is surely such advice as should not be neglected, neither at the time of coming to the Sacrament nor any other when we are under any fear or reasons of doubt concerning the state of our souls.[134]

Francis White, writing in 1624, wrote a text entitled *A Reply to Jesuit Fisher's Answer to Certain Questions Propounded by His Most Gracious Majesty, King James,* in which he explains the difference between "Papal" confession and the practice of the Church of England:

> The difference between the Papals and us in this question is not about the thing itself, considered without abuses, but concerning the manner and also the obligation and necessity thereof.

> First, they require of all persons, being of age, a private and distinct confession of all and every known mortal sin, open and secret, of outward deed and inward consent, together with the circumstances thereof, through obscene and odious to Christian ears, to be made a least annually to some Roman priest authorized.

---

[134] Anglicanism ed. by Paul E. More and Frank L. Cross. Morehouse Publishing Co., Milwaukee, Wisconsin. 1935. 513.

Secondly, our tenet is that auricular confession is not absolutely necessary to remission of sins after baptism, neither is the same generally in respect of all persons commanded or imposed by divine Law, and the rigorous urging thereof according to the Popish Doctrine is not Orthodox or Catholic faith. Neither is Penance a Sacrament of the New Testament like unto Baptism and the Holy Eucharist.

The true ends of private confession are these which follow: first, to inform, instruct, and counsel Christian people in their particular actions. Secondly, if they be delinquents, to reprove them and make them understand the danger of their sin. Thirdly, to comfort those that are afflicted, and truly penitent, and to assure them of remission of sins by the word of Absolution. Fourthly, to prepare people to the worth receiving of the Holy Communion.

And if private confession be referred and used to these ends it is a work of godly discipline, consonant to the Holy Scripture and anciently practiced by the Primitive Church. Bishops and Ministers of the Church are Shepherds, Stewards, and Overseers of God's people committed to their charge. They have received the keys of the Kingdom of Heaven and power to loose and bind sinners.

If Christian people must confess their sins and acknowledge their faults to one another, then also when there is a cause, why should they not do the same to the Pastors of their souls?[135]

White clearly saw private confession as optional, but as a good and proper thing to do.

Bishop John Cosin (1594-1672), writing in his *Notes and Collections on the Book of Common Prayer,* which was published in 1710 after his death, wrote concerning confession:

The Church of England howsoever holdeth not Confession and Absolution Sacramental, that is made unto and received from a Priest, to be absolutely necessary, as without there can be no remission of sins, yet by this place it is manifest what she teacheth concerning the virtue and force of this sacred action. The confession is commanded to be special. The Absolution is the same that the ancient Church and the present Church of Rome useth ... The truth is, that in the Priest's Absolution there is the true power and virtue of forgiveness, which will most certainly take effect, Nisi ponitur obex, as in Baptism.[136]

---

[135] Ibid, 514-515.

[136] Ibid, 515-516.

From these brief samples, we witness the overall understanding of the Church of England at this time to be one where confession of sins was optional, yet commended for guilty souls, particularly before receiving the Eucharist. These authors all seem to understand that confession was ancient, and useful, yet not according to the requirements of the Roman Church after Trent, and none of them consider confession to be a sacrament. In the midst of the Puritan age, which accompanied many of these writings, the writing of the Church of England is fairly anti-Roman, although it is most interesting that even among those who sought to put away the practices of confession promulgated by the Council of Trent, there remains a desire for the antiquity of the confessional system, and the endurance of clerical or "godly" guidance for souls in need of assistance achieving true repentance.

The Oxford Movement (1833-1845) of the nineteenth century sought to define the theology of the Church of England on historically catholic terms. It was an attempt to revive the historic faith and worship of the Church through sermons, articles, and tracts distributed for the stimulation of thought and sacramental practice. Several of the tracts address confession and penance and demonstrate the perceived theology of the Church of England, at least in Oxford, at a time of this theological revival.

Tract 71, which was written anonymously, was titled *On the Controversy with the Romanists,* in which the author lists several grievances with the Roman church. The third grievance is as follows, regarding confession:

3. The Necessity of Confession.

By the council of Trent, every member of the Church must confess himself to a priest once a year at least. This confession extends to all mortal sins, that is, to all sins which either are done willingly or are of any magnitude. Without this confession, which must be accompanied by hearty sorrow for the things confessed, no one can be partaker of the Holy Communion. Here is a third obstacle in the way of our receiving the grace of the Sacraments in the Roman Church, which surely requires our diligent examination, before it be passed over. That there is no such impediment sanctioned in

Scripture, is plain, yet to believe in it is a point of faith with the Romanist. The practice is grievous enough; but it is not enough to submit to it; you must believe that it is part of the gospel doctrine, or you are committing one of those mortal sins which are to be confessed; and you must believe, moreover, that every one who does not believe it, is excluded from the hope of salvation. But, not to dwell on the belief in the necessity of confession itself, consider the number of points of faith which the Church of Rome has set up. You must believe every one of them; if you have allowed yourself to doubt any one of them, you must repent of it, and confess it to the priest. If you knowingly omit any one such doubt you have entertained, and much more if you still cherish it, your confession is worse than useless; nay, such conduct is considered sacrilege, or the sin against the Holy Ghost. Further, if, under such circumstances, you partake of the Communion, it is a partaking of it unworthily to your condemnation.[137]

The primary grievance, in addition to the process itself which the author states is not scripturally warranted, is the fact that if one did not agree with the Roman system, that too was a sin, and had to be confessed.

In the controversial *Tract 90*, which was written by John Henry Newman (1801-1890) on the Feast of the Conversion of St. Paul in 1841, Newman addressed the teaching of the Catechism on the Sacraments. In this context, he writes briefly of penance within a grouping of the other five sacraments in section seven of the tract concerning Article XXV of the 39 Articles:

7. The Sacraments

Article XXV—"*Those five, commonly called Sacraments, that is to say, Confirmation, Penance, Orders, Matrimony, and Extreme Unction, are not to be counted for Sacraments of the Gospel, being such as have grown, partly of the corrupt following of the Apostles, partly from states of life allowed in the Scriptures; but yet have not like nature of sacraments with Baptism and the LORD'S Supper, for that they have not any visible sign or ceremony ordained of GOD.*"

This Articles does not deny the five rites in question to be sacraments, but to be sacraments in the sense in which Baptism and the Lord's Supper are

---

[137] "Tract 71." Accessed March 9th, 2013. http://www.anglicanhistory.org/tracts/tract71.html

sacraments; "sacraments of the Gospel," sacraments with an outward sign ordained of God.

They are not sacraments in any sense, unless the Church has the power of dispensing grace through rites of its own appointing, or is endued with the gift of blessing and hallowing the "rites or ceremonies" which, according to the Twentieth Article, it "hath power to decree." But we may well believe that the Church has this gift.

If, then, a sacrament be merely an outward sign of an invisible grace under it, the five rites may be sacraments; but if it must be an outward sign ordained by GOD or CHRIST, then only Baptism and the LORD'S Supper are sacraments.

Another definition of the word sacrament, which equally succeeds in limiting it to the two principal rites of the Christian Church, is also contained in the Catechism, as well as alluded to in the above passage:— "Two only, as generally necessary to salvation, Baptism and the Supper of the LORD." On this subject the following remark has been made:—

The Roman Catholic considers that there are seven [sacraments]; we do not strictly determine the number. We define the word generally to be an "outward sign of an inward grace," without saying to how many ordinances this applies. However, what we do determine is, that CHRIST has ordained two special sacraments, as generally necessary to salvation. This, then is the characteristic mark of those two, separating them from all other whatever; and this is nothing else but saying in other words that they are the only justifying rites, or instruments of communicating the Atonement, which is the one thing necessary to us. Ordination, for instance, gives power, yet without making the soul acceptable to God; Confirmation gives light and strength, yet is the mere completion of Baptism; and Absolution may be viewed as a negative ordinance removing the barrier which sin has raised between us and that grace, which by inheritance is ours. But the two sacraments "of the Gospel," as they may be emphatically styled, are the instruments of inward life, according to our LORD'S declaration, that Baptism is a new birth, and that in the Eucharist we eat the living bread.[138]

---

[138] "Tract 90." Accessed March 9th, 2013. http://www.anglicanhistory.org/tracts/tract90/fulltext.html

Here, Newman introduces a thought which he perceives to be supported by the wording of the Catechism, in which Baptism and Eucharist are undoubtedly sacraments, while the others are still somewhat sacraments (albeit not instituted of Christ or God in the scriptures), depending on the definition of "sacrament". Although Newman concedes that the Church of England does not strictly number the sacraments as the Roman Church does.

Edward Pusey (1800-1882) who was considered the leader of the Oxford Movement, or the Tractarian Movement, largely because of his seniority in age and reputation among the others, wrote several times on confession. These writings were not, however, numbered among the tracts. In a sermon entitled *Entire Absolution of a Penitent,* preached at Oxford on the First Sunday of Advent in 1861, Pusey defends penance and confession by any means the penitent truly and humbly makes them, while uplifting private confession for the troubled soul:

> In my last sermon, I dwelt upon that authoritative act, whereby God, through the ministry of man, conveys His own sentence of pardon to the soul of the penitent, sets him free from the guilt of his past sins, opens to the blessed influx of His grace the channels which sin had stopped, and often pours at once large grace and love into the soul. But, since the efficacy of Absolution depends upon the penitence of him who receives it, the deeper that penitence, the fuller will be the grace. And so, since special confession, gathering into one before the soul all its greater sins, until it shrinks and recoils and sickens at the miserable sight, mostly brings with it a lowlier self-abhorrence, deepens its cry for mercy, and issues in greater love for Him Who loved it amid such loathsomeness and misery, special confession will mostly obtain more grace and have more assurance of pardon. And this I say, not (God forbid!) to lessen the comfort of such as have not been led by Him to desire any other than the general Absolution of all true penitents in the whole congregation, when confession has been made to God only, but as a source of increased comfort to laden or anxious souls who feel that they need what is more special to themselves. The Church (I am compelled to repeat) allows us both ways. In particular cases, she recommends special Confession, and Absolution in form more authoritative. For in the Visitation of the Sick, she directs her Priests to "move the sick person to

make a special confession of his sins, if he feel his conscience troubled with any weighty matter.[139]

Here, Pusey asserts that, "the Church allows us both ways," demonstrating again that confession was seen as useful, but not necessary to the piety of the penitent in the Church of England in the nineteenth century. Dr. Pusey only refers to Penance as a sacrament once in this text, although he defends the understanding that absolution is offered by God alone, and that the clergy are only mediators of the sacrament to the people:

> The Church, our Mother, would not bring all her children, with their varied tempers, needs, languishings, sicknesses, under one rigid, unbending, rule. She shows, in the Exhortation to Holy Communion, that she would deal, not with laden consciences only, but with timorous, scrupulous, doubting, tender, souls, the lambs of the flock of Christ, otherwise than she would with those who seem to themselves, or are, the strong or the whole. One thing only she excludes, when she excludes any thing, compulsory confession; "any man should be bound to the numbering of his sins;" "as if," adds Hooker, "remission of sins otherwise were impossible." But, short of this, in that Exhortation, she strives, with an austere, anxious love, to rouse the conscience, not only as to overt, but as to secret, mental, sins, "if any of you be in malice, envy, or any other grievous crime;" and then, after words, which may well shake the soul through and through, "lest after taking of that Holy Sacrament, the devil enter into you, as he entered into Judas, and fill you full of all iniquities, and bring you to destruction both of body and soul," she straightway insists on the necessity of "a quiet conscience," and invites such as cannot otherwise quiet theirs, to open their griefs, that by the ministry of God's Holy Word, they may receive the benefit of absolution. "By the ministry," she says, "of God's Word, for," (as I said more at large before,) "all forgiveness of sin, by whomsoever, or howsoever it comes to us, is from Him." "God alone forgiveth sin." The Word of God is the authority by virtue of which the Priest acts; "men," St. Ambrose says, "supply their ministry" only; or as he says again, "Sins are remitted through the word of God, of which the Levite is the interpreter and a sort of executor: they are remitted also through the office of the Priest, and the sacred ministry."[140]

---

[139] "Entire Absolution of a Penitent." Accessed March 9th, 2013. http://www.anglicanhistory.org/pusey/pusey6.html
[140] Ibid.

It is most interesting that in his later brief tract *Hints on Making a First Confession*, published in 1851, Pusey does not even use the word "sacrament" once. However, in his last paragraph, he does refute, to some degree, the Roman teaching on making a confession, and being barred from communion until one has made a confession to the priest:

> There is no reason to debar yourself from Holy Communion while preparing for the Confession. You have not been debarred before. It seems misplaced that you should now debar yourself, when you are seeking the fuller favour of God. I do not mean that a person might not, on the deeper humiliation of himself, and out of a sense of deep unworthiness, abstain for a time from that Heavenly Food. But, ordinarily, when a person has been a Communicant for many years, there seems to be no reason why he should excommunicate himself, when he is returned to his Father's house, and is wishing only to make his Confession more perfect. What is done in intent, and delayed only in order to make it less imperfect, and more according to the Mind of God, God regards as done.[141]

To close this section on theologians of the Church of England, it is worth mentioning that two in particular wrote extensive books on the subject of penance, with the singular goal to vehemently refute the Romanist use of the practice through very detailed examinations of the history of the confessional. The first, Edward William Jelf (1811-1875), was a contemporary in Oxford of the Oxford Movement, but was not in favor of ritualism, and wrote against the efforts of the Tractarians and the Romanists alike. He was an esteemed graduate of Oxford, tutor of Christ Church at Oxford from 1836-1849, and closely attached to Oxford, becoming the Proctor and Senior Censor of the University's publications in 1843 until his departure in 1849. Due to his position as censor, and his short temper with undergraduates, he was not very popular among his contemporaries, which is a likely reason his theological writing is not well known, although his Greek Grammar was quite well known and published. In his text, *an Examination into the Doctrine and Practice of Confession* written in 1875, Jelf witnessed to the

---

[141] "Hints on Making a First Confession." Accessed March 9th, 2013. http://www.anglicanhistory.org/pusey/pusey1.html

vast disarray of praxis among the clergy in the Church of England at the close of the nineteenth century:

> Thus some writers in defending confession content themselves with proving absolution. Some maintaining absolution, think their point is established if they believe that they have shown confession to be useful or necessary to the spiritual life. Some identify absolution with the absolute forgiveness of sin, or a juridical power of forgiveness; others speak of it as having the promise of forgiveness of sin, or as an assuring or absolving grace, or grace of absolution, or an authoritative grant, or assurance of forgiveness; others, as the channel through which forgiveness *ipso facto* flows; some as the application of the Blood of Christ to the soul for the remission of sins. Some call confession a divinely appointed means of cleansing the soul; others, a divinely appointed condition of pardon; some hold it to be indispensable, others only beneficial; some universally obligatory, others universally optional; some as obligatory only in some cases, optional in others—some as beneficial only to persons of a peculiar temperament, or only for grievous sins; others, for all persons and for all sins—some hold that every sin must be laid before the priest; others that only particular sins must be disclosed—some hold confession to be an essential part of the forgiving ordinance; others, only as necessary to it, either for a complete repentance, or as enabling a priest to judge of the sincerity of a repentance for forgiveness—to fix the amount of penance to be appointed after it, so that he may be able to arrange the terms on which God's mercy may be obtained!

> Some learned men say that the difference between confession in the Church of England and the Church of Rome is, that in the latter it is habitual and obligatory, and in the former occasional and voluntary; laying especial emphasis on its not being compulsory in the Church of England, as if anything of the sort could be compulsory in our Church, except in proportion as people were told that they could not do without it. In fact, there are not as many of its advocates or apologists who do not at one time advance one thing, and at another something else.[142]

Jelf's witness offers us a perspective on a variety in practice and teaching, and even a perceived wavering on the subject by certain parties who apparently changed their position on confession over time.

---

[142] An Examination into the Doctrine and Practice of Confession by Edward William Jelf. Longmans, Green, and Co. London, 1875. 17-18

His overall perspective was that, although the practices of the Church of England differed from those of Rome in the manner of making confession, i.e. a mandatory and frequent requirement *versus* the English way of making it voluntary, although encouraged, the practices remained fundamentally the same, which he held to be contrary to the practice in the ancient Church:

> We have now arrived at which is technically called Auricular or Sacramental Confession, that is, confession received by a priest in the exercise of his sacerdotal office with a view to, and to be followed by, a formal and personal forgiveness of sins, in the exercise of a sacerdotal power attached to that office, but which, in the parlance of the school, is generally called confession, without any addition to distinguish it from the earlier and more innocent stages; to confound it with which is the result, if not the design, of the usage of this word.

> My readers can scarcely fail to see that, while this differs essentially from pastoral intercourse, it differs little, at least in its extreme development, from the pseudo-sacramental Romish practice; that the change from the one to the other would be little more than nominal and accidental.[143]

This raises a good point. If the Anglican Church is to distinguish confession, as it has attempted to do through making it voluntary, or optional, and yet uses the same terminology, and even the same patterns of making confession, there is little reason not to some confusion over the distinction, particularly when the clergy are calling the practices by the one and the same name of "confession" or "penance." Perhaps this was also the motive for naming the contemporary rite: "The Reconciliation of a Penitent" rather than "Confession."

The second author to consider, who is of the practice of the Church of England, and yet is an American, is John Henry Hopkins (1792-1886). Although Hopkins was born in Ireland, he immigrated to the United States as a child in 1801, and eventually became the first Bishop of Vermont, and eventually the eighth Presiding Bishop of the Episcopal Church in the United States of America. Although a contemporary of the Oxford Movement in his lifetime, Hopkins wrote

---

[143] Ibid, 24-25

in America concerning *The History of the Confessional*. Hopkins, who like Jelf, sought to demonstrate the discrepancies between the ancient Church and the Roman practice of his day, used detailed citations from the Canons of the early Church councils, many of which have been cited earlier in this study, along with his observations, in which he demonstrated that the confessional practice of the Roman Church was not of divine authority, nor of antiquity a common practice. He made the same arguments as the Reformers, only offering more detailed citations and commentary. In his concluding chapter, Hopkins offered a view of the practice of his day, but rather in the Episcopal Church of the United States.

> I frankly own, therefore, that I cannot imagine how such an innovation, even if it were possible to establish it, could ever be expected to improve the piety either of our clergy or our people. As it is, we have all the means of grace, and all the holy privileges appointed by our Lord, and administered by his inspired apostles. As it is, the members of our flocks are constantly led to confess their sins to Him who is the searcher of hearts, and before whose awful tribunal they must stand in judgment. As it is, they have the grace of pardon connected with the faithful reception of the sacraments and the regular absolution of prayer, the only form employed by the Church until the thirteenth century. As it is, they are freely invited to come to their pastors and "open their grief," whenever they feel that they, "can not quiet their own consciences, and need further comfort or counsel." And it is impossible to add any real improvement to these privileges by borrowing the form of words introduced through the despotic influence of the fourth Lateran Council.
>
> We have been taught by all the standard writers of our venerated Mother Church to regard that form with little reverence. Her clergy have never considered it as an active element of ministerial duty. Her laity scarcely know if its existence; and her divines speak of it, not in the language of praise, but rather in terms of reluctant apology. It was most wisely left out of our ecclesiastical system, and never can be grafted upon it hereafter.[144]

This perspective, only a century past, leaves us with little wonder at the state of the confessional in the Episcopal Church today. Not only

---

[144] The History of the Confessional Hopkins. 268-269.

was the Episcopal Church largely founded to be a Protestant Church, operating autonomously from the polity of the Church of England, from this we can also witness a vehement refutation of the practices of Rome.

Although it will not be addressed in depth beyond this conclusion, the perspectives expressed in this section by Anglican Theologians against the practice and authority of the Church of Rome following the Council of Trent were all the more cemented after the First Vatican Council which concluded in 1870, in which the Roman Church pronounced the Pope to be infallible. Furthermore, within the same century, Pope Leo XIII denounced Anglican Holy Orders as "absolutely null, and utterly void" in his papal bull *Apostolicae Curae* of 1896. In this light, it is of little wonder why the Anglican Church of the twentieth century and following were not, as a majority, naturally inclined to accede to the practices of the Roman Church, let alone the pronouncement of her Councils on the doctrine and discipline of confession. We may furthermore conclude that the majority of the Anglican Divines who wrote on confession did not view it as a sacrament, at least not as Trent defined it, did not uplift it as an obligatory practice, and yet in many places actually did maintain some semblance of the practice as being good for the troubled soul, although not universally required nor promulgated.

Archbishop Cranmer And Liturgy

Prior to the first Book of Common Prayer printed in 1549, the clergy utilized various kinds of manuals for ministerial purposes. Depending on the service being rendered, the priest would gather the marriage manual, or the penitential manual, or the burial manual, and meet the family or individual at the gate of the Church with the proper "liturgy" in hand. Without uniformity, local customs provided for a variety of approaches to liturgies, and confession was no different. As we have already discussed, there are numerous manuals for confession or penitentials to be chosen from in any given place. Unless the local bishop had a "customary" for ministry, which was not uncommon even as early as the Medieval period, as the clergy were often ordained without proper, let alone exhaustive training, the clergy lacked guidance on how to teach and minister to those in their charge. So it is no wonder that the practices of confession varied greatly in the whole Church, let alone the Church of England. The liturgies for confessional or penitential opportunities also came in differing forms, depending on the context. One form of confession was used in preparing a catechumen prior to be baptized; another form was used for readmission of penitents to the fold after a grave sin; yet another form was used to remedy a smaller sin confessed before one was allowed to advance to the altar rail to receive communion; and another form was utilized when one was on their death bed and preparing to make a final confession and receive viaticum or extreme unction. As we will see, even in the context of the Prayer Book, the confession finds its home in various places, again, depending on the context.

Thomas Cranmer

Thomas Cranmer's (1489-1556) influence on the worship and practice of the Church of England is beyond measurement. Generally speaking, his goal was simple: to make things easier, and to bring people closer to a loving God by shaping the people into a deeper faith through penitence, but not a penitence which was as practiced in the Roman system. The manner in which Cranmer achieved these goals was, however, influenced by several factors of polity and politics. Cranmer was also influenced deeply by Erasmus and Humanism, and by the works of the Reformers, particularly Luther. In the midst of serving several monarchs, and among many bishops, each of whom had their own preferences and agendas, Cranmer had a hand in formulating several statements of the faith, not all of which perfectly reflected his own theology, nor the theology of the whole of the Church of England.

In this section we will review many of the formularies Cranmer played a part in, and discuss how they influenced the prayers and prayer books he composed for the Church of England.

Cranmer began his first Book of Common Prayer with a preface stating plainly that his motive for creating a new liturgy was to simplify the ritual and make it accessible to the clergy and public:

> There was never any thing by the wit of man so well devised, or so sure established, which in continuance of time hath not been corrupted: as, among other things, it may plainly appear by the common prayers in the Church, commonly called Divine Service: the first original and ground whereof, if a man would search out by the ancient fathers, he shall find, that the same was not ordained, but of a good purpose, and for a great advancement of godliness: For they so ordered the matter, that all the whole Bible (or the greatest part thereof) should be read over once in the year, intending thereby, that the Clergy, and especially such as were Ministers of the congregation, should (by often reading, and meditation of God's word) be stirred up to godliness themselves, and be more able to exhort others by wholesome doctrine, and to confute them that were adversaries to the truth. And further, that the people (by daily hearing of Holy Scripture read in the Church) should continually profit more and more in the knowledge of God, and be the more inflamed with the love of his true religion.[145]

Time, in Cranmer's eyes, had corrupted the practice of the Church, and he argued that the original fathers of the Church had intended that the entire Bible be read at least once over in each year so to stir up the clergy and the people to godliness. As such, he sought to make a prayer book that would be so easy to use with few plain instructions so to bring the worship of the Church of England into some level of uniformity, with an ultimate goal of bringing the people into a deeper holiness.

Cranmer had a significant hand in the various formularies that defined the practice of the Church of England during the reign of Henry VIII, and continuing through the reign of Edward VI, until his death under the reign of Mary. While it may seem that Cranmer's theology changes over time, we must consider that he was also under significant pressure from monarchs and bishops to produce materials

---

[145] The Book of Common Prayer (1979) 866.

suitable to their likings, and he was also torn between the Catholic leanings of two of the monarchs under whom he served and his own Protestant leanings. John Ashley Null, a contemporary Oxford scholar on Cranmer, summarizes Cranmer's influences and pressures in his book *Thomas Cranmer's Doctrine of Repentance* in this way:

> In the light of Cranmer's unitary vision of history, the recantations of his last days seem not so much a sign of fear inspired theological instability as an indication of penultimate despair that the course of events in England had apparently failed to vindicate the Gospel he served. Whereas Edward's ascension appeared to validate Cranmer's cautious and compromising path toward reform under Henry, the boy-king's early death did the exact opposite. This obvious observation could not have been too far from Cranmer's mind during the intense campaign of intellectual pressure and emotional manipulation conducted by the Marian authorities to bring about his complete capitulation in the months leading up to his execution. Eventually, the dissidence between Cranmer's beliefs and his circumstances became too much for him.

> If Cranmer's belief in the power of divine love at times left his life looking inconsistent, this fundamental tenet gave coherence to the trajectory of his theological development and its eventual doctrinal maturity.[146]

In short, Null argues that if there were inconsistencies in Cranmer's writings over the years, they were not all of his own making—he had other pressures and influences.

Now, let us review the formularies composed in part or in full by Cranmer. *The Ten Articles* published in 1536 were likely the work of Cranmer, and came with the sanction of the crown. The first five of the articles pertain to the doctrines of the Church, and the last five to the ceremonies of the Church. The third article, which is on the *Sacrament of Penance*, contains the language that would also be contributed to the text published the following year: *The Institution of a Christian Man*, commonly called "The Bishop's Book", and which further contained the Creed, the Lord's Prayer, the Ten Commandments, as well as defining the sacraments and other religious acts to be performed. This

---

[146] Thomas Cranmer's Doctrine of Repentance By Ashley Null. Oxford University Press, Oxford. 2000. 250.

fuller text was created by a committee of forty-six divines, also headed by Cranmer. Within this text, Penance is spoken of as a sacrament, and is defined as follows:

> As concerning the sacrament of penance, we think it convenient, that all bishops and preachers shall instruct and teach the people committed into their spiritual charge that they ought and must most constantly believe that the said sacrament was instituted by God in the New Testament, as a thing so necessary for man's salvation, that no man, which after his baptism is fallen again, and hath committed deadly sin, can without the same be saved, or attain everlasting life.

> That like as such men, which after baptism, do fall again into sins, if they do not penance in this life, shall undoubtedly be damned; even so, whensoever the same men shall concert themselves from their naughty life, and do such penance for the same as Christ requireth of them, they shall without doubt attain remission of their sins, and shall be saved.

> That the sacrament of perfect penance, which Christ requireth of such manner persons, consisteth of three parts; whereof the one is contrition, the other is confession, and the third is the amendment of their former life, or the new obedient reconciliation unto the laws and will of God, that is to say, exterior acts and works of charity, according as they be commanded of God, which be called in scripture fructus digni poenitentia, the worthy fruits of penance.[147]

Then after explaining the elements of contrition and confession, the passage continues:

> Wherefore, as touching confession, we think it convenient, that all bishops and preachers shall instruct and teach the people committed unto their spiritual charge, that they ought and must certainly believe, that the words of absolution pronounced by the priest be spoken by the authority given to him by Christ in the Gospel. And that they ought and must give no less faith and credence to the same words of absolution, so pronounced by the ministers of the church, than they would give unto the very words and voice of God himself, if he should speak unto us out of heaven, according to the saying of Christ, Whose sins soever you do forgive, shall be forgiven: whose sins soever you do retain, shall be retained. And again, in another place, Christ saith, Whosoever heareth you heareth me.

---

[147] Formulations of Faith Put Forth During the Reign of Henry VIII ed. by Charles Lloyd. Oxford University Press, Oxford. 1856. 96-97

That the people may in no wise contemn this auricular confession, which is made unto the ministers of the church; but that they ought to repute the same as a very expedient and necessary means, whereby they may require and ask this absolution at the priest's hands, at such time as they shall find their consciences grieved with the mortal sin, and have occasion to do so, to the intent they may thereby attain certain comfort and consolation of their consciences.[148]

We see in these passages that the teaching of these Bishops under the reign of Henry was very much in line with auricular confession according to the Roman doctrine, except on the following points: they did not favor indulgences, but rather penances were to be works of charity or mercy, and this system did not require the people to make a regular annual confession, nor require the people to make a confession to their own parish priest. Rather, this text requires that the use of the confessional be taught and encouraged among the people as a good and holy practice, and as a sacrament of the Church. But nowhere does it say that auricular confession was required of the people; rather, it is a good thing to remedy those under the burden of a mortal sin.

In 1538, Henry entertained a coalition of three German theologians, Francis Burkhardt, George von Boyneburg, and Freidrich Myconius, who attempted a peaceful conference with the English bishops in order to try to discover common points of faith at which they would agree in the midst of Reformation debates. After months of deliberating, the Germans were unable to convince the Anglican bishops of their proposed articles of faith that had been based on the Lutheran Confession of Augsburg. In the course of time, they found that the Anglican bishops could not come into agreement with the continental Reformers, although they also could not reconcile themselves to the theology of Rome, despite the fact that Cranmer himself tended to side more with the Germans. Henry, who leaned closer to the Roman doctrines, disbanded this conference, and in 1539 he convened Parliament for the first time in three years. Parliament then created a committee to examine and formalize a statement on the doctrine of the

---

[148] Ibid, 98.

Church of England. Within eleven days, it was resolved that they could not come into agreement on anything, but resolved to discuss six key points of contention that eventually became the basis for the *Six Articles Act* of 1539. The six points were: transubstantiation, withholding the cup from the laity during communion, clerical celibacy, the observance of vows of chastity, private masses, and auricular confession. Under the *Six Articles Act,* anyone who taught anything contrary to the practice of auricular confession, as already defined above, as well as any of the other sacraments, should be considered felons, and be condemned to death:

> VI. And furthermore be it enacted, by the authority of this recent Parliament, that if any person or persons, preach in any sermon or collation openly made to the King's people, or teach in any common school or to other congregation of people, or being called before such judges and according to such form as hereafter shall be declared, do obstinately affirm, uphold, maintain, or defend...that auricular confession is not expedient and necessary to be retained and continued, used and frequented, in the Church of God...be and shall be, by authority above written, deemed and adjudged a felon and felons; and that every offended in the same, being therefore duly convicted, shall therefore suffer pains of death...and shall forfeit lands... [and etc.] [149]

Now auricular confession was not only policy, it was to be taught and upheld under penalty of death under the authority of Parliament and the King! This was difficult for Cranmer, who sought to bring penitence to the Church, but not under a threat of death. Cranmer emphasized the love and mercy of God, according to the more Humanist perspective, rather than the angry medieval God who allegedly required self-flagellation and extensive penances.

Three years later, the "Bishop's Book" was re-published in 1542 under a revised title: *A Necessary Doctrine of Erudition for any Christian Man*, although it was known as "The King's Book." The language concerning penance varies a bit, and is rather softened to the end of sounding less legalistic, and more pastoral in its outlook:

---

[149] Select Documents of English Constitutional History ed. by George B. Adams and H. Morse Stephens. The Macmillan Company, London. 1939. 257.

For the clear understanding of this sacrament, it is to be considered what penance is, and also what is the sacrament of penance.

Penance is an inward sorrow and grief of the heart for the sins by us done and committed, and an hatred and detestation of the same, with an earnest desire to be purged from them, and to recover again the grace and favour of God by such means and remedies as God hath appointed for the attaining thereof, with a steadfast purpose and mind never to offend again. For he that saith that his is sorry for his offenses committed against the high majesty of God, and yet still continueth or intendeth to continue in the same, is no penitent person, but a dissembler or rather a derider of penance. And this is penance commonly taken in the scripture, as well in the New as in the Old Testament. And this penance is a thing so necessary for man's salvation, that without it no man that offendeth God can be saved, or attain everlasting life.

The sacrament of penance is properly the absolution pronounced by the priest upon such as be penitent for their sins, and so do acknowledge and show themselves to be. To the obtaining of that which absolution of sacrament of penance be required contrition, confession, and satisfaction, as ways and means expedient and necessary to obtain the said absolution. [150]

Here, the formularies remain the same, and yet the authors have made a point to define penance, something which Calvin had accused the Romanists of having neglected in the *Institutes*, which had been published in 1536 and likely influenced this second book. Despite this influence the definition of sacrament is very much the same as it had been in the previous book only five years earlier. One significant addition is the last paragraph of the section that defines whether absolution can be received if there is no priest to offer absolution:

Finally, it is to be remembered, that notwithstanding this way before described is the ordinary mean for penitent sinners to obtain remission of sins, and to be reconciled to the favour of God, yet in case there lack a minister to pronounce the words of absolution, or in time of necessity, when a sinner hath not sufficient leisure or opportunity to do the works of penance before declared, if he truly repent him of his sinful life, and with all his heart purpose through God's grace to change and amend the same, he shall undoubtedly have pardon and forgiveness of all his misdoings.[151]

---

[150] Ibid, 257.

[151] Ibid, 261.

Here we see that the bishops of this time considered auricular confession to be the normative means of seeking forgiveness of sins, but not absolutely required for a soul to obtain the pardon of God and the remission of their sins.

Five years later, in 1547, Henry died and his nine-year-old son Edward VI assumed the throne. During Edward's reign, Cranmer had significantly more influence over the King, and more freedom to formulate the doctrine and discipline of the Church of England. By 1552 Cranmer, who held a significantly more Protestant view of the faith than Henry, had principally authored the *Forty Two Articles* which were intended to summarize the Anglican faith as he saw it, with the support of the now teen-aged king, who, unlike his father, leaned more towards Protestantism than Rome. These articles were intended to be shorter and more direct definitions of the doctrine of the Church of England. The articles were never really enforced, as Edward died the following year, and Mary fully intended to return the Church of England to the practices of the Roman Church. Despite the short life of these articles, they demonstrate the tone in which Cranmer intended to direct the Church, particularly on confession:

Article XXVI Of the Sacraments

Our Lord Jesus Christ hath knit together a company of new people with sacraments, most few in number, most easy to be kept, most excellent in signification, as is Baptism and the Lord's Supper.

The sacraments were not ordained by Christ to be gazed upon, or carried about, but that we should rightly use them, and in such only as worthily receive the same, they have an wholesome effect and operation, and yet not that of the work wrought, as some men speak, which word, as it is strange, and unknown to Holy Scripture; so it engendereth no godly, but a very superstitious sense. But they that receive the sacraments unworthily purchase to themselves damnation, as St. Paul saith.

Sacraments ordained by the Word of God (of Christ), be not only badges or tokens of Christian men's profession; but rather they be certain sure witnesses and effectual signs of grace towards us, by the which he doth work invisibly in us, and doth not only quicken, but also strengthen and confirm our faith in him.

There are two sacraments ordained of Christ our Lord in the Gospel, that is to say, baptism and the supper of the Lord.

Those five commonly called sacraments, that is to say, confirmation, penance, orders, matrimony, and extreme unction are not to be counted for sacraments of the Gospel, being such as have grown partly of the corrupt following of the Apostles, partly are states of life allowed in the scriptures; but yet have not like nature of sacraments with baptism and the Lord's supper, for that they have not any visible sign or ceremony ordained of God. [152]

This language would be retained in the redacted *Thirty-Nine Articles* published in 1563:

XXV. Of the Sacraments.

Sacraments ordained of Christ be not only badges or tokens of Christian men's profession, but rather they be certain sure witnesses, and effectual signs of grace, and God's good will towards us, by the which he doth work invisibly in us, and doth not only quicken, but also strengthen and confirm our Faith in him.

There are two Sacraments ordained of Christ our Lord in the Gospel, that is to say, Baptism, and the Supper of the Lord.

Those five commonly called Sacraments, that is to say, Confirmation, Penance, Orders, Matrimony, and Extreme Unction, are not to be counted for Sacraments of the Gospel, being such as have grown partly of the corrupt following of the Apostles, partly are states of life allowed in the Scriptures, but yet have not like nature of Sacraments with Baptism, and the Lord's Supper, for that they have not any visible sign or ceremony ordained of God. The Sacraments were not ordained of Christ to be gazed upon, or to be carried about, but that we should duly use them. And in such only as worthily receive the same, they have a wholesome effect or operation: but they that receive them unworthily, purchase to themselves damnation, as Saint Paul saith.[153]

---

[152] Documents of the English Reformation ed. by Gerald Bray. James Clarke & Co. Cambridge. 1994. 298-299

[153] The Book of Common Prayer Church Publishing Incorporated, New York. 1979.

The final redaction of these articles, which would make their way into the 1662 Book of Common Prayer, cemented the language and theology of the Church of England on confessional practice. The twenty-fifth article does not say explicitly that these five were not sacraments, but rather not sacraments "of the Gospel." In addition, they were:

> ... such as have grown partly of the corrupt following of the Apostles, partly are states of life allowed in the Scriptures: but yet have not like nature of Sacraments with Baptism and the Lord's Super, for that they have not any visible sign or ceremony ordained of God.[154]

It is of little wonder, then, that auricular confession does not find a real place in the liturgy of the Church for hundreds of years to follow.

Now, having reviewed the formularies composed in part or in whole by Cranmer, it is necessary to identify where his personal theology made room for penitence in the course of the liturgy. While Cranmer did not include a stand-alone liturgy for auricular confession, John Ashley Null, a modern Oxford scholar on Cranmer's penitential doctrine, argues that Cranmer did weave his penitential theology into the forms of the absolutions which accompanied the Daily Office and the Eucharist, with the goal of gently guiding the prayers of the people back to God, and to shape their understanding of God's love and mercy through the formularies of the absolutions and eucharistic liturgies. Null argues that he did so because exclusion from the Eucharist (excommunication) was the principle means of regulating sin at the time:

> If the Forty-Two Articles were the fullest public exposition of Cranmer's theology, his liturgical work was the most moving expression of his beliefs. In his prayers for the English people Cranmer gradually enshrined turning to God in repentance and faith as the chief effect of saving grace and its chief means. In the process, excommunication came to supersede auricular confession as the normal means of church discipline.

872.

[154] Ibid.

In 1548, the Catechism he set forth taught two kinds of ecclesiastical penance. Absolution by the power of the keys was numbered as one of three sacraments, and its purpose was to quiet troubled consciences. Excommunication, however, was an additional function of the power of the keys for disciplining doers of "open synnes." Although the Catechism insisted that absolution should not be despised, two other products from Cranmer's pen made it evident that auricular confession was no longer compulsory...

That the new formulary denied any biblical warrant for the necessity of sacramental penance was, as Dixon noted, "the first open stroke that was made by authority against secret or auricular confession."[155]

In short, after consulting with his clergy, and discovering that it was most difficult to compel the people to make use of the confessional, particularly in light of the negative perception that the Roman system had given to confessional practice, Cranmer sought to bring the spirit of penitence to the Eucharist, because excommunication from the Lord's table had become the only real practical mode of church discipline for clergy.

Null, who is a proponent of Cranmer's theology, argues in favor of his true penitential doctrine as found in the various absolutions of the prayer book and in the rearrangement and wording of the Eucharistic liturgy. He argues that these formularies follow the more Lutheran mode of "justification by faith," but also teach a perspective of penance which is based on the mercy of God rather than the purely Roman expiating understanding requiring contrition, confession, and satisfaction. In his argument favoring the penitence propounded in the absolutions, Null asserts:

In the following year [1549] Cranmer outlined his mature understanding of poenitentia in his contribution to the Croydon commentary on Matthew. Saving penitence was defined as a sorrow for sin for having offended God joined with a hope of gaining forgiveness through Christ and the intention of amending one's life with his help. The true saving confession that always accompanied complete penitence was not the enumeration of sins and the

---

[155] Thomas Cranmer's Doctrine of Repentance Null, 236-237.

explication of their circumstances but rather a hatred for sin from a true recognition of the heart before God coupled with a fervent prayer for their forgiveness...Dating from 1549, this is the doctrine to which Cranmer sought to conform the prayer book's presentation of confession and penance.

Therefore, all the absolutions in the prayer books of 1549 and 1552 contained a description of forgiveness of sin through justification by faith: 'Almighty God our heavenly Father, who of his great mercy hath promised forgiveness of sins to all them, which with hearty repentance and true faith turn unto him' (the absolution from the communion); 'Our Lord Jesus Christ, who hath left power to his Church to absolve all sinners, which truly repent and believe in Him' (the absolution of the sick), 'Almighty God.... pardoneth and absolveth all them which truly repent, and unfeignedly believe His holy Gospel' (the absolution added to the daily office in 1552). Likewise, the fruit of repentance was described as amendment of life, rather than making satisfaction: 'Forgive us all that is past, and grant that we may ever hereafter serve and please thee in newness of life, to the honour and glory of thy name' (the general confession prior to the communion in 1549 and 1552); 'Confirm and strengthen you in all goodness' (the absolution which followed); 'Grant...that we may hereafter live a godly, righteous, and sober life, to the glory of thy holy name' (the general confession added to the Daily Office in 1552); and 'Grant us true repentance and his Holy Spirit, that those things may please him which we do at this present, and that the rest of our lives hereafter may be pure and holy.'[156]

As for the rearrangement of the prayer book to accommodate and promote more genuine penance, Null cites the following revisions and changes:

The same liturgical revision in 1552 which lessened the role of auricular confession also greatly increased the emphasis on repentance. In keeping with the great notebook's propositional heading, "God ought always to be asked so that he may forgive sin, even those belonging to godly sons which are already all forgiven," Cranmer added a penitential opening to the Daily Office, and to the end of the Litany he appended prayers which promised repentance in order to mitigate divinely sent punishments. He also inserted a recitation of the Ten Commandments at the beginning of the Lord's Supper which aptly expressed his understanding of repentance as turning

---

[156] Ibid, 237-239.

to God to be turned by God, for in response to hearing the commandments read, the people were to say, "Lord have mercy upon us, and incline or hearts to keep this law." [157]

Null's argument here is that in exhorting the people to repent of their sins, and to confess them in the context of the various liturgies, there was ample opportunity to offer redemption in a way that was more accessible than auricular confession. And by having the Ten Commandments read, the examinations done in the confessional could be done publicly in the context of the Mass, in which the people immediately responded with pleas of mercy, asking God to help them "keep these laws." This, Null argues, was Cranmer's means of bringing the confessional process to the people in a far more approachable way that did not bear the baggage of the Roman auricular confession, yet had the one and same goal: to redeem and redirect the souls of sinners.

In spite of all of this, Null argues that Cranmer's strongest contribution toward penance was in the Eucharistic liturgy:

> Yet the most significant change in the 1552 prayer book was Cranmer's complete reordering of the Communion service to fit the protestant understanding of what made repentance possible.
>
> Cranmer dropped the explicit epiclesis over the elements and made their reception the immediate response to the words of Institution. As a result, the receiving of the sacramental bread and wine, not their prior consecration, was the liturgy's climax. Now the sacramental miracle was not the changing of the material elements but drawing human hearts to the divine, not increasing personal righteousness but strengthening the communicants' "right-willedness." In so doing, Cranmer removed the prayer of oblation from the canon altogether, using it as a post-communion prayer instead. The community now offered nothing themselves to propitiate God but simply responded after the Communion with praise, thanksgiving, and a life of service because of the 'full, perfect, and sufficient sacrifice, oblation, and satisfaction' of Christ 'once offered' on their behalf.
>
> By these changes Cranmer enshrined the responsive nature of the Christian life as taught by the protestant doctrine of the affections in the very heart of his last Eucharistic liturgy.[158]

---

[157] Ibid, 241-242.

[158] Ibid, 242-243.

By these changes, Null argues that Cranmer brings to the Communion liturgy the perspectives necessary for participation in the body of Christ, which were founded on his personal Protestant theology of justification by faith, and "an understanding of what made repentance possible." Overall his argument is that although Cranmer's new liturgies only referenced private confession briefly, he infused a penitential doctrine within the context of the most frequented liturgies of the Church so to shape the minds of the people toward a more repentant faith and allow access to true repentance through the Eucharist.

Having now established Cranmer's influence on the formularies and liturgies of the Church, from here we will examine the appearance, or lack thereof, of liturgies provided to deal specifically with penance in the prayer books from the English Litany, written just prior to 1549, until now.

Confession in the Liturgy of the Church

Before entering into examination of the English liturgy, we should take notice of the popular contemporary liturgies from which the vernacular liturgies departed. In the medieval Sarum Rite, confession first appeared as the priest and ministers approached the altar. They would stop at the first step and say what we know as the *Confiteor:*

> And lead us not into temptation, but deliver us from evil. Let us confess unto the Lord, for He is gracious; for His mercy endureth forever. I confess to God, to Blessed Mary, and all the Saints, and to you; I have sinned exceedingly in thought, word, and deed, through my fault. I pray holy Mary, all God's saints, and you to pray for me.[159]

They were then absolved by the assisting ministers saying,

> Almighty God, have mercy upon you, and forgive you all your sins, deliver you from all evil, preserve and strengthen you in goodness, and bring you to everlasting life. Amen.[160]

---

[159] Liturgies and Offices of the Church by Edward Burbridge. Thomas Whittaker, New York. 1886. 91-92.

[160] Ibid, 92.

The "ministers," or assistants, would then make the same confession the priest had made, and the priest would then absolve them saying,

> Almighty and merciful God, grant you absolution and remission of all your sins, space for true repentance, and amendment of life, and the grace and consolation of the Holy Spirit. Amen.[161]

They would then share the peace and the Mass would continue. Edward Burbridge, writing on this early and popular form of the Mass, commented:

> The laity were instructed, at this time, that the absolution was pronounced for the benefit of all who were willing to confess; and that they were bidden to confess their sins privately, and add other devotions, while the priest and ministers were repeating the public forms.[162]

The worship of the Sarum Rite is here mentioned because, in 1543, Henry ordered that the kingdom should be of a single use, and this was to be the Sarum Rite, which was one of the two most popular Eucharistic liturgies. The Sarum rite became the basis for the formulation of the first Book of Common Prayer in England. The Sarum Rite had already been influential by its common usage in many of the Churches. Invariably, the people of any generation dislike change in their liturgies, and conformity to new forms is often slow, and not without much resistance and hostility. This liturgy was also among the many books in Cranmer's library when he made an exhaustive study of the liturgy so to prepare his own prayer book.

Two years after the publication of *The King's Book*, Cranmer was directed by the King to write an English Litany. This litany was published in 1544, and contains the devotional spirit of Cranmer. Along with being almost entirely penitential in nature, it also contained rubrics which instructed that it be read aloud in such as voice as the people could plainly hear it, which was far different from the nearly inaudible liturgies in use at the time. The people usually prayed privately, while

---

[161] Ibid.

[162] Ibid, 93.

the priest said the Mass in a low tone at the altar. As we will also see, the final line of the litany speaks against the "tyranny of the bishop of Rome," indicating that a break has occurred between the King and the Pope. This break gave Cranmer additional license towards his own ends, which were aimed more Protestant than Roman.

The Litany

O God, the Father of heaven:
> have mercy upon us miserable sinners.

O God, the Father of heaven:
> have mercy upon us miserable sinners.

O God the Son, redeemer of the world:
> have mercy upon us miserable sinners.

O God the Son, redeemer of the world:
> have mercy upon us miserable sinners.

O God the Holy Ghost, proceeding from the Father and the Son:
> have mercy upon us miserable sinners.

O God the Holy Ghost, proceeding from the Father and the Son:
> have mercy upon us miserable sinners.

O holy, blessed and glorious Trinity, three persons and one God:
> have mercy upon us miserable sinners.

O holy, blessed and glorious Trinity, three persons and one God:
> have mercy upon us miserable sinners.

Holy Virgin Mary, mother of God our Saviour Jesu Christ.
> Pray for us

All holy Angels and Archangels and all holy orders of blessed spirits.
> Pray for us.

All holy Patriarchs, and Prophets, Apostles Martyrs, Confessors,
> & Virgins, and all the blessed company of heaven:
> Pray for us.

Remember not Lord our offenses, nor the offences of our forefather, neither take thou vengeance on our sins: spare us good Lord, spare thy people, whom thou hast received with thy most precious blood, and be not angry with us for ever:
> Spare us good Lord.

From all evil and mischief, from sin, from the crafts and assaults of the devil, from thy wrath, and from everlasting damnation:
> Good Lord deliver us.

From blindness of heart, from pride, vainglory, and hypocrisy, from envy, hatred and malice, and all uncharitableness:
> Good Lord deliver us.

From fornication and all deadly sin, and from all the deceits of the world, the flesh, and the devil:
> Good Lord deliver us.

From lightning and tempest, from plague, pestilence and famine, from battle and murder, & from sudden death:
> Good Lord deliver us.

From all sedition and privy conspiracy, from the tyranny of the bishop of Rome and all his detestable enormities, from all false doctrine and heresy, from hardness of heart, and contempt of thy word and commandments:
> Good Lord deliver us. [163]

Four years later, in 1548, another book was published for *The Service of the Mass,* which was largely still in Latin, but afterwards included *The Order of the Communion* in English. This English *Order for Communion* called for the priest to exhort the people a day in advance, to prepare to receive communion. Within this preparation, the people were directed, as follows, to make a confession:

> Dear friends, and you especially, upon whose souls I have cure and charge, upon _____ day next I do intend by God's grace to offer to all such as shall be thereto Godly disposed, the most comfortable sacrament of the body and blood of Christ, to be taken by them in the remembrance f his most fruitful and glorious Passion: by the which Passion we have obtained remission of our sins...and to forgive other as you would that God would forgive you. And if there be any of you whose conscience is troubled and grieved in any thing, lacking comfort or counsel let him come to me, or to some other discreet and learned Priest taught in the law of God, and

---

[163] The Oxford Guide to the Book of Common Prayer Ed. by Charles Hefling and Cynthia Shattuck. Oxford University Press, Oxford. 2006. 24.

confess and open his sin and grief secretly, that he may receive such ghostly counsel, advice and comfort that his conscience may be relieved, and that of us, as a minister of God and of the Church, he may receive comfort and absolution, to the satisfaction of his mind, and avoiding of all scruple and doubtfulness: requiring such as shall be satisfied with a general confession, not to be offended with them that doth use, to their further satisfying, the auricular and secret confession to the Priest; nor those also which think needful or convenient for the quieting of their own consciences particularly to open their sins to the Priest, to be offended with them which are satisfied with their humble confession to God, and the general confession to the Church; but in all these things to follow and keep the rule of charity, and etc.[164]

It is peculiar that this exhortation not only calls people to repentance, but also calls for those who make only a general confession not to be offended with those who make an auricular confession, and vice versa. Clearly the tensions over these practices were quite evident to Cranmer, who acknowledged this tension within the first English Eucharist of the Church.

In the first Book of Common Prayer, officially titled: *The Booke of the Common Prayer and Admininistracion of the Sacramentes, and other Rites and Ceremonies of the Churche after the use of the Churche of England,* published in 1549, the order *The Supper of the Lord, and the Holy Communion, Commonly Called the Mass,* also allowed for a general confession, which remained, pretty much in its first form, in all subsequent English books up to and including the 1928 Book of Common Prayer (American). The liturgy began, as it had in the Sarum rite, with the Lord's Prayer and the Collect of Purity prayed by the priest and his ministers privately in the sacristy, followed by the Introit or Psalm, then the Kyrie, the Gloria, and the call to prayer and the Collect of the day. After the Sursum Corda and the Sanctus came the Prayers for the Whole State of Christ's Church. This then led to the Canon of the Mass, the Lord's Prayer, now bidden to be prayed by the whole congregation, followed by the Peace. Then, quite contrary to our

---

[164] Liturgies and Offices of the Church Burbridge, 155-156.

current rites, came a bidding prayer to confession which read as follows:

> Christe our Pascal Lambe is offered up for us once for all, when He bare our sinnes on His body upon the crosse. For He is the very Lambe of God that taketh away the sinnes of the worlde; wherefore let us kepe a joyfull and holy feast with the Lorde.[165]

Then came the invitation, "You that do truly and earnestly repent… and etc." followed by the Confession, Absolution, which is the same as the form in the 1928 Book of Common Prayer (American), and followed by the Prayer of Humble Access. Here, the confession is nestled between the Peace and the Prayer of Humble Access, just before the people are to receive communion.

Beyond the general confession, the only other place in this prayer book which made mention of a confession was in the liturgy for the visitation of the sick, which was very long. Charles Hefling comments:

> The modern reader can only wonder at the stamina of the sick in former times. Even the 1552 form, which was much abbreviated from 1549, would tax many a healthy person. Both forms included brief prayers, a lengthy exhortation, and examination of the faith and conscience of the sick person, and if necessary the writing of a will.[166]

Within this rite, which was titled *The Order for the Visitacion of the Sicke, and the Communion of the Same,* after the opening greeting and a recitation of a psalm followed a brief litany as follows:

> Remember not Lord our iniquities, nor the iniquities of our forefathers. Spare us good Lord, spare thy people, whom thou hast redeemed with thy most precious bloud, and be not angry with us for ever.
>
> Lorde have mercye upon us.
>
> Christe have mercye upon us.
>
> Lorde have mercye upon us.
>
> Our father, whiche art in heaven, &c. And leade us not into temptacion.
>
> Answere. But deliver us from evill. Amen.
>
> The Minister. O lorde save thy servaunte.

---

[165] Ibid, 161.

[166] The Oxford Guide to the Book of Common Prayer, Hefling, 36.

Answere. Whiche putteth his trust in the.
Minister. Sende hym helpe from thy holy place.
Answere. And evermore mightily defende hym.
Minister. Leat the enemie have none advauntage of hym.
Answere. Nor the wicked approche to hurte hym.
Minister. Bee unto hym, o lorde, a strong tower.
Answere. From the face of his enemie.
Minister. Lord heare my prayer.
Answer. And let my crye come unto thee.[167]

This was followed by two prayers and a very lengthy exhortation, which concluded with a full rehearsal of all the articles of faith, by which to examine one's sins. The priest is instructed to then go over the opening of the baptismal rite, "Doest thou believe in God the father almyghtie?" and so on. Then came the following rubrics on confession:

Then shall the minister examine whether he be in charitie with all the woride. Exhortyng hym to forgeve from the botome of his herte al persons, that have offended hym, and yf he have offended other, to aske them forgevenesse: and where he hathe done injurye or wrong to any manne, that he make amendes to hys uttermoste power. And if he have not afore disposed his goodes, let him then make his will. (But men must be oft admonished that they set an ordre for their temporall goodees and landes whan they be in helth.) And also to declare his debtes, what he oweth, and what is owing to him: for discharging of his conscience, and quietnesse of his executours. The minister may not forget nor omitte to move the sicke person (and that moste earnestly) to lyberalitie towarde the poore.

Here shall the sicke person make a speciall confession, yf he fele his conscience troubled with any weightie matter. After which confession, the priest shall absolve hym after this forme: and the same forme of absolucion shalbe used its all pryvate confessions.[168]

This is the only place in which instruction is given on hearing private confessions, saying in the final sentence: "the same form of absolution shall be used by all private confessions." Then followed the

---

[167] The Book of Common Prayer, 1549. Accessed March 12th, 2013. http://justus.anglican.org/resources/bcp/1549/BCP_1549.htm

[168] Ibid.

absolution, which is surprisingly Roman in nature given that the priest is to say "I absolve thee...," which was one of the points of contention for the reformers who argued that the priest had no power to absolve, rather only the power to assure the penitent of God's forgiveness. It is somewhat surprising that this form remained:

> Our Lord Jesus Christ, who hath lefte power to his Churche to absolve all sinners, which truely repent and beleve in hym: of his great mercy forgeve thee thyne offences: and by his autoritie committed to me, I absolve thee from all thy synnes, in the name of the father, and of the sonne, and of the holy gost. Amen.[169]

The absolution is followed by a collect which was intended for the reassurance of the penitent, but also serves to demonstrate the penitential understanding of the Church at this time:

> O most mercifull God, which according to the multitude of thy mercies, doest so putte away the synnes of those which truely repent, that thou remembrest them no more: open thy iye of mercy upon this thy servaunt, who moste earnestly desireth pardon and forgevenesse: Renue in hym, moste lovyng father, whatsoever hath been decayed by the fraude and malice of the devil, or by his owne carnall wyll, and frailnesse: preserve and continue this sicke membre in the unitie of thy Churche, consyder his contricion, accepte his teares, aswage his payne, as shalbe seen to thee moste expedient for him. And forasmuch as he putteth his full trust only in thy mercy: Impute not unto him his former sinnes, but take him unto thy favour: through the merites of thy moste derely beloved sonne Jesus Christe. Amen.[170]

The 1552 Book, which only had a short life following the accession of Mary to the throne in July 1553, amended and abridged this form of the visitation of the sick, so that any reference to private confession was omitted. Hefling comments on this change, stating: "In 1552 the reference to private confessions was omitted. Evidently Cranmer had no wish to give sacramental status to what he no longer considered a sacrament."[171] Instead, what remained was as follows:

---

[169] Ibid.

[170] Ibid.

[171] The Oxford Guide to the Book of Common Prayer, Hefling, 36.

Then shall the Minister examine whether he be in charitie with al the world: Exhortinge him to forgeve from the bottome of his hearte al persons that have offended hym: and yf he have offended other to aske them forgevenesse: And where he hath done injurie or wrong to any man, that he make amendes to the uttermost of his power. And yf he have not afore disposed hys goodes, let him then make his wyl. But men must be of be admonished that they sette an ordre for theyr temporall goodes and landes whan they be in health. And also declare his debtes, what he oweth, and what is owing unto him, for discharging of his conscience, and quietnesse of hys executours.

These words before rehearsed, may be said before the Minister beginne his prayer, as he shal see cause.

The minister may not forgeat nor omitte to move the sicke person (and that most earnestly) to lyberalitie towarde the poore.

Here shal the sicke person make a special confession, yf he feele his conscience troubled wyth any weyghtie matter. After which confession the Priest shal absolve hym after thys sorte.[172]

Note, that the reference to "private confession" has changed to "special confession" and it was to be made at this time. The absolution then followed the same pattern as the 1549 book.

Despite this revision, another penitential detail added to this book was a liturgy towards the end of the book called A Comminacion against sinners, with certain praiers to be used divers tymes in the yere. This liturgy was to be used at certain times of the year, following the recitation of the English Litany, and then the priest was to assume the pulpit and read an exhortation:

Brethren, in the primitive church there was a Godly discyplyne, that at the begynnyng of Lent suche persons as were notorious synners, wer put to open penaunce and punished in thys world, that their soules might be saved in the day of the lorde, and that others admonished by theyr example, myght be more afrayed to offende. In the stede wherof, untyl the sayd discipline may be restored againe, (which thing is much to be wyshed,) it is thought good, that at thys tyme (in your presence) should be read the general sentences of God's curssyng against impenitent sinners, gathered

[172] The Book of Common Prayer, 1552. Accessed March 12th, 2013. http://justus. anglican.org/resources/bcp/1549/BCP_1549.htm

out of the xxvii. Chapiter of Deuteronomye, and other places of scripture: and that ye shoulde aunswere to every sentence, Amen. To thintent that you, beyng admonished of the great indignacion of God agaynst synners, may the rather be called to earneste and true repentaunce, and may walke more warely in these daungerous daies, fleeing from such vices, for the which ye affirme with your owne mouthes the curse of God to be due.[173]

This exhortation was followed by a brief litany of anathemas, saying "Cursed is he that letteth..." and so on. The priest then reads another long exhortation to recall the minds of the people to penitence of David and others, followed by a reading of Psalm 51. This liturgy is the forerunner of the Ash Wednesday service which would be retained in the books to follow, in various forms.

Beyond this, the sentences, exhortation, confession, and absolution we moved from their position, which had been immediately prior to the communion, forward to the liturgy for Matins. This way, the service began with a call to holiness, to consider one's sins, and to confess them and be absolved of them well before the Eucharist. This allowed for those who did not come to the Eucharist to also have an opportunity to confess, as not all people stayed past the sermon.

Of course, as previously stated, this 1552 book was short-lived, but the character of it would return in the 1559 Prayer Book under the reign of Elizabeth. This new prayer book was more conservative than the previous book, attempting to make it somewhat less Protestant by dropping the "black rubric," synthesizing the wording of the Eucharist from the previous two books, dropping the final prayer against the Pope from the English litany, and allowing for traditional vestments to be used in the daily offices. The liturgy for the visitation of the sick was essentially identical to the 1559 book, still allowing for a "special confession" rather than the "private confession" of the 1549, and it retained the same prayers of absolution from the previous two books.

The 1662 Book of Common Prayer witnessed various additions, however not to the liturgy of the visitation of the sick, and no liturgy was added for a private confession. Certain additional prayers were

---

[173] Ibid. Chapter XX.

added for various occasions, and the minister was permitted to omit certain prayers if the sick person was in such poor heath as to be unable to respond. However, the rubrics on the confession remained the same. This prayer book added the Coverdale translation of the Book of Psalms. The Psalms, which we have already discussed, have a deep penitential value. The Thirty-Nine Articles of Religion were also added, which of course made mention of the sacrament of penance. It was this prayer book that would first come to America, and bring with it the same concerns on confession.

The 1789 Book of Common Prayer was the first American edition of the prayer book, and would remain in service until the 1892 revision. However, there were several editions of this book, which corrected several printing errors, and slight adjustments made over the years by the General Convention of the Protestant Episcopal Church of the United States. Therefore there were several different editions, which varied in format and type set, and appeared in several shapes and sizes. While this book made several changes for American usage, it was largely based on the 1662 book. It added separate forms for the baptism of infants and children, prayers for those at sea, an order for confirmation, and it also retained the Thirty-Nine Articles of Religion. The prayers for the visitation of the sick were nearly identical, only they finally omitted any reference to confession at all. What began as "private confession," and had been changed to "special confession," was now completely gone. Despite this omission, a liturgy was added for *The Visitation of Prisoners*. This liturgy, contrary to the previous, restores a charge for confession, and actually bids the prisoner to make what is called a "particular confession." Towards the end of the exhortation it states:

> Since therefore you are soon to pass into an endless and unchangeable state, and your future happiness or misery depends upon the few moments which are left you, I require you strictly to examine yourself, and your estate both towards God and towards man; and let no worldly consideration hinder you from making a true and full confession of your sins, and giving all the satisfaction which is in your power to every one whom you have wronged or injured; that you may find mercy at your heavenly Father's hand, for Christ's sake, and not be condemned in the dreadful day of judgment.[174]

---

[174] The Book of Common Prayer 1789, Accessed March 12th, 2013. http://justus. anglican.org/resources/bcp/1789/BCP_1789.htm

The rubric then follows:

Here the Minister shall examine him concerning his faith, and rehearse the Articles of the Creed, Dost thou believe in God, &c.

And the Criminal shall answer,
All this I steadfastly believe.

Then shall the Minister examine whether he repent him truly of his sins, exhorting him to a particular confession of the sin for which he is condemned; and upon confession, he shall instruct him what satisfaction ought to be made to those whom he has offended thereby; and if he knoweth any combinations in wicked-ness, or any evil practices designed against others, let him be admonished to the utmost of his power to discover and prevent them.

After his confession, the Priest shall declare to him the pardoning mercy of God, in the form which is used in the Communion Service.[175]

This prayer book also added a "Catechism" with the subtitle: *An instruction, to be Learned by Every Person Before he be Brought to be Confirmed by the Bishop.* In this catechism, there is absolutely no mention of penance or confession. Rather, the following was the common teaching of the Church on sacraments:

Question: How many Sacraments hath Christ ordained in his Church?
Answer. Two only as generally necessary to salvation; that is to say, Baptism and the Supper of the Lord.[176]

The wording which usually followed this teaching in the Thirty-Nine Articles is nowhere to be found here, although the thirty-Nine Articles were included in this prayer book in their original form. It is curious that despite the omission of reference in the catechism to the other five so-called "sacraments," this book retained liturgies from the previous book for confirmation and matrimony, and after 1810 added an ordinal, but did not include any prayers or liturgies for extreme unction or confession, and the order for *The Visitation of the Sick* does not make any mention of unction or holy oil at all.

---

[175] Ibid.

[176] Ibid.

The 1892 Book of Common Prayer differed only slightly form the 1789 book. All of the elements addressed in the previous book were retained verbatim, although the ordinal was officially added, and a Penitential Office was designated for Morning Prayer on Ash Wednesday, redacting the *Commination* from the 1662 book into a much shorter form. This abbreviated form, however, included a brief general confession which read:

> O Lord, we beseech thee, mercifully hear our prayers, and spare all those who confess their sins unto thee; that they, whose consciences by sin are accused, by thy merciful pardon may be absolved; through Christ our Lord. Amen[177]

This book was replaced only thirty-five years later in 1928 with a far more elaborate revision.

The 1928 revision was far more radical of a change than either of the first two American books. *The Visitation to Prisoners* liturgy, which had been the only mention of confession in the previous book, was dropped. The various baptismal liturgies were redacted to a single liturgy. The communion service was rearranged in an attempt to more closely resemble the 1549 book. What was called a Catechism in the 1892 book was shifted to the end of the 1928 book, although a form similar to it was amended slightly and put in its place, now called the *Offices of Instruction*, in which the language concerning the sacraments remained the same as the previous book's *Catechism*.

The order for the visitation of the sick was relatively the same; however the rubrics were changed slightly, making it much shorter by omitting the recitation of the articles, the need to make a will, and restoring some relatively familiar language of confession as follows:

> Then shall the sick person be moved to make a special confession, if he feel his conscience troubled with any matter; after which confession, on evidence of his repentance, the Minister shall assure him of God's mercy and forgiveness.[178]

---

[177] The Book of Common Prayer 1892, Accessed March 12th, 2013. http://justus.anglican.org/resources/bcp/1892/BCP_1892.htm

[178] The Book of Common Prayer 1928, Accessed March 12th, 2013. http://justus.anglican.org/resources/bcp/1928/BCP_1928.htm

Here we see the words "special confession" have returned, however the tone of this rubric is such that the confession is completely voluntary, rather than the penitent being exhorted to do make a confession. The Thirty-Nine Articles remained unchanged, and were appended to this book as well.

The most radical change came in the form of the *1979 Book of Common Prayer*. This book retained the general confession in the Mass, although it allowed for two "traditional language" masses called *Rite I*, and introduced four modern English liturgies for the Eucharist called *Rite II*. However all of these liturgies share the same general confession, only diverging after the peace into the various forms for the canon of the Mass. In addition to the expounded liturgies for the Eucharist, each form was prefixed with a *Penitential Order*, allowing for a reading of the Decalogue, and a general confession prior to the beginning of the *Liturgy of the Word*. These were an attempt to mirror the 1552 book which had moved the confession from just before the Eucharist to the beginning of the service. The exhortation, which had been just before the reception of the Eucharist in the 1549 book, but moved to matins in the 1552 book has been honored in this book by restoring an Exhortation to the beginning of the Rite I Eucharist. This exhortation is likely seldom used, yet contains a modern translation of the 1549 exhortation, including the following:

> Examine your lives and conduct by the rule of God's commandments, that you may perceive wherein you have offended in what you have done or left undone, whether in thought, word, or deed. And acknowledge your sins before Almighty God, with full purpose of amendment of life, being ready to make restitution for all injuries and wrongs done by you to others; and also being ready to forgive those who have offended you, in order that you yourselves may be forgiven. And then, being reconciled with one another, come to the banquet of that most heavenly Food.

> And if, in your preparation, you need help and counsel, then go and open your grief to a discreet and understanding priest, and confess your sins, that you may receive the benefit of absolution, and spiritual counsel and advice; to the removal of scruple and doubt, the assurance of pardon, and the strengthening of your faith. [179]

---

[179] The Book of Common Prayer 1979, 317.

After hundreds of year of omission, this prayer book acknowledges private confession and the benefits to be gained from the practice.

This book also introduced not one, but two separate rites for private confession. In his text *Commentary on the American Prayer Book,* Dr. Marion Hatchett (of blessed memory) identifies the inspiration for including confessional rites in the 1979 book:

> Recent revisions in other provinces of Anglicanism have contained a form for private confession, normally modeled on that of the Roman rite. The absolution has customarily been the one included in the English Books since 1549. The present book gives two forms. Form One is like the forms in other recent revisions in the various Anglican provinces. Form Two a much fuller rite, containing material similar to the Byzantine form for confession and other material similar to the recently revised Roman Catholic form. Possibly it is better suited than Form One for the penitent who has come to confession when such an action marks a radical turning point in that person's life.[180]

Prior to the confessional forms in the 1979 book there has been added a single page of instruction entitled *Concerning the Rite.* This page, which according to Dr. Hatchett was composed by The Rev. Donald L. Garfield, was put into place to attempt to bridge the gap of misunderstandings between those who had never known confession to be a part of Anglican liturgies, and the current text. For those unfamiliar with this page, its instructions are as follows:

Concerning the Rite

> The ministry of reconciliation, which has been committed by Christ to his Church, is exercised through the care each Christian has for others, through the common prayer of Christians assembled for public worship, and through the priesthood of the Church and its ministers declaring absolution.

> The Reconciliation of a Penitent is available for all who desire it. It is not restricted to times of sickness. Confessions may be heard anytime and anywhere.

---

[180] Commentary on the American prayer Book By Marion J. Hatchett. The Seabury Press, New York. 1981. 452-453.

Two equivalent forms of service are provided here to meet the needs of penitents. The absolution in these services may be pronounced only by a bishop or priest. Another Christian may be asked to hear a confession, but it must be made clear to the penitent that absolution will not be pronounced; instead, a declaration of forgiveness is provided.

When a confession is heard in a church building, the confessor may sit inside the altar rails or in a place set aside to give greater privacy, and the penitent kneels nearby. If preferred, the confessor and penitent may sit face to face for a spiritual conference leading to absolution or a declaration of forgiveness.

When the penitent has confessed all serious sins troubling the conscience and has given evidence of due contrition, the priest gives such counsel and encouragement as are needed and pronounces absolution. Before giving absolution, the priest may assign to the penitent a psalm, prayer, or hymn to be said, or something to be done, as a sign of penitence and act of thanksgiving.

The content of a confession is not normally a matter of subsequent discussion. The secrecy of a confession is morally absolute for the confessor, and must under no circumstances be broken.[181]

It is of note that nowhere in this page is the rite referred to as a sacrament, nor is it required of all people. Commenting on the content of the first paragraph, Hatchett summarizes:

The first paragraph and the first sentence of the second are analogous to the section on confession in the exhortations of the English Prayer Books. Private confession is available for all who desire it, but it is not compulsory. The Anglican attitude has been summarized: "All can; some should; none must."[182]

Concerning the confession attached to the rite for *Ministration to the Sick*, this rite includes a general confession as a part of the rite, which is identical to the general confession from the Rite II Eucharist, but it also allows for the other under a rubric, which speaks of it with old familiar language: "The Priest may suggest the making of a special

---

[181] Book of Common Prayer 1979. 446.

[182] Commentary on the American Prayer Book, Hatchett, 453.

confession, if the sick person's conscience is troubled, and use the form for the Reconciliation of a Penitent."[183]

Finally, to conclude the innovations of the most recent *Book of Common Prayer*, we must take notice of the change in the catechism from the previous books. Where all three previous prayer books restricted discussion of the sacraments to either Baptism and the Lord's Supper, or to the language of the Thirty-nine Articles, which are also appended to this text, the catechism of the current book ventures to call confirmation, ordination, holy matrimony, reconciliation of a penitent and unction "sacramental rites." The portions pertaining to *Reconciliation of a Penitent* are cited here:

Other Sacramental Rites

Q. What other sacramental rites evolved in the Church under the guidance of the Holy Spirit?

A. Other sacramental rites which evolved in the Church include confirmation, ordination, holy matrimony, reconciliation of a penitent, and unction.

Q. How do they differ from the two sacraments of the Gospel?

A. Although they are means of grace, they are not necessary for all persons in the same way that Baptism and the Eucharist are.

Q. What is Reconciliation of a Penitent?

A. Reconciliation of a Penitent, or Penance, is the rite in which those who repent of their sins may confess them to God in the presence of a priest, and receive the assurance of pardon and the grace of absolution.[184]

Commenting on the justification for this addition, Hatchett defines the pedigree of the restoration of these other five sacraments as such:

The word "sacrament" (oath or pledge or earnest), sometimes used as a translation of the Greek word "mysterion," became a part of the Christian vocabulary probably at the end of the second century or the beginning of the third, in relation to many rites or signs of spiritual significance.

---

[183] Book of Common Prayer 1979. 454.

[184] Ibid, 860-861.

Not until the twelfth century did Peter Lombard designate seven rites as the sacraments of the church, an enumeration which was affirmed at the council of Florence (1439) and the council of Trent. Various English Reformation formularies and the Elizabethan homilies speak of marriage or the reconciliation of a penitent, as well as Baptism and the Eucharist, as sacraments. Article XXV (p.872) asserted that there were two sacraments ordained by our Lord, and that the five other rites "commonly called Sacraments," are partly "states of life" (for example, marriage or ordination) or arose in part from the "corrupt following of the Apostles," for example, the unction for healing of the early church became the "Extreme Unction" of the late medieval period). The section on the sacraments, added to the catechism of 1604, asked the question "How many Sacraments hath Christ ordained in his Church?" The answer was "Two only, as generally necessary to salvation; that is to say, Baptism and the Supper of the Lord."

The present Book treats Baptism and the Eucharist as "the two great sacraments of the Gospel, given by Christ to his Church." The "minor sacraments" of the late medieval enumeration are listed as "other sacramental rites" to be distinguished from the sacraments of the Gospel in that they are not necessary for all persons.[185]

In summary, the rite or "sacrament" of confession, as it is interchangeably referred to, has been through a variety of placements, inclusions, exclusions, endorsements, and omissions, only to be established by the current book, not only as a sacrament, but one with antiquity, and with multiple rites provided, depending on the need of the penitent. It is not safe to say that Anglican doctrinal theology has been consistent on this matter. However, it seems to have been resolved that this is an optional practice for those who have need of spiritual guidance, relief of conscience, and reassurance of absolution from the priests hearing the confessions. It is of little wonder that this practice has not really caught on, as it is of such recent addition to the prayers of the Church. The Anglican Church, particularly that vein in the United States which uses this current prayer book, seems to have been slow to incorporate this liturgy into the life of the Church, if at all, with exception of a few places. Even so, confession or *Reconciliation of a*

---

[185] Commentary on the American Prayer Book, Hatchett, 581-582.

Penitent has found a place in the prayer book, and may be utilized better by those who value the opportunity it avails the troubled conscience, and the sin-sick soul.

CHAPTER SEVEN
Conclusion to the Theological Study

We have now witnessed, in brief, a survey of the transitions from the Old to the New Testament systems of atonement, the use of these systems by early Church, the rigor of the Patristic Church, the changes which followed the "Peace of Constantine," the increase of penitential discipline brought about by the rise of monasticism, penitentials, and other factors in the late patristic period, the transition toward a more "sacramental" understanding of penance following a major shift at the Fourth Lateran Council, the effects of this change on the Medieval period and the abuses that accompanied them, the Reformation which attempted to reform these abuses of medieval practice and theology, and the fallout which followed through the eyes of Anglican theologians and the liturgy of the Church of England from the Reformation to today. In an attempt to demonstrate these evolving trends, the following graphic may be helpful. This demonstrates the shift between atonement of a community versus the individual, and whether this atonement was accomplished publically or privately over the course of time.

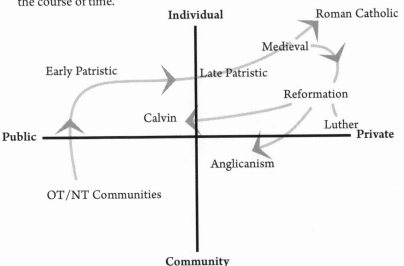

It is not safe to say that the results or trends are cyclical in nature. However, among the Reformers, particularly Calvin and Hooker, there is seen a desire to return to communal atonement and accountability, while questioning the sacramental system for atonement (as then understood) to varying degrees. Others, like Luther long for confessional accountability to be made to individuals in the community, but ultimately to God, rather than to a priest. Anglicans attempt to enjoy "the best of all worlds" containing monastic spirituality, Reformed theology closer to Calvin or Luther, while also in some places sacramental confession and very western Catholic practices. Anglicanism today seems to encompass one of three modes for atonement or confession: first, and seemingly most popular, the general confession in the communal context of the eucharist or Morning Prayer; secondly, in some places auricular confession is practiced in forms which closely resemble the Catholic rites; and finally, confession to a spiritual counselor or other mature Christian, either in the context of a community, or sometimes to a monastic where available, although this practice seems to be even more rare than auricular confession. Most Anglicans desire to make a confession privately, if at all, and to make it to either God alone, to a fellow "mature" Christian, or in some limited cases to their priest or spiritual director. This three-fold system will also come into to play when we look at the clerical and lay studies to follow, which illustrate the practice in the Diocese of Fort Worth today. However, it is useful to map out briefly where the Church has moved from the biblical pedigree until now.

In summary, the Church has made many transitions over time, yet there seems to be a real longing, at least among scholars and modern Protestant church movements, to return to the communal penitential practices which echo those of the Old Testament, the New Testament, and the early Patristic Church. The shift of penance to a sacramental practice in the Medieval period seems to have never really caught on outside of the Roman Church, particularly after the Reformation. Although the net result of the Reformation was to some extent the reduction of abuses in the Church, such as a diminished emphasis on the sale of indulgences, the overall result was invariably the splintering of the Church into factions, all of which hold their own traditions when it comes to the application of reconciling their people to God. Protesting from one extreme or another, the whole Church seems to be in flux over what invariably is the witness of each tradition. Even within Anglicanism, there is great variation from church to church, concerning the practice of hearing confessions or offering spiritual direction, or even the a need for atonement with God at all. Despite the Roman influence on the Church of England from the Medieval period to the Reformation—particularly in King Henry VIII's defense of the Roman system—the overall view of Anglican theologians is one of confusion over the identity of confession in the life of the Church. As such, there is no uniform Anglican synthesis on the theology or practice of confession today. The Articles of the Faith, which were intended to clarify these points, offered the Church little authority or guidance, as they came about as a result of dissent over these practices, and did not bear any antiquity or true expounded scholarly defense with which to support their claims as real authoritative Articles of Faith. While most Anglian authors defend the sacrament of penance as something that is useful, and good for the soul, they have really not thrown their weight behind the necessity for the practice for all Christians, and as such have not promulgated the Roman sacramental view of the practice. At the same time confession has been listed in the articles of faith among the "other sacraments," without providing any liturgical guidance on the subject until the most recent American prayer book.

As for the true doctrine, discipline, and praxis of "the modern confessional," which is the ultimate target of this study, it is difficult to arrive at a consensus within a faith tradition, let alone within a single diocese. The wealth of material written on confession since the Reformation has largely been published in the Roman Catholic tradition, although Anglicans have contributed considerably to this library of world literature, as we have found ourselves on the battleground between those who think us more inclined to the Protestant veins of Calvinism and Lutheranism, versus those who are more Roman Catholic in their outlook. As for other faith traditions, Gary Moon and David Benner's contemporary text *Spiritual Direction and the Care of Souls* identifies seven major contemporary traditions in which confession and spiritual direction are emphasized: the Orthodox Church, the Roman Catholic Church, the Episcopal tradition, the Reformed tradition, the Wesleyan-Holiness tradition, the Social Justice tradition, and the Pentecostal/Charismatic tradition.[186] They also identify what they call "the three major voices of soul care" which are: spiritual direction and psychotherapy—conceptual, spiritual direction and psychotherapy—ethical and spiritual direction and pastoral counseling. Without expanding on all of these disciplines, it is worthy of note that many of our clergy and people have been exposed, to some degree, in all of these traditions and manners of therapy. It would be difficult for any tradition, in this day and age, to claim that their tradition is purely one or another, given that our people and our clergy, with varying frequency, shift from one tradition to another and bring with them the doctrine, discipline, and praxis of the churches in which they are reared, trained for the ministry, and in which they occasionally worship with other family members and friends. Our society has become far more mobile, and as such it is not uncommon for a family to live in several different geographical areas in the course of a lifetime, and to be exposed to several different traditions or ways of doing things within the same doctrinal framework.

The Anglican veins of the Church are currently in a state of theological and doctrinal realignment, although it is safe to say that the statements made earlier by Bishop Hopkins and John Jewell illustrate the complex diversity of praxis in the Church of England, the Anglican Communion, and in the Episcopal Church in the United States over matters of confession are not new. Our liturgies contain both a general confession, as well as multiple rites for offering a private confession.

[186] Spiritual Direction and the Care of Souls by Gary Moon and David Benner, Intervarsity Press, Downers Grove, Illinois. 2004.

However, nowhere is confession required, and it is scarcely practiced, taught, or even offered in training by seminaries to the clergy of a tradition that has historically upheld the value of making a good confession for the troubled soul. It is the opinion of this author that this subject, for the good of the Church, must be raised at a "grass roots" level in the seminaries. The seminary is our only potential common ground, as it has the potential to educate our people and clergy on the history of atonement and confessional practice, and to encourage them to seek out confession, in whichever form is most comfortable, accountable, and effective at adequately assisting them with conquering their sins, and growing in a life of virtue as individuals and as a community. Without this education, we can expect little change on the status of the confusion over these matters. Without the encouragement of ecclesiastical authorities within dioceses, or consistent training for the clergy, we should not expect the laity to conclude on their own that confession should be practiced.

PART II: A CASE STUDY IN CONFESSION

CHAPTER EIGHT
Clergy & Laity Study Results

An anonymous response survey was conducted within an "Anglo-Catholic" Diocese in the United States of America in summer of 2012, in which forty-three clergy participated in a ten-question survey about their current confessional practice, provided certain demographic information, and answered questions about the traditions which primarily trained them for the ministry. The Diocese had ninety-seven licensed priests, fifty-five of whom were active in parish ministry; two were military chaplains, eleven were non-parochial, and twenty-nine were retired. The diocese contained forty-seven parishes, missions, and mission stations, of which only three had any form of confessional "booths."

Furthermore, eight focus group studies of laity were conducted within the same diocese between November and December of 2012. The focus groups were assembled by the Rectors or Vicars of seven parishes based on the requirement that all participants should have made a confession or have participated in Spiritual Direction at least once in their lifetime, and the focus groups were then conducted without the presence of the Rector or Vicar. Studies were conducted in two urban parishes, three sub-urban parishes, and two rural parishes. One separate study was conducted with various youth from the same demographic spectrum of parishes representing urban, rural, and sub-urban parishes. In this study, thirty-six people participated, twenty-nine of whom were thirty years of age and above, and nine of whom were between the ages of fourteen and twenty-nine. The ages of the participants ranged from teenagers to those in their nineties. All of these studies were recorded and transcribed, and the transcriptions are available in the original dissertation version of this document, available at the Nashotah House Library. This was a qualitative study in which the following eight questions were asked to all lay focus groups:

1. How do you feel about formal confessions?
2. In making confession, did you find that the confession brought relief to your soul, or guided you in the right direction?
3. How much teaching do you think your parish ought to have on confession?
4. How do you feel about spiritual direction in a casual setting versus confession in the Church?
5. If you have already done spiritual direction, what did you find useful about it?
6. How much teaching do you think your church would need on spiritual direction?
7. When you made a confession or went in for spiritual direction, did you feel as though the priest was adequately trained to guide you?
8. What, in your eyes, is the biggest problem with the modern confessional?

The responses of the laity will be integrated within the responses of the clergy, so to give the reader a clearer idea of what the clergy are saying (or think they are saying), and in direct correlation, what the people claim they are hearing. However, in general, it is of note to mention here that the laity are actually in favor of confession. This study has shown that the lack of use of the confessional by the laity is not entirely a matter of will or desire of the laity alone. Many other factors influence the use of the confessional by the laity, many of which are related to the behaviors, desires, and training of the clergy. Limited opportunity, a lack of teaching on confession and/or spiritual direction, and certain individual biases (mostly on the side of the clergy) all play a role in the laity's use of the confessional. Since there really is no category in which the clergy could weigh in on the perspective of the laity as regards confession, we will begin by simply showing the data that indicate their interests before looking into how to evaluate and improve the practice.

Laity on Q.1:
How do you feel about formal confessions?

This question was aimed at evaluating the "gut emotional reaction" of the laity on the mere subject of confession. This question generated four popular responses, which can be described overall as thirty-one positive, and six negative comments. These comments were divided into the following categories:

I. **I like confession**
   a. I completely like it (15 Responses)
   b. I go out of a sense of discipline, for the process, or because of the sacramental nature of it. (11 Responses)
   c. I have trepidation going in, but still like it. (5 Responses)

II. **I dislike confession**
   a. I dislike it, but find it necessary (4 Responses)
   b. I discontinued using the confessional due to a bad experience (1 Response)
   c. I do not go to formal confession (1 Response)

Under the first general category "I like confession," the first sub-category: "I completely like it," drew fifteen responses, and people were overall quite thankful for what confession added to their spirituality. A sample quote representing this category is: "I think it's very necessary to my soul, otherwise things begin to pile up inside you, and you begin to feel terribly guilty." Many people view confession as a gift of the Church that helps them put sin away. A few common threads that were found in this first section were comments such as: "I will not confess to my own parish priest." This theme was repeated four times in this section of the responses, and seven times total under this question. There is some level of personal familiarity that actually turns away potential penitents, particularly novice penitents, and there is also a desire for greater anonymity for the penitent in the confessional process, particularly for first confessions, although not exclusively for first confessions.

The second most popular response under "I like confession" shared a common theme of "going to confession out of a sense of discipline, for the process, or because of the sacramental nature of confession." There were eleven responses, all of which said things pertaining to the necessity of the sacrament, or spoke in some positive way about the structure of the confessional process. "I like the structure of it," was a common response. Some spoke to the "official" nature of it with comments such as, "I like the credibility of an ordained priest," or, "It's what God wants you to do."

The third and final positive group of responses shared a common theme of "I have trepidation going in, but still like it." Five people shared responses indicating that they are always nervous entering the confessional but very relieved on the other side of absolution. One person even commented, "It is difficult but worth it. It shouldn't be easy." All of the people who responded this way demonstrated a level of reverence for the sacrament, which is why this is listed as a positive response; however, they all indicated a common theme of trepidation or fear in approaching confession. This section acknowledges a certain level of "holy fear" which comes into the process of auricular confession. The laity demonstrated this holy fear in that they are willing to approach a frightening subject because of the positive benefits of relieving themselves of sin. There is, in our society, a certain fear of the unknown, and a fear of trusting our private matters to a third party. This is true in medicine. People are often afraid of the doctor, although the doctor is a professional who prescribes remedies. But this is not the limit of this kind of trepidation. People are equally as afraid to take their car to a mechanic, for fear of what the repairs might cost. Rather, they will often, quite dangerously at that, drive a car with smoke coming out of the engine, bright red lights flashing on the dash-board, and every possible indicator that there is a problem with their car, knowing the whole time that the remedy is around the corner at the local mechanic. This kind of fear seems to be universal across ages and demographics. But this portion of the study might be encouraging if reported to lay people by other lay people who can encourage one another to be brave and to seek the healing that is offered—particularly in that confession is free, and as such, cheaper than the doctor's office, or the mechanic's shop.

Now, shifting toward the comments of those who do *not* like confession, clergy should be most attentive to these comments among those who dislike or do not use the process. Among those in the negative responses, only 16% of this study (six total) indicated that they disliked the confessional, and for specific reasons: four said they "dislike confession but still find it necessary," one said they, "discontinued the practice after a bad experience," and one said, "I do not make a formal confession." Among the first four comments that said, roughly, that they "dislike going in, but find it necessary," there was a common theme of respect for the sacrament, yet they commented that it indeed was a heavy burden. Yet, despite this perception of dislike and burden, all continued to go out of a sense of discipline. There is a fine line between those who do not like confession and yet still go because they know the benefits and enjoy it as such, versus those who adamantly do not like confession, but find it necessary, still not liking it in the end, yet partaking nonetheless. In one sense, these responses come across somewhat positively in the use of the practice, yet not in the morale or motivators behind pursuing the practice.

The two unique responses could potentially be put together, but for differing reasons. The first unique response indicated: "I had a bad experience in the Roman Catholic Church and discontinued going after that." This individual felt that the priest gave them harmful guidance that negatively affected the penitent's marital relationship in a major way. This person had been a regular penitent, yet stopped going once there was a breach of trust in the reliability of the counsel given by their confessor, largely because the confessor brought a third party into the confessional process by prescribing a penance that took the confession outside of the confessional. The second unique response, similar to the first, was that this individual does not want to make a formal confession, not because of a bad experience in the confessional, but rather, due to a bad perception of the confessional implanted in their mind as a child. Later in the study, this individual indicated that the confessional was used as a threat to them as a child, and that this perception of the confessional, used as a punishment, prevailed into their adulthood. This individual also uniquely commented on their use of the general confession in a positive way, saying that they felt the general confession did bring them relief. This portion of the study, although unique, is probably not uncommon in the experiences of our society at large. People come to our churches with all kinds of baggage from other Churches—some good, and some bad. It is important to teach the people that the confessional is a place of healing and integrity, and that their private affairs will remain private after their confession. Penances, particularly those that are aimed towards encouraging the penitent to make restitution to someone they have harmed, must be carefully administered. The confessional is a place for the penitent to receive healing and guidance for themselves, not for others. Likewise, the confessional is a place for people to reveal their own sins, and not those of others. If the confessor encourages a penitent to do something to "make up" for their sins in a way that ties someone else into the confessional experience, this has the potential to become a breach of the integrity of the confessional. The participant who revealed their negative experience with the confessional said it was not actually the result of a confession they made, but rather, their spouse had made a confession and was directed by the confessor to confess their sin to their spouse (this respondent), which produced a harmful result in their relationship.

Addressing the second unique comment of the individual who was threatened with confession as a child, a common trick people use in society to make something less comfortable by making fun of it, thereby removing some of its power of fear. This behavior is common among those who would make fun of the confessional by using it as a threat. I often go to parties or gatherings of our secular friends who joke that I need to set up a confessional booth in the closet for their friends who are all sinners and need to make a confession, or something similar to this script. Of course, the people who usually say such things should probably be first in line if I were to set up a confessional at their parties. But the threat of the confessional has also has been common among those of previous generations in which the threat of the confessional was quite real. Parents have often, in times past, used the threat of the confessional to keep their kids walking the "straight and narrow" line at home. Teachers in parochial schools also seem to have been regular culprits of this practice, particularly those who were habited religious teachers (nuns) in Catholic parochial schools. Parents also seem to do the same thing at Christmas, using reports to Santa Claus as the threat to keep their kids in line. This is a dangerous tactic, as children come to fear that with which they have been threatened. Although they seem to out-grow the fear of Santa bringing them a lump of coal, the fear of the confessional has been deeply rooted in some people within our society. Once again, the confessional needs to be taught and promoted as a place of healing, rather than a place of punishment for bad deeds. Public perception is quite important to the success of the confessional, and the integrity, privacy, and positive aspects need to be emphasized to overcome some of these deeply rooted negative perceptions of the confessional.

In summary, the majority of the responses to the confessional were positive, in that thirty-one out of thirty-seven people (84%) felt it was a positive practice. The remainders were either hesitant out of fear, bad experiences, or an overall negative perception of the confessional that was not actually based on a confessional experience so much as the perception of confession as a scary thing. It is entirely likely that these negative responses are more prevalent in the Church than this study represents.

Laity on Q.2
: Did you find that confession brought relief to your soul or
guided you in the right direction?

A natural follow-up question to a qualitative study on whether people like the practice of confession was to ask, roughly, "Did it bring relief or guide you in a better direction?" This question generated three common themes, which can simply be categorized as: twenty-nine positive, five "mixed feelings," and only two negative responses. Overall, it appears that those who go to confession benefit from the practice, and are relieved in mind, body, and soul.

Among the majority of twenty-nine responses who said it brought relief, there were divisions among those who found that it brought positive relief and good direction to follow, those who commented that they "felt nervous going in, but great coming out," and those who "felt a relief, yet commented that the direction to follow was sub-par or poor."

First, twenty-one of the participants (72%) spoke very positively about the effects of confession saying things in common such as, "It's like the weight of the world is off of my shoulders." This quote appeared verbatim three times, and all in separate studies. Three others indicated a common theme that they were actually very surprised if not shocked by the power that making a confession had on their lives. Comments such as these could be quite useful to clergy seeking to encourage their people with the voices of the laity rather than their own. Lay people can often dismiss the voice of the clergy when they disagree on a certain subject. However, when other lay people say the same thing, it has a different effect on how the data are received by people of similar peer-groups—that is, non-clergy. A sub-theme, which appeared four times in this question, indicated that their relationship with the priest made a positive difference in the confessional process. Either they indicated that having a regular confessor made an accumulative difference over time, marked by spiritual progress, that they did not dread it as much because of repetition, or that knowing that they would be going back to the same confessor was an incentive to not sin in the same way again. Several found that confessors who knew them personally offered more specific advice and remedies based on their knowledge of the individual's spiritual life, and the practices they keep. All of these benefits seem to be dependent upon having a regular confessor who knows us, rather than someone who is always a stranger. There was also one positive yet unique comment here about confessing, not only to the clergy, but also among a group of peers or a twelve-step support group, who reported that such experiences were very relieving and brought in an extra layer of love and support. This is significant, in that the fifth step in the "Alcoholics Anonymous" program, as well as in other similarly modeled twelve-step recovery programs, is confession. People seem to find relief where they honestly admit their sins to a confessor or to a peer group and face their sins by committing themselves to the discipline and accountability of others who are outside of their own mind and conscience. This practice sounds a lot like the early public confession models practiced during the early centuries of the Church.

Next, among those four participants who indicated in common tone that they felt nervous going into a confessional situation, yet great coming out, there was also a common theme of elation, only counterbalanced by an extreme fear or nervousness going into the confessional. One participant said, "I was scared at first, but felt almost holy coming out." This tone of nervousness, which was addressed above, was also indicated in one response, in knowing that they have to go through that again was an incentive to not repeat the previously confessed sin. The net result of these responses is simply summarized as: "forgiveness feels good!" When we unburden ourselves of sin, we should feel better, in some sense, about our spiritual health. Of course, this elation is likely proportional to the amount of sin being laid down. Those who are carrying a heavier burden are likely to feel more relief than those who lay down smaller burdens. The overall goal is a clear conscience, and a clean soul. The muddier and dirtier the soul, the more likely one is to feel elation once it is clean. This seems to account for the variance among those who experience different levels of joy following a confession. Regular penitents seem to feel less joy and elation, yet they do express a real sense of comfort as a result of the confessional process, and have learned that the secret to relief is to not pick up the same burdens we have just laid down. Over time, this leads to spiritual maturity, and less potential for committing grave sins by closely guarding the newly cleansed soul.

The final four participants who gave a positive response to this question also made common comments about the direction offered after the confession, which was "sub-par." Comments such as, "The guidance was sound, yet not very insightful," or "Giving me a psalm to read didn't do much for guidance," may offer confessors some insight into how they are directing their penitents after the confession. "Assigning Hail Mary's alone doesn't feel complete," was another unique comment. It appears the people want something that will put them in the right direction, and give them a goal or duty to come away with, which will put them on the path toward replacing their sin with virtue, and challenges them to be a better person with a task aimed at personal holiness. It may also be of value to confessors to realize that the people have generally reported that they do not know what to expect in the confessional. Perhaps if they are taught that the penances should be easy and that they are meant to express the great mercy of God, then their expectations of heavier penances will be minimized. Also, perhaps some penances need to be heavier than assigning a psalm or canticle for particular sins. Some people want to do something good to "pay" for their sin, and although this is not entirely necessary to the process, it is something of which to be aware in the confessional. In the public realm, people are often offered opportunities to do "public service" rather than to pay a fine. While not requiring such acts as contingent on their forgiveness, a confessor might suggest that a remedy to a sin such as selfishness could be to go out and do some community service, or to suggest that they come and see you in the office sometime to talk about what they could do to better serve the church or their community.

When St. Benedict said in his rule, "Idleness is the enemy of the soul," he knew that people often get into trouble when they have nothing else going on in their daily lives. This might be helpful for guiding new penitents toward better holy living, through direction offered in the confessional, yet not making the absolution offered contingent on the acts themselves. People want to put things right, and the direction portion of the confessional could probably be stronger in some parishes than it is currently.

Finally, there were two participants who said that the confessional experience brought no relief to their souls, but for varying reasons. One individual indicated that they never found the penances to be that serious. One comment heard earlier by one who did find relief in the confession said: "It seemed like it wasn't enough." Another participant said, "Others told me I would feel awesome if I made a confession, but I didn't." Perhaps, from this comment, we might consider whether initial expectations have anything to do with the process. If people are assured of relief, and yet don't feel relief, is that an indication of failure of the process, the clergy, or the penitent? It this case, it appears the expectation was that they would feel "awesome" and yet after the confession that was not the case. They could not qualify why this was the case—it just was not the feeling that they were promised. People bring a lot of expectations to the confessional, and it cannot be assumed that the experience of one person with a varying list of sins making a confession to one confessor will be mirrored by a completely different person with different sins offering a confession to a different confessor. The experience is unique in each instance, based on the sins being laid down, the quality of the confessor, the quality of the advice or remedies offered, the reception of these things by the penitent, the stress of the penitent and their ability to receive the advice given while in a state of anxiety, and the grace working throughout the process in the perception of the penitent. Overall, what can be taken from these responses is the fact that we should teach those who have not made a confession that their confession will be unique to them, and that they should simply approach the confessional by preparing using some form of an examination of conscience, being as honest as possible to the process, and to be attentive to the advice being offered and the forgiveness of God to be obtained. The feelings, results, and aftermath of the process will be what they will be. However, there are many who have had consistently positive experiences, and sharing those experiences (not the content, just the quality of the experience) can be helpful in encouraging others to make a confession. But no promises should be made as to how they will feel afterwards. One cannot tell another how to feel, but may comment on how it made them feel. Such things can clearly change the perception of new penitents entering the confessional for the first time.

In summary, most people who responded to this question did so in a favorable or positive manner. This teaches us that although auricular is not the most popular mode of confession in the current life of the Church, it is quite useful and seems to be doing some good in the lives of our people.

Clergy Questions

The following questions were posited to the clergy. Results follow each question, from which we may draw some conclusions based on the raw data alone, but will also offer commentary in light of the historical study's conclusions.

Question 1: How regularly do you sit to hear confessions in the Church or confessional?

fig 1

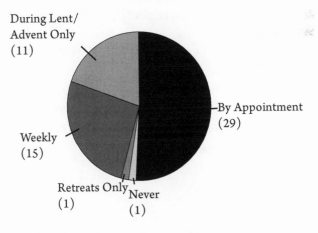

How regularly do you sit to hear confessions in the church or confessional?

During Lent/ Advent Only (11)

By Appointment (29)

Weekly (15)

Retreats Only (1)   Never (1)

From this data we can draw a few conclusions: First, none (0%) of the clergy are sitting daily to hear confessions. Secondly, the vast majority, 67.4% of the clergy, only hear   confessions "by appointment", leaving the responsibility for scheduling confessions to the laity. This also demonstrates one of the points discussed earlier at the conclusion of the historical section, that most clergy are depending on the general confession to do the work of atonement, and as such are not regularly sitting to hear confessions, or leave it to their people to determine when their sin is worthy of scheduling an appointment. This is not to say that the people are completely inept at making this decision. However, the laity have consistently reported throughout the study that they will not make an appointment to make a confession due to some sense of: "my sin is bad, but not bad enough to make an appointment," or "making an appointment is scary." The clergy have seemingly used this "by appointment" policy as a means of not having to sit for regular confessional hours under the guise of being a better use of their time to meet the people when they are available to meet. However, the people have revealed in this study that they will not make an appointment, and would actually be significantly more likely to come if there was a regularly set time, and if the time and name of the confessor was well advertised. A common thread woven throughout the laity responses to this subject, were comments such as "I will not make an appointment to have father hear my confession." This seems to be particularly true for first time penitents, but was also fairly prevalent even for experienced penitents. There are some things said in the confessional that the laity simply cannot bring themselves to sharing with familiar clergy. This is where bringing in a guest confessor, trading confessional hours with another local parish priest, or simply referring our people to another local parish's confessor can be handy tools to alleviate some of the fear of this stigma—or perhaps eliminate the excuse.

Third, the next largest field is among those clergy who have regular weekly scheduled confessions, which make up 34.9%, or just over a third of the clergy who responded. This is significant, in that this is considered rare, and that just over a third of the clergy who responded are regularly scheduling and hearing confessions. Those who do sit regularly also say that they do not get much regular business in the confessional, although a few of them do have a line waiting for them out the door. In these parishes where the priest has been a regular confessor with posted and advertised confessional hours and who also regularly preach on the subject, their people are far more in favor of the practice, and consider it significantly important to their spiritual lives. These parishes also seem to boast more than the usual number of "mature" Christian leaders among their laity, who also serve to meet the needs of those in the congregation who need support and encouragement in this area.

In the lay study, seven people indicated that increasing the availability of confessional opportunities would be an incentive for them to practice it more, and to make it known in the parish that it is a practice of the Church. It seems although we have identified three major modes of confession, the general confession is perceived to be the only mode in many places. To this point some said, "If it's a sacrament, then it should be offered weekly," while another said, "If I knew someone was there, I would be more likely to go." Among the comments offered at the end of the laity study, which will be included below under the heading: "The best advice of the laity for the clergy," several indicated the need for more frequent opportunities to make a confession, a need for a variety of confessional opportunities such as anything other than Saturday mornings, and even the possibility of offering a variety of confessors, or referring the people to neighboring churches when anonymity or availability are an issue. The people give an overall sense that they want to make a confession during regular confessional hours, but they have to be available to be utilized.

Fourth, roughly a quarter (25.6%) of the clergy only hear confessions during penitential seasons such as Lent or Advent, which only accounts for six weeks in the spring, and four weeks in the winter, leaving forty-two weeks of the year without offering a regularly scheduled time to make a confession. The priests in this field revealed that this practice does not seem to draw much business. The laity have clearly said, "if it is only a once in a while practice, that to them it does not seem as important," although the clergy did reveal that they do get some business during these seasons, and the people who come find it helpful. One portion of the laity study reveled that the clergy sometimes announce confessional hours during Advent and Lent as their "required duty" but that the clergy were somewhat dismissive about their expectations that anyone would come. It should be noted that if the clergy are dismissive about this practice, the laity will pay it no mind, and are unlikely to come to confession if the priest presents it as a burden or a waste of their time.

Fifth, this leaves the remainder, only two clergymen of the diocese who responded, who only hear confessions on retreats, or not at all. These, it would seem, are those who consider the general confession sufficient to this end, and have no intention of ever offering auricular confession in their parishes. Clergy comments that support this assertion are listed below in response to a sub-question to this part of the survey. To those clergy who believe the general confession sufficient to the needs of the laity, they might be surprised to learn that a common thread that appeared several times in the study, in reference to the general confession as said in the context of the Sunday Eucharist, saying that they felt it was inadequate. One even said, "I don't always feel forgiven in the general confession." Another said, "[Confession] is a lot better than the general confession because it kind of focuses on the accountability that you have to your faith, and helps you follow through on it, more so than confessing it on your own, or among a group of people in the Church." These responses are most intriguing, in that they address the first and most popular mode of confession in Anglican Churches—the general confession—as inadequate to their spiritual needs. While some believe the general confession is a good thing, and needs to remain in its proper place, they acknowledge times in their own spiritual journeys in which they needed something more, and auricular confession was the remedy. In support of this premise, eleven people commented on the positive aspect of having a process that assures them of forgiveness, and said that auricular confession brought a level of credibility to their confession. It seems people like to be assured of their forgiveness, and auricular confession meets this need, more so than the general confession, which offers no assurances or accountability to the penitent beyond their own conscience. This not only raises the relevance of auricular confession, but should also inspire the interest among the clergy as to whether they should be offering more than one mode of confession in their parishes.

Conclusions to be drawn from these data are simply that of the overall limited availability of the exercise around the diocese. We can deduce that if the confessional is not made available, then the people must therefore request an appointment with the clergy to make a confession, which is something that they have said they are very unlikely to do. In those places where confession is frequently offered, it is more frequently utilized by the laity—not a majority of the laity, but it is more frequent where the practice is offered and well-advertised and supported with sermons and teachings on the practice.

A sub-question was offered to this first question, which may be of some value to the reader, which read: If you answered "not at all", how do you handle "confessional" moments or "spiritual direction"? Also, feel free to comment on the "demand" of the people for confession/ spiritual direction as you see it in your context. These were the raw responses:

    a. During penitential seasons, monthly, and on request.

    b. We have taught this so poorly the world has moved beyond us.

    c. There is very little demand for personal confession, though the demand I do receive is very significant. Most appointments are for spiritual direction in a general sense.

    d. More demand for pastoral counseling/spiritual direction than anything else. Topics run from dealing with sin to being surprised and confused by a spiritual situation such as an immediate, unexpected answer to prayer.

    e. Personal counsel.

    f. I have only received one request for confession in the past five years. Most appointments are for general counseling.

    g. On demand, whenever it occurs. In fact, I would guess that I hear more occasional 'on demand' confessions than formal ones.

    h. I will be answering based on my situation having been the rector of the same church for the 34 years. I have known the benefit and grace of sacramental confession since I was 22 years of age when I started making my confession regularly and have continued so to do to this day. "Regular" has meant at least every two months and before major feasts, and in between when in special need, such as having committed mortal sin. Now retired, I am probably making my confession once a month or every two or three weeks. Many years in my active ministry I was making my confession weekly. With this as background, I taught and preached about the benefit and grace of sacramental confession regularly at my church. As a curate of mine once said, "Father, you're a real Mass, Mary, and confession priest". And the parish priests, in my early years, sat for confessions every Saturday, from Noon to 12:30pm, whether or not anyone came; we could certainly use the time to pray for our people's growth in repentance and holiness of life. But over the years, often enough, at least one person would show up for confession. And before Christmas and Easter we had to schedule multiple sittings for confession (each one for an hour or more), because of the numbers.

Based on these responses, we can say that the experience of the clergy is clearly mixed. Some are not getting much action in the confessional, while others are. One in particular indicated that they have only had one request in five years or confession, although they only hear confessions by appointment. One other has conceded that: "We have taught this so poorly the world has moved beyond us." A couple of the clergy have indicated that they are being approached more for spiritual counsel than confession, the frequency of which will be covered by a later question. This also supports the lay perspective, which said overwhelmingly that they are unlikely to schedule a confession. The clergy have likewise said that the people have not been making any appointments for confession, but when they make appointments, it is more for a general state of "guidance" than for a formal confession.

Overall, we may conclude that regular hours of hearing confessions are not being kept by a majority of the clergy. The majority (67.4%) prefer to hear confessions by appointment only. Although just over a third are offering regular confessional hours, and are hearing confessions during that time.

Question 2: How regularly do you get approached in public for "Spiritual Advice"?

The purpose of this question was to ascertain whether clergy are receiving regular requests for spiritual counsel in public as opposed to the Church setting.

fig 2

How regularly do you get approached in public for spiritual advice?

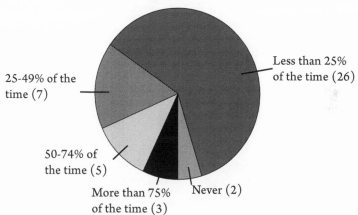

These results indicate that many of the clergy are not getting approached in public with any regularity, though it does happen. A total of 18.6% of the clergy indicated that they are being approached by people for spiritual counsel greater than 50% of the time they go in public. It seems people are approaching clergy when they see them, and in some places are very willing to even make a confession or discuss spiritual matters and concerns while sitting in public with someone they have never met, yet recognize them as clergy.

Natural questions arise from these results, such as: do the clergy wear clericals or other clergy garb in public? Another way of asking this question is: can the people tell that they are clergy? Are the clergy going to places where people have the opportunity to approach them, such as sitting in a social environment like a coffee shop, restaurant counter, a bar, or other place in which they are seen and seem approachable? Are they staying long enough to be approached? Many public places are quite busy, or crowded, and it is difficult to approach someone for a personal matter in a crowded or noisy place, or in a fast-food or take-out venue. While it is difficult, if not impossible, to quantify these last two questions, as most clergy are not accustomed to systematically recording the number of times they go into public, or how long we stay there; it is however possible to ask the clergy how often then wear clericals in public.

Overall, despite little discussion of what these results reveal, it does seem that people have an interest in seeking spiritual guidance, and will even approach a clergyman in public to discuss their concerns rather than asking to make an appointment in the Church, which seemingly would be more private. It is the experience of the author that more people approach me in the public sphere than in the Church about spiritual guidance. Many times, I have been approached and even interrupted in the middle of a meal or a conversation by someone who has a burning need to talk about something, which I find usually to be related to sin or a fairly serious spiritual matter. Such is the hunger of the average person on the street to make a confession to a stranger in public, rather than to ask for an appointment, or to seek out counsel in the church itself. As for our laity, it seems that their expectation is to find the priest in Church, and to find confession in the confessional space. Several have indicated that they are willing to "drop by the office" when they have a burning spiritual need, and may not wait for the prescribed confessional hours. However, there are a number of people in the public realm who have no other recourse than to catch clergy when they are in public spheres. As such, they take advantage of speaking to clergy as the opportunity presents itself, so the clergy might endeavor to be prepared to be asked anything when in public. Although it seems the people in our parishes will seek us out at the Church, which is our expected venue of church-business.

Question 3: How often do you wear 'clericals' or other identifying 'clergy garb' in public?

It should be of note to this question that the customary of the diocese surveyed requires all active clergy to wear cassocks in the office, or other such acceptable clergy garb when they are in the office or public sphere, such as a black suit with a black clergy shirt and clerical collar.

fig 3

How often do you wear "Clericals" or other identifying "clergy garb" in public?

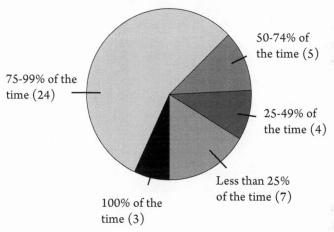

These data indicate that the vast majority of the clergy are wearing clericals when they go about in public places. None (0%) of the responses indicated that they never wear clericals. This would lead us to conclude that the majority of our clergy, when in public, are likely identifiable as "clergy" by their common dress, and as such, the people in the public sphere among the places where our clergy serve, eat, and shop are extremely likely to recognize them as clergy.

While we cannot quantify the value of wearing clericals in public, this practice may be of value for those ministers of traditions that do not wear clothing that identifies them as clergy in public places. There is some benefit to being identified as clergy to strangers who meet them in public. Many of our clergy report that they are regularly approached in public by strangers who recognize that they are clergy according to their "uniform." These data may also be of some benefit to clergy of traditions that traditionally wear clericals, but whose clergy may not be of the habit of wearing them on a regular basis or when they are not "in the office" or otherwise at the Church.

Those who do regularly wear clericals in public have revealed that this practice serves as an invitation, indicating that they are willing to be approached about spiritual matters. There is also a factor in the research of "the science of persuasion" that reveals that people are significantly more likely to trust a person in uniform, and to lend more credence to their expertise in any and all matters. I have also found that I get approached in public while wearing clericals by people who assume I work wherever it is that I am, even a restaurant or a dollar store, simply because I look like someone in authority. When people see a uniform, or even just a well-dressed individual, they assume authority, trust, and reliability, and therefore, respond accordingly.

The laity were not asked specifically about the use of clericals, nor about approaching their priest or any priest in public, and as such, there is little reflection to be shared here. However, the laity did indicate that although they are at times reluctant to make a confession to their own priest, they would be willing to make a confession to an unfamiliar or guest confessor, who would also be identified as clergy by their dress, or by the fact that they have been licensed or allowed to hear confessions in their home parish as a guest confessor.

Question 4: What is the proportion of public confessions/counseling requests you receive, versus formal confessions the Church setting?

fig 4

What is the proportion of public confessions/counselling requests you receive versus formal confessions in a church setting?

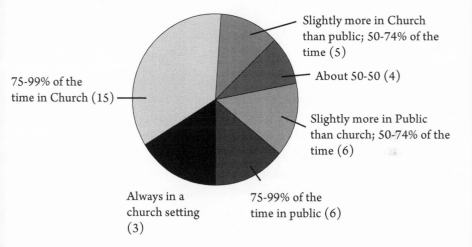

These data support the fact that the majority of the confessions heard by the clergy are heard in a church setting versus a public setting. It may also be of note that fifteen clergy indicated that they hear more confessions in Church than in public, while at the same time, fifteen clergy responded to question one saying that they sit regularly to hear confessions on a weekly basis. This may indicate that when the confessional is regularly advertised and open for business, this may be the place where clergy are most likely to hear the most confessions. While this may seem redundant, as clergy are far more likey to be found in a church or church office than in a public place, the data indicate something extraordinary: over a quarter (28.6%) of the clergy reported that they hear confessions more in public than in private. A few (9.5%) of the clergy said that they hear around the same amount in public as in private (50/50%), while 14.3% said that they hear a few more in public than in Church, and an equal 14.3% indicated that they hear exceedingly more confessions in public than in Church. These are remarkable data which support the assertions found in response to the previous questions, that non-churched people are increasingly more likely to approach us publicly than to make an appointment, although our own people will be more likely to speak to us in the Church if we are there.

The laity were posed a question on spiritual direction in opposition to confession to determine, if possible whether it is the formality or contextual setting of confession that may turn people away, and whether or not the people would be more comfortable making a confession or receiving spiritual guidance in a casual or face-to-face encounter, rather than in a confessional-booth, or other such formal confessional setting. Admittedly, the conjecture by the author in this portion of the interviews was that there was something about the setting that was keeping people away. However, the results were contrary to this assertion.

First, fourteen people (38.88%) said that they preferred the confessional setting. Bear in mind, none of these respondents churches have actual confessional booths, but they are describing the more formalized confessional practice in which confessions are heard in the church setting (e.g. within the altar rail, or in the rector's office). One said, "I don't think of spiritual direction as a 'real confession.'" Another indicated a reason: "Confession feels more complete or 'full circle.' Spiritual direction seems 'open-ended.'" Another indicated, "We should do sacramental things in the sacramental place—the Church." Of these fourteen, four in particular indicated that they felt they got plenty of spiritual direction within the context of the confessional. Three people actually called for a return of the confessional booths, a practice long thought to be out of vogue.

One participant said, "If I had it my way, I would reinstall the confessional booths, and it would be offered regularly." Similar to this comment, three people said this in a different way, indicating that they don't want to encounter the priest for confession in a "face-to-face" encounter. One in particular said, "I don't like looking at the priest while confessing. The back of his head is fine." Many people indicated throughout the study that they would not be likely to go to someone other than the priest to make a confession. The interesting conclusion to be drawn from these responses was that the people are actually in favor of the formal setting, and the more private the better. Many, as we have already witnessed, actually called for a return of the confessional booth. This teaches us that not only is the second mode of confession, auricular confession, a valid mode, but that it is perceived by a large portion of this study as more relevant or effective than the third mode, and capable of achieving the same goals in a different context, while still vastly different than the general confession.

Now, to expound on the middle of the spectrum, seventeen people (47.22%) said that they thought "both practices were good," and that each had its place in the life of the Church. Many said things such as, "Different needs call for different answers or solutions." Five of the participants indicated that their comfort was a factor in choosing how to approach their spiritual needs. Some addressed the nature of the conversation: "Sometimes it's nice to have a casual conversation," while others addressed the setting: "Sometimes I'm more spiritually comfortable where I'm also physically comfortable." The same person also said, "The formal [context] with the screen is nice." This leaves one to wonder, is the confessional booth actually a more comfortable option than the church pews, or a chair? Perhaps a side-note is to make sure the chair used for confessions, whether in or out of a "booth" is a comfortable chair. That is, of course, unless you use a kneeler or a prie-dieu, in which case, the padding on the kneeler might need to be addressed. From these responses, we witness a continual support for the confessional as an appropriate mode of confession, while also allowing that sometimes the third mode of private spiritual direction is helpful, depending on the spiritual need of the penitent. Comfort also seems to come into play in a large way with these responses in particular. The people have said clearly that they will share their sins where they are most comfortable, and that the varying modes offer varying modes of comfort. We can deduce from these responses that clergy should be attentive to the comfort level of their confessional and spiritual direction spaces, as these directly correlate to the frequency of usage among some people.

The qualitative nature of this part of the study may be indicating more about the comfort of those who want to confess in a more casual setting, versus those who prefer that we "bring back the booths." The people seem to be in favor of confessions in the formal setting, or would gladly go either way, so long as it is in a comfortable setting and meets their spiritual needs. Only a very few indicated that they absolutely preferred the more casual setting, and there really is not a consistent reason beyond personal preference or "comfort." Privacy is a consistent concern, and to some degree the priest's office or another private place seems to offer a higher sense of privacy in some settings, while in others the priest's office is perceived to be just as public as people can see when the penitents come or go. However, from these responses we have seen that the perception is: if a more private place were offered in the church, such as a sound-proofed confessional, the people seem to be far more in favor of that setting for a formal confession.

One unique response indicated that the most beneficial thing to them was the anonymity of the process. They spoke specifically of partaking of spiritual direction with someone who was not their priest: "In spiritual direction, I can go to someone who is not my priest." Once again, this theme of anonymity has come up, in which the person finds comfort in someone who they do not have to see on a regular basis in the parish. This raises the point that if this is truly a recurring theme throughout the study, perhaps the clergy should have available alternative sources for confession and spiritual direction for their people who bear this hindrance. While many have indicated that having a regular confessor is actually more beneficial, there seem to be many, at least for their first few confessions, who would prefer to share their sins with someone that they do not have to see as often. It is difficult to gauge the motive behind this need, other than as a matter of comfort for the penitent. However, in attempting to address the needs of the people, having alternative confessors or spiritual directors from time to time may allow for some people to come to confession or spiritual direction who would otherwise not be as likely to partake.

This is a side note on comfort, but perhaps there is something to the counseling office model of having a separate entrance and exit for those seeking confession or spiritual guidance. Professional counselors often implement this system in their offices of offering a separate waiting room or those expecting to enter for counseling, and a quite separate exit door to the counselor's office for those who have already received counseling. A question to be considered might be: what if we offered a confessional booth that had a separate entrance and exit? If privacy is a major issue, perhaps aiming for the highest level of privacy would benefit the use of the confessional, or increased use of spiritual direction in the private offices of the clergy. Of course, the argument might also go the other way, in that the people waiting to make a confession might be encouraged by the positive looks of those leaving he confession, and perhaps be a little less afraid to enter when it is their turn. But nonetheless, the people's responses were overwhelmingly in favor of more privacy, rather than influencing those in the waiting area.

Another repeating theme was found in the qualitative study under how people who like confession first came to the confessional, in which three people commented that they were brought to the confessional for the first time through the encouragement of other lay people at a renewal weekend or non-parish-church environment. This is a theme that also repeated several times in other parts of the study. Other penitent-laity can play a significant role in the spread of the practice of confession. This is one of the areas in which the clergy could benefit from the help of experienced laity by giving them a voice to the non-confessing laity concerning confessional practice. Spiritual retreats or renewal weekends are usually attended by those who are already in a mode of seeking something new to add to their spiritual lives. One piece of advice given here was to encourage the clergy to ask certain regular penitents to speak up when talking in a group setting about confession, and asking to share the nature of their experience, not the content. Then the clergy could give their talk about the practice, and simply say, "Is there anyone in the room that would like to say something about their confessional experience, without bringing up what they actually discussed in the confessional." This then gives them a window of opportunity to speak up, and to encourage others in the room to give it a try. Several clergy have reported that when this opportunity accompanies their teaching, the number of first-time penitents is exponentially larger than if the clergy were the sole speakers on the subject.

As a sub-question to this particular survey question the clergy were asked: "Is there a specific place you hear the most public confessions such as prisons, retreat centers, monasteries, and etc.?" These were the responses:

a. Youth Camps, bars, restauruants, Happening, renewal events, Youth Fall Rally.
b. In public, when in clericals, I get approached more for other things (money) than confessions.
c. Prisons and retreats
d. No specific location (2 identical responses)
e. Funeral Homes
f. Hospitals, retreat centers, camps, restaurants, and major department stores.

These responses tell us that people on religious retreats are also likley candidates for confessional opportunities, if offered, while there are also many opportunities for confessional moments in hospitals, restaurants, department stores, and other seemingly unlikely places for confessions to be heard. It is also of note that some of these places must be sought out by the clergy, such as prisons.

Question 5: How many years have you been serving as a priest, chaplain, or other form of minister?

This question's main objective was to obtain basic demographics from among the clergy for the sake of the reader, but perhaps to also identify whether clergy of a certain tenure in the ministry were more likely to hear confessions than recently ordained clergy. While the data do not support any such conclusion, as the majority of the clergy identified here are of the practice of hearing confessions, the data support the fact that the clergy in this particular diocese are of consistent practice of offering to hear confessions regardless of length or tenureof experience. This may also be the result of a generation of clergymen being trained primarily by the same seminary.

fig 5

How many years have you been serving as a priest/chaplain/minister?

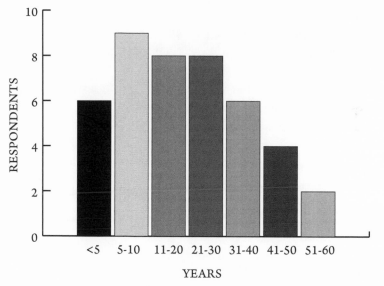

The laity made several comments throughout the study pertaining to the confessional skills of the clergy, saying things such as: "Some priests are better than others." Similar comments repeat throughout this study, indicating that the people perceive that there is a variance in the guidance being offered by the various clergy confessors, which is recognizable to the penitent laity. Suffice to say that the people are fairly charitable to the clergy as a whole for offering them guidance, even if it is not quite what they expected, or not as good as they receive "back home." Overall, the people want more direction, and perceive a difference in the confessional practice of various confessors. Five people offered answers to this question of the quality of the confessor, which said that they had "mixed experiences with relief and guidance in the confessional." This picks up on a common theme from before, in which four out of the five said that, "the selection of a confessor makes a big difference." These people have gone to confession to multiple confessors, and have noticed over time that some priests are quite good at hearing confessions and offering direction, while others simply are not. Another mentioned that the personality of the clergyman made them feel as though they would not make a confession to him. But with their current priest, the relationship is such that they felt the priest has, "a closeness to God that makes me want to open up." This information should be important to clergy who are preparing to hear confessions, and to know that their life outside of the confessional does influence, to some degree, the willingness of some of the people to make a confession to them. There is another factor to be discussed here, which this survey does not reflect, which is that the diocese interviewed for tis study does a really good job at mentoring younger clergy in the praxis of the ministry, including confession. These mentoring opportunities come in different forms, from diocesan curacies where newly ordained clergy spend two years under the mentorship of a senior clergyman, to regular "new clergy" gatherings which offer lectures on various subjects for the benefit of new clergy and the renewal of the others. These clergy also have various opportunites to work together on retreats, at summer camp, and in other contexts where the young or newly-ordained clergy have ample opportunites to grow in the practice of ministry. In places where clergy are more isolated and insular, this is probably less likely to happen. While this Diocese does not really indoctrinate the clergy to a single mind-set, there are various opportunites for collegiality, open discussion, and sharing of pastoral resources for the benefit of the whole. Those who do not have such an opportunity might consider whether seeking out a group of local clergy peers, even of other denominations, such as in a community "ministerial alliance", may be of value to the isolated clergy. Also, there is great benefit in continuing education, even for the seasoned clergyman as offered by various seminaries.

Question 6: What is your current age?

Like the previous qustion, this was a matter of obtaining demographics, and did not lead to any conclusions as to whether clergy of a certain age are more likely to hear confessions than those of a younger age, although it does demonstrate the variety of ages active within the diocese. It is also interesting how many active clergy within the diocese are over seventy years old, given that the mandatory retirement age is seventy-two. This is merely an indication of how many devoted clergy we have who are willing to continue to offer their services as an assistant or chaplain after they have retired from full-time ministry. Senior clergy are a true inspiration in our Diocese, and often lead retreats and lectures for the benefit of the younger clergy.

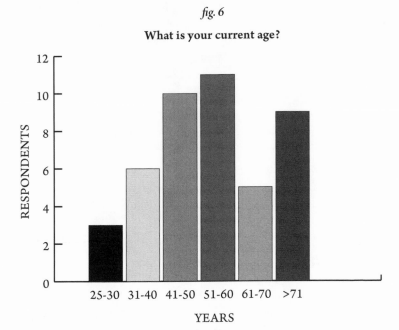

fig. 6

What is your current age?

Question 7: In which Faith Tradition were you born and raised?

The purpose of this question was to determine if the tradition in which the clergy were born and raised was of influence on whether they were of the practice of hearing confessions. The assumption here is that clergy who were raised in a tradition which offered confession would probably be more likley to become clergy who would offer to hear confessions. The clergy were offered the following twenty-one selections of faith traditions (based on other common surveys regarding faith traditions in the United States): Roman Catholic, Eastern Orthodox, Episcopal/Anglican, Lutheran, Methodist/Pietist, Baptist, Presbyterian, Disciples of Christ, Assemblies of God, Mormon/Latter Day Saints, Adventist, Christian Science, Communal, European Free Church (Brethren, Mennonites, Quakers, Amish), Holiness, Independent Fundamentalist, Judaism, Pentecostal, Spiritualist, Non-Denominational, and Other. These are the results:

fig. 7

In what faith tradition were you born and raised?

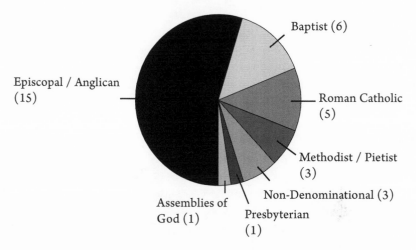

This question also allowed for an "Other" category, which had two responses:

a. None.

b. Converted to Christianity from nothing at age 18.

The majority of the clergy of the diocese surveyed (56.1%) grew up as Episcopal or Anglican children, and another sizable group (12.2%) were from the Roman Catholic tradition, which also is of the regular practice of offering auricular confessions. There remain roughly one-third (34%) of the clergy who grew up in a different tradition, or more than one tradition, which were not known to be of the regular habit of offering confessions as a tradition.

It would seem, in this particular Diocese, that the assumption asserted is supported by this data, in that clergy who were reared in a more Protestant tradition, tend to hold to more Protestant practices, or to lean more towards the Protestant theologies and tendencies within Anglicanism. The clergy who were raised in Episcopal/Anglican or

Catholic traditions tend to lean more towards confessional practice and the more Catholic theological leanings. In addition, this Diocese seems to have had more of an Anglo-Catholic pedigree, in that the majority of the clergy sent to seminary from this Diocese were trained in Anglo-Catholic seminaries, and as such, their piety is reflective of more traditional confessional praxis. This is significant, in that many of the clergy in the diocese are "home-grown" or were fairly local to the area in their youth.

Question 8: In what faith tradition were you primarily trained for the ministry?

The purpose of this question was to determine whether the clergy were trained for the ministry by faith traditions that are known to offer training in hearing confessions, as not all of our clergy began their ministry in the Episcopal or Anglican Church. The same twenty-one faith traditions listed in the previous question were offered for this question. These were the results:

fig. 8

In what faith tradition were primarily trained for the ministry?

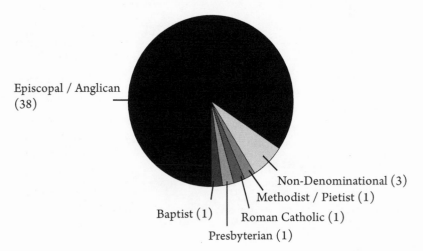

The vast majority (88.4%) of the clergy serving in this diocese were trained in an Episcopal Seminary. The first conclusion to be drawn from these data, in light of the previous question as well, is that while the majority (51.6%) of our clergy were reared in our tradition, even more (88.4%) were trained by our tradition for the ministry.

While the laity were not asked to determine whether they thought the faith tradition of the clergy made an impact on the confessional teaching in their parish, as they all generally assume their clergy were trained by Anglican or Episcopal seminaries if they are working in such parishes, a question was to the laity to ascertain the people's overall perception of the education or training of the clergy when hearing confessions or offering spiritual guidance. The laity were asked specifically, "When you made a confession or went for spiritual direction, do you feel as though your priest was adequately trained to guide you?" The people approached this subject from varying viewpoints, but overall answered: "yes," "no," or "I have had mixed experiences." In general, it seems the people are quite charitable with the clergy, and do in fact trust the clergy to guide them, even if the guidance was not very deep or profound.

Overwhelmingly, twenty-eight (77.77%) of the participants said "Yes," the clergy were adequately trained. Some approached this from a technical standpoint such as "the clergy said all of the things in the sacrament that they were supposed to say." While others related their answers to the guidance they received. Many did not make these distinctions, but simply answered: "Yes." Of the twenty-eight who said yes, four of them indicated a very small anomaly in which the priest was not educated or was "sub-par" to handle the problem, based on their experience, but acknowledged that this was a rare occurrence. Three others indicated that although they felt the priest was educated enough, "Some [clergy] are simply better than others," or, "I relate better to some than others." This was not an indictment against the education of the clergy, but rather their individual preferences for more educated or more relational clergy, depending on their personal situation and personality preferences. One peculiar answer added, "With their higher learning, they need to be sensitive to the fact that I need to relate to what they're saying." Another peculiar instance was of a parishioner who said, "I had one bad experience when I was in a long line of confessions, and the priest wasn't attentive. But that was another parish. I felt, 'If I've prepared for this, then the priest should too.'" Here, two conclusions may be asserted—first, that the clergy need to make sure that the people in the confessional or spiritual direction session understand what they are saying and that they are confident that they can follow-up on the instruction given, or that it has at least been understood. Secondly, the people want to perceive that the clergy are taking their spiritual care seriously, and that they are willing to treat each instance separately and with dignity, as the penitent only knows of the content of their own confession. While the clergy may have just heard five confessions in a row, each one is new, and requires our complete attention. We should be offering guidance specific to the needs of the penitent, rather than simply telling all of them to "say three *Hail Mary's*, and two *Our Fathers,* and go in peace." The people want to perceive that we have heard their concerns, and offered them not only absolution, but also some kind of advice or encouragement specific to their problems.

Only two (5.55%) of the comments said "No." One was more of a philosophical viewpoint: "No priest will ever be completely adequate for all needs at all times. The Holy Spirit is what makes and forms them into something that they are not by nature." The other response was negative as to the training for their specific need, but said in the positive, "Not really, not for what I went in for, but his kindness made up for any lack of training." Here, we see that most of the people think the clergy are well trained, and the only two negative comments have more to do with the breadth of advice the priest had to offer in their particular instance, one of which was hypothetical. We may also extract from the latter of the two comments, a common theme from previous answers which leads us to understand that if the clergy are kind in the confessional, and can indicate that they are listening and offering the best advice they have to offer, while also saying that there might be other solutions, and that the penitent might find a more direct answer to their need if they consulted someone else suggested by the clergy, the people are willing to forgive ignorance of the clergy concerning their specific problem, if the clergy are friendly and emotionally supportive.

Six respondents indicated that they had mixed experiences, which were beyond single anomalies, and left them to respond accordingly. Two of the six indicated that the problem might have been in how they communicated with different priests. "Most of the time—yes. I don't like leaving with a feeling of 'if' in my mind. I'm not sure they always understood me." The other said, "I think they all have the training, but perhaps it is how I communicate that leads to a bad experience. I'm not sure they always get what I'm saying." Another person indicated, uniquely, that the education needed for confession should be fairly simple, yet for spiritual direction they thought the clergy would need significantly more education or training than a confessor. The remaining three simply stated that their experiences were "hit and miss." One was happy with their home confessor yet disappointed outside of their home parish. Another indicated, "Some [clergy] seem well trained; others just don't seem to hit the nail on the head." These perspectives seem to weigh heavily upon the experiences of the penitents, some of whom compared their peculiar experiences to the comfort of their home confessor. First, we should note that clarity is important to a confession or spiritual direction session. No matter how good the advice may be, if it is not understood, it is useless. Perhaps confessors could add to their confessional process a simple question at the end, "Has everything I've said made sense to you?" or "Do you feel as though we've answered all of your concerns today?" This offers the penitent an opportunity to say no, and to explain what continues to confuse or baffle them, or to seek more clarity. Secondly, it seems that those who attend parishes that offer regular confessional hours have a real attachment to their home confessor, and as such, seem to hold others pale in comparison. This is the perception of the author, in that I know that this diocese has a few "All Star" confessors who are truly gifted, and some who probably should not be hearing confessions without more training. It is difficult not to compare one confessor to another, particularly once you have developed an emotional and spiritual bond with a good and godly confessor. Whether this is perfectly true or not, it is true that the perception of regular penitents will change with a change of regular confessor. At any rate, if the confessor is sincere, and doing what they can to offer good guidance and absolution, forgiveness comes, and God can use the Holy Spirit in various ways to achieve direction where the confessor may fail.

Overall, it seems the vast majority of the people making confessions and attending spiritual direction are pleased with the education of their clergy. There are a few people who have had different experiences, but do not attribute all of the blame on the clergy. Kindness, it seems, is the secret to covering any gaps.

The data also support the fact that there are a number of clergy actively ministering in our diocese who expereinced a breadth of training from other traditions, many of which are not known to be traditions which offer or emphasize confession or private spiritual direction.

While this portion of the survey does indicate the faith traditions which primarily trained the clergy for ministry, it does not indicate conclusively whether the education offered in the seminaries actually included any training in hearing confession or offering spiritual direction. Furthermore, these data do not indicate whether the clergy trained in any tradition may have continued to expand their education outside of the seminary, either by attending continuing education courses or seminars, or by reading on subjects in which they found that they needed more edification. These concerns will be addressed in the following question.

Question 9: What was the proportion of training you experienced in spiritual direction versus confessional training?

fig. 9

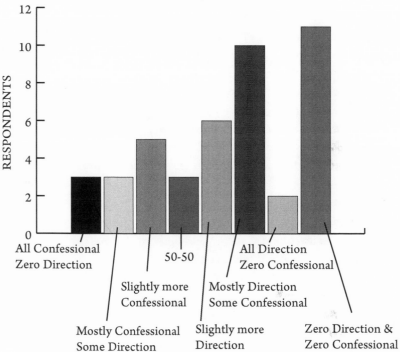

What is the proportion of training you received in spiritual direction versus confessional training?

The data here support several conclusions, many of which are suprising, given that local Episcopal/Anglican traditions are historically known to offer confession, and that our prayer books offer liturgies for hearing confessions. Anglo-Catholic clergy are especially known to be regular confessors, and the Diocese surveyed boasts having a majority of Anglo-Catholic clergy.

First, approximately a quarter (25.6%) of the clergy indicated that they have received no (0%) education in either confessional practice, or in offering spiritual direction. This is astounding, given than some of these clergy are likely offering to hear confessions and spiritual direction with absolutley no training in either field. Although we may assume that they do offer some kind of Christian-based direction, given their training in Biblical morals and ethics and so on, it is distressing that so many claim to have not been trained in either practice by their seminaries.

The data reveal that a total of 42% of the clergy who say they were trained in one or the other claim that the majority of their training favored spiritual direction rather than confession, to varying degrees. Roughly a quarter (25.6%) reported that they were trained primarily in confessional practice to varying degrees, leaving a small margin (7%) of those surveyed who said they were trained fairly evenly in both disciplines. The conclusion we may draw from these data is that the majority of those surveyed were given either more emphasis on spiritual direction over confession, or they were not trained at all. We may further deduce from these data that perhaps the reason many of the clergy do not offer regular confessions is simply that they do not really know how to do so, and as such, have not been teaching the people in their parishes to seek out such practices.

This question highlights another common refrain of this study which should be noted: the seminary is the place to begin a revival or renewal of confessional practice. The people are clearly hungry for some means of putting away their sin, and as we are in the "getting rid of sin business" we should probably spend some time learning how to help people to be better penitents, and better disciples of Jesus, by teaching them to conquer their sins, and offering them our support in doing so.

A sub-question was offered to the clergy under this question, which read: "Have you continued to study confessional practice or spiritual direction since seminary, and if so, please name texts or resources that have been helpful to your studies? These were the responses:

a.   Yes (three identical responses)
b.   Yes and my work with other priests and with this attached to Holy Orders primarily.

c.   Yes, through scripture, narrative studies, clergy retreats, advanced pastoral care studies, and numerous clergy seminars.

d.   Yes, THE BIBLE, especially the Psalms, is still my best resource.

e.   I have not studied confessional practice or spiritual direction since seminary beyond cursory reviews of the practice before appointments.

f.   Hearing Confessions by Kenneth Ross is a classic and still pertinent; Elements of the Spiritual Life by F.P. Harton is very useful when diagnosing various spiritual conditions; Christian Proficiency by Martin Thornton. These are old "war-horses" but they get to the heart of the matter. Luke 15:11-32.

g.   Yes, Meditation from Henri Nouwen, and I plan to get the new book drawn from his writings on spiritual direction. W. Paul Jones, The Art of Spiritual Direction.

h.   I am a graduate of that "whore of Babylon" seminary, Episcopal Divinity School. Who cared about the soul?! Well, I did, at least about mine! And I got myself quickly to the then Superior of the Cowley Fathers (when it was still a wonderful monastic order) – Fr. Pederson -- and he took me under his wing as both my spiritual director, confessor, and mentor in both. What a fantastic blessing it was!

i.   I've had to study confessional practice and spiritual direction since seminary as it was not part of my formal training.

j.   A Priest's Handbook

k.   Healing the Wounded Spirit - John and Paula Sanford.

l.   Confession - St. Severin Community Confession in the Church of England by St Alfonsus Ligouri, John Paul II, Benedict Greoschel, and Michael Ramsey.

m.   A couple of seminars, discussions with other clergy (CCU, SSC, etc.) and a couple of books which were recommended by them - do not remember the names at this time. Also spent time with a couple of excellent spiritual directors discussing practices, etc. one a lay person and one a cleric.

It is of note here that several clergy have continued their studies, although only a third of the clergy responded to this sub-question, which makes us wonder whether continuing education has been neglected in their ministries, particularly on this subject. It seems that the apathy of the clergy may have come into play here, in that use of the idiom: "the squeaky wheel gets the grease," or perhaps another: "where there is no demand, there is no supply." It is easy to neglect study of things that are not in demand from our people. However, we hope to encourage the reader to continue studies in areas in which you may be uncomfortable. Confession, for many, is an uncomfortable subject. If we are willing to teach our people, familiarity makes that which is uncomfortable more comfortable, and might even lead a few souls closer to Jesus, but only if we are bold enough to suggest that such a thing is necessary. However, this will require more learning and teaching on the clergy's part.

Question 10: How often do you teach your people about confession and/or spiritual direction?

This question was aimed at determining the actual practice of teaching on either the discipline of confession or spiritual direction within the parishes by the clergy. These data, in light of the previous question's findings, are most interesting.

fig. 10

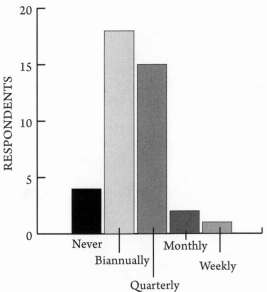

How often do you teach your people about Confession or Spiritual Direction?

To begin, 10% of the clergy openly conceded that they never teach their people about confession or spiritual direction. We may deduce from this that the parishes led by those clergy offer no regular times for confession, and are likely not in the practice of offering spiritual direction, and may not have been trained in offering either discipline.

The majority of the responses (45%) indicate that the clergy are teaching the people about confession or spiritual direction once or twice a year. Given the other data collected, we might assume that this trend follows the pattern mentioned earlier, of offering confession only during the penitential seasons of Advent and Lent. While all clergy seem to think of Lent as a penitential season, some do not consider advent to be a penitential season, leaving only one brief season of the year in which these disciplines are discussed in many of their parishes. The laity revealed in their study that the less something is spoken about, the less important it seems. To some, it seems like confession is like a traffic accident that happens from time to time. We don't like it, don't expect it, and given warning, we can avoid it, even if it happens for six consistent weeks. The rest of the time, if they are not encouraged to make a regular confession, the opportunity eludes them, or is more easily ignored by them as unimportant, otherwise it would be discussed more fully and more frequently by the clergy.

A little over one third (37.5%) of the clergy claimed to be teaching on confession or spiritual direction once every quarter, or every three months or so. This also appears to be supported by the data, which demonstrate that some clergy are actually regularly sitting for confessions, and as such are regularly advertising the practice and supporting it with sermons or Sunday school classes or other teaching forums to further promote the practices. These churches seem to be more effective in retaining regular penitents, and, according to the lay studies, have not been perceived as over-teaching the people, or burdening them with guilt over not going to confession. Rather, they have been consistent in reminding the people that the opportunity exists, and refreshing them in teaching on the practice on a subtle yet consistent basis. In these places, the perception is that it is important, and attendance in the confessional is higher.

Interestingly, a small margin (5%) of the clergy further indicated that they are teaching on the practice on a monthly basis, and one lone clergyman is teaching on it on a weekly basis. While this may seem extreme, the diocese has a few parishes which are known as "confessional churches," and although these data are not directly linked to the demographic information within the diocese, what is most interesting is that this diocese is home to only three churches with confessional booths, and here we see three priests reporting to teach on the practice on a weekly or monthly basis. In these churches, the confessional seems to have been integrated into the regular life of the parish, and those who frequent their confessionals are seemingly quite happy and eager to do so.

Laity on Spiritual Direction

The laity were aksed separate questions about their perceptions of needed teaching on spiritual direction and confession. We will first begin by discussing their responses to teaching on spiritual direction. The laity were asked, "How much teaching do you think the Church needs on spiritual direction?" This question addressed the need for teaching specifically on spiritual direction, either in the parish, or in the greater Church. The spectrum of responses included: "more teaching," "we have adequate instruction," or "less teaching." Thirty-one comments were made (86.11%) which said that we need to be offering more teaching on spiritual direction. Eight people indicated that if the clergy utilized the voices of the laity in teaching and promoting spiritual direction, this would likely help promote the practice more than if the teaching came solely from the clergy. One of these eight spoke of a class being taught by the local "Episcopal Center for Renewal," which already offers classes on spiritual direction. Another said, "When the results are seen in changed lives, other people will learn from those who have had good experiences." Others spoke more generally of mutual support and encouragement of the practice among peers.

It is interesting that eight people (22.22%) indicated that they don't really know anything about spiritual direction, yet seven of those eight answered that they preferred one over the other to a previous question. If this indicates anything it is that there needs to be more clarity on the nature and distinction between spiritual direction and confession. One participant said, "I don't know enough to differentiate the differences between confession and spiritual direction."

Seven people specifically addressed the need for more education by offering specific suggestions of how to increase awareness, which included: "Explain what it is"; "Define along with it what sins are, and why you need direction"; "Utilize Diocesan-wide programs and the Renewal Center's *School of Spirituality*"; "Define what a spiritual director does for you"; "Produce a brochure on it"; and "Perhaps an instructed confession or mock spiritual direction session during a sermon would be helpful." There are all good ideas that the lay people seem to be willing to embrace and attend if offered.

Under the heading of "more teaching" there arose a common thread of people indicating the inter-relationship between the two modes of confession: auricular confession and spiritual direction. Four separate people indicated that one tends to promote the other. Half say, "Confession leads to more spiritual direction;" and other half, the inverse, "If you taught more on spiritual direction, a natural byproduct would be a better understanding of confession." Either way, there seems to be an opportunity to teach the laity about these two modes in a way which promotes all three modes as adequate, depending on the spiritual needs of the penitent. It would seem that promoting only one over the other seems in appropriate, as all three according to the laity, have their place in the life of the Church. If teaching were consistent about the nature of the three modes, and their inter-relationship in the life of a penitent, then perhaps the two less popular modes would receive more attention, and serve a larger place in the life of the Church.

Only five people (13.88%) of the participants claimed that their parish was adequately teaching on spiritual direction, but for different reasons. One said it was blended into confirmation class, and that was adequate. Another said, "It's adequate here, because we have a lot of holy people around." One addressed again a sense of supply and demand, "If the people aren't seeking it, then not many step up to offer it." Two participants attributed the adequacy to the personality of the priest, saying things such as: "The personality of the priest makes me feel I could approach him with anything."

It appears that there is a great deal of teaching to be done, as many people claimed that they could not define, or did not know enough about spiritual direction to respond to this question. This is perhaps an indicator that this third mode of confession, being spiritual direction, is indeed the least prevalent of the modes.

Laity on Confession Teaching

The laity were also asked: "How much teaching do you think your parish ought to have on confession?" In a broad-stroke, the answers fell into one of three categories: "more teaching," "we have adequate teaching," or "we need less teaching on the subject." The vast majority, thirty participants (83%), answered consistently that we need more teaching on auricular confession. There was no need to create sub-categories for this answer, although there were many consistent themes that emerged from these requests for more teaching. In the positive, people generally indicated that they wanted to hear more about confession, or that they have heard absolutely nothing about it in recent experience. Some said things such as: "I didn't grow up in this tradition so it's new to me."

An additional seven participants indicated a desire to see it taught more to children at a younger age and throughout the Sunday-school curriculum for all ages. One in particular commented: "Teaching [on confession] should come at an earlier age, so it's not scary when you encounter it as a teenager." This perception addressed an earlier concern regarding the perception of the confessional. If we only seem to talk about it once people are already grown, it is harder to implement. Rather, if it is taught at an early age, and consistently throughout the ages of children and over time, the perception is that it has always been there, even from youth.

Four participants shared comments about the encouragement they received from other lay people to go to confession, and the desire to see open-ended discussions among lay-people on their positive experiences in the confessional in order to foster more use of the confessional within parishes. One participant said, "There needs to be more open discussion among all ages, to take away the 'scare factor.'" Another said (quite positively) that "There needs to be more teaching, and more encouragement among peer groups. We should not be afraid to use confession to strengthen us. We need to admit that we need this and stop blaming society for our problems. Let's start with ourselves, and let our example rub off on others." We cannot underestimate the power of the influence of laity on other laity. If people were given opportunities to share their positive experiences with those for whom this practice is not common, it can have a dramatic effect on the openness of new penitents to the confessional.

Two lay people in the study indicated a sense that the clergy are afraid to teach on confession. One said, "It seems you have to twist the arms of the clergy to talk about confession. They should be more direct." Another said, similarly, "The priests only mention it in passing, as a duty to report, and then they move on." This comes to addressing a point that is beyond the scope of the laity, and completely in the hands of the clergy: if the clergy are afraid, or feel under-educated to speak on confession, where else are the people to hear about it? Perhaps in some places the clergy have felt outnumbered by the laity who have leaned on them to stop teaching on confession, or perhaps there is just a general fear of approaching difficult subjects with the laity. This is a fear that must be overcome for the good of the people. Perhaps this is one of the devil's keenest tricks: to make good things seem taboo, or unnatural, and as such, to conquer our desire to talk about the things that can bring us closer to God. Whatever it is, and wherever the fear is rooted, it must be conquered. If the clergy will not address the spiritual health of the people beyond a "come if you want" stance, the people have said that they will tend to be equally dismissive of the practice. They need to be told that it is good for them, and that it is not something to be afraid of, but rather that harboring sin is the thing to be feared.

In summary, the people across this diocese, from all kinds of parishes, and across all ages, want to hear more about confession, and to see the practice spread in their parishes. There is a real willingness to learn, and for the lay people to support the clergy in teaching this practice for the good of the parish. Absolutely no one said that their Churches or that the Church in general needs less teaching on confession. However, six people (16%) indicated that they felt the teaching in their parishes was in fact adequate. These answers did not all come out of the same churches, and there was some variance even among those parishes where confession is regularly taught, in that there was still an appetite to always learn more, a desire to integrate new people into the parish's confessional practice, and to see it spread across the diocese. Among the six people who responded that the teaching was adequate, there was also a recognition that sacramental confession is a neglected practice, even where it is well advertised, scheduled, and taught by the clergy. While there were not a lot of identical repeating answers or themes, there were comments consistent with those who wanted more teaching in the previous section. One said, "We need to 'de bunk' the misconceptions. I think this could be done with lay-people talking about it." Another said something pertaining to the willingness of the clergy: "If the priest leads, the people will follow. If he isn't embracing confession, the people won't either." These are themes we have already addressed, but are clearly supported by the responses and perceptions of the laity.

Clergy Follow-Up

A sub-question was also offered for this subject which read: "If you do not regularly teach or preach on the need for confession or spiritual direction, what have you done to otherwise promote the use of confession or spiritual direction for your people? Do your people know that they are expected to make a confession in any way?" These were the responses:

a. It's written about in the parish newsletter during penitential seasons and taught in confirmation prep and adult and youth Sunday school.

b. The topic surfaces often in sermons, DOK work, EYC work. Hard to say how often.

c. Sin and salvation, grace, forgiveness, penitence, restitution through Jesus Christ is always preached. Private, auricular confession must be held up in terms of 1st John 2:1-2 (My little children, I am writing this to you so that you may not sin; but if any one does sin, we have an advocate with the Father, Jesus Christ the righteous; and he is the expiation for our sins, and not for ours only but also for the sins of the whole world.), and 1st Timothy 1:15 (The saying is sure and worthy of full acceptance, that Christ Jesus came into the world to save sinners. And I am the foremost of sinners.). Today, both clergy and laity have written off sin, so why need confession?

d. Not always.

e. As a retired priest, if approached in public at a church gathering or anywhere else, I usually seize the moment by having a brief pastoral visit, offer spiritual direction, cross them with a blessing and pray for their needs whether we are sitting or standing. I then add them to my personal prayer list. It is important to seize the moment if an individual has approached you because it may be the only opportunity you will have to meet their spiritual needs. Confession presents itself to clergy in many forms and situations.

f. The congregation that I serve is much older than normal (50 to 80+) and have no need for prompting.

g. While neither confession nor spiritual direction is emphasized in particular, per se, the *general confession* is a consistent topic of sermons, in whole or in part. Further, many sermons issue a plea to the congregation to engage the clergy for pastoral care beyond the context of the worship service, should it be required. For example, in preaching on marriage, I will issue the invitation for counseling. In preaching on sexual sin, I will issue the invitation for counseling. I will also add that being a fairly new congregation, our focus is still largely on establishing the "big picture"; that is, the general principles that will guide the parish over the long term. Digging deeper on any particular concern, whether it be sacramental, liturgical, or otherwise, is more difficult absent a permanent venue in which to shape the habit of those practices. In time, those points of particularity will find their place in the parish life.

h. Confession must be held before the people at every opportunity. Many more people should avail themselves of this blessing. Confessions must be scheduled WEEKLY. If they are not publicly scheduled, do not expect to hear many. When penitents do not appear, use the time for spiritual reading.

i. None of the categories above really apply to what I did, because the blessing of sacramental confession and spiritual counsel weave in and out of much of my preaching.

j. This survey might be 'contaminated' by someone nearly 83 years old, having been ordained in 1959 and now 'retired' over 10 years. Back in the old days I made private confession a matter of some importance to the congregation, and would hear confessions as asked. I must say that the content of most seemed fairly rote to me, without any depth to the sort of spiritual self-examination I would have hoped for, but there were the occasions when I felt the power of the Holy Spirit in a work of spiritual cleansing. Alas, there seems in our day a too casual view of the necessity of confession at all, along with the feeling that all it takes is a bit of acknowledged regret to achieve reconciliation with God ("cheap grace" Bonhoeffer).

k. I talk about it in my newcomer's classes, confirmation classes, etc. Occasionally, I will write an article about one of the subjects in the newsletter.

l. The *general confession* suffices.

m. I teach on the use of the *general confession* while explaining the use of private confession for spiritual direction. I promote in general a life of corporate spiritual direction. I handle private spiritual direction only upon request which is rare.

n. Newsletter.

o. Many of my sermons call for regular times of confession (daily or more often) and include times of reflection, direction, and if need be - directed confession / spiritual direction. I also note that I make my confession in various ways on a regular basis and use practical examples.

From these raw responses, we can see a variety of understanding on confessional practice, as well as various approaches which directly mirror the conclusions drawn from the historical study, which were that Anglicanism today seems to encompass one of three modes for confession:

1. The *general confession* in the communal context of the eucharist or morning prayer;
2. Auricular confession closely resembling the Catholic rites
3. Confession to a spiritual counselor or other mature Christian either in the context of a community, or sometimes to a monastic where available.

The majority of the clergy seem, without much opposition, to be depending on the general confession and the private morality of their people to achieve atonement with God. The closest we come to the biblical model of confession, as a community, is the general confession, which may be why some of the clergy have stated plainly, "The general confession suffices." While some teach on the necessity of the confessional practice, others emphasize the general confession as the first means of confession while also supporting confession and spiritual direction as a "next-level" or "as needed" practice for those who determine that their sins are in greater need of direction. Of course, this method appears to leave the diagnosis of what a "notorious sin" is to the person with the sin. One respondent somewhat cynically acknowledged a problem, which seems to be that both the people and the clergy have "written off sin," and if this is the case, then why bother offering confession? Despite the sarcasm, this does make the point that some clergy have perceived an apparent lack of discussion among Christian people about sin, and as such, have also stopped talking about the remedies to sin. Perhaps this leads us to believe that there may be a fear among the clergy in talking about uncomfortable subjects such as sin.

Those who fall into the second category of offering auricular confession in their parishes seem to be few in number, because the training on the subject seems to be limited, and interest seems to be directly rooted not only in the education of the clergy, but also in the pedigree of their life experiences. If the church they grew up in did not teach confession, they do seemingly not promulgate it later in life. I also grew up in a parish that did not ever speak about confession. However, I came to it through a mentor who was Anglo-Catholic, and I have come to know the benefits. Therefore, the confessional has become a large part of my ministry, although the parish I serve has also not been one that had a pedigree of confessional practice. Perhaps another question or factor that could come into play here, beyond the training and upbringing of the clergy, is the history of the teaching in the parish or parishes in which they serve. A clergyman who comes from a vacuum of confessional praxis, and a vacuum of teaching in seminary, and then arrives to serve a parish that expects them to hear confessions would likely find themselves either learning the practice retrospectively, or bucking the trend. While a clergyman who grew up in a church with regular confessional practice, who also learned something of it in seminary, and yet is called to work in a parish that has no history of confessional practice is also just as likely to find themselves bucking a trend or going against the grain of the people when they preach on the subject. Each church absorbs, to some degree, the heritage of the clergy who serve them. It should be acknowledged that it is most difficult to institute a change in a place that has gone so far for so long without a confessional in place, but it is possible.

Finally, as rare as auricular confessional practice is in our Churches, spiritual direction seems to be even more scarce. The clergy seem to have been taught so very little about the practice of spiritual direction, and the absence of a vibrant monastic community in our area does not lead us toward guiding others to obtain the benefits to be found therein. However, it does seem from the lay-study that there are several "renewal programs" taught locally in the art of spiritual direction for clergy and laity, and this could offer some potential for future growth in this area. There is a genuine interest in a few parishes in increasing the lay-involvement, under clergy supervision, by training lay spiritual directors. While this practice seems to be fairly new, and minimal in implementation, it may be either an indicator of spiritual maturity among some of the laity, or perhaps a need to establish a monastic order for those who may be feeling a vocation to the religious life. It is possible that we just have a few laity who are otherwise simply gifted in these areas, and could be utilized by the clergy in the parishes in which they serve. While the Anglican tradition has boasted such monastic traditions in the past, this seems to be significantly waning in the current strata of the Anglican tradition, particularly in this Diocese.

As for the advice given by the clergy on existing praxis, some of the clergy responses suggest that confessions should be regularly scheduled weekly opportunities within the parish, while others clearly have no intention of offering confession outside of the general confession offered within the liturgies on Sunday Morning. One senior clergyman suggests that many moments arise in the context of ministry, and that these moments when people talk to us about their spiritual woes are perfect opportunities for guidance, absolution, and a time for prayer to offer support to our people. This approach requires an actively attuned ear, and a heart and mind that are prepared to offer direction in the moment, but this is the place where much of our pastoral ministry will be done if we do not offer regular confession times and seek to teach our people to take advantage of them.

Concerning teaching on the parish level, a great variety exists here as well. Some clergy are simply writing newsletter articles, which many clergy believe are not commonly read by our parishioners. Others are occasionally weaving the subject of confession into their sermons. Others still are teaching it in membership or confirmation classes, assuming that those lessons are remembered perpetually. This raises the question, "How much teaching is enough?" We might also be led to ask: "How much teaching is too much?" The laity seem to say that "once a quarter is about right." But we cannot assume that they will hear it every time we preach about confession. Confession is one of those subjects that some of the laity have reported "cues them to tune out." But once again, unless it is consistent, and not over-bearing, it will be considered unimportant, and therefore ignored. When preaching on sin, there is a delicate balance between offering an opportunity for healing to our people, by encouraging them to reap the benefits of the confessional, and burdening them with guilt, in an effort to get them to show up on Saturday mornings. The people have a genuine natural interest in being closer to God, but they also bear the guilt of their sin, which is adequate alone to keep them from talking to their priest. Gentleness seems to be most important tactic in this respect, and clergy should not only seek to gain the knowledge and skills of a good confessor, but also be shrewd in how they advertise the opportunities of the confessional to their people in a very positive and encouraging manner.

The survey results reveal that the clergy have not been uniformly trained in either practice, and there does not seem to be a Diocesan expectation of the practice from the Bishop, either that the clergy offer confessions or be trained in offering spiritual direction. Not to say that the practice is either discouraged or not actively encouraged, but rather that it is not required by Canon or other such "rule" within the diocese. The Bishop is quite supportive of the practice itself, and has said as much at clergy gatherings, and also makes ample opportunities for clergy to make confessions at large clergy gatherings and retreats. However, that being said, the education of the clergy on these matters is paramount, as the people we serve will only likely be as educated as their clergy train them to be. Some of our laity do attend seminars on spiritual healing, and are encouraged at renewal events to make a confession and to learn more about the practices of spiritual direction in their home parishes. If the clergy are uncomfortable with their education on certain matters, it is no large jump to assume that they are equally as unlikely to offer any teaching on the practice, particularly if they believe that asking for forgiveness within the context of the general confession is sufficient to the cure of their people's souls.

In the next chapter, we will examine the perspective of the laity by sampling small groups from among the people of the diocese in various places, and from this material we should be able to clearly ascertain what the people hunger for confession and spiritual direction at a spiritual level, and whether they believe more teaching or education is needed on the subjects of confession or spiritual direction. Perhaps if the clergy can witness a hunger from their people for something more in the way of spiritual direction, they might be more inclined to seek out and offer more teaching on the subject.

Unique Responses And Best Advice To Clergy From Laity

There remain several unique comments from the laity study on the processes of confession and spiritual direction that did not adequately fit into the questions listed above, as such, they will be included below. Furthermore, the laity studies were also concluded by asking them to offer their best advice to the clergy on the use of the modern confessional. Although this material is somewhat redundant to the content of this chapter, we felt it best to offer those things that the laity chose to highlight to the clergy as a whole for the benefit of clergy readers.

Unique responses

Four people indicated something quite interesting, that they would also be as likely to receive spiritual direction from a lay-person they knew to be "spiritually mature." One indicated: "It's easier to establish a spiritual relationship with a peer than with a priest." Two similar, yet independently unique comments addressed the problem of those who attempt to be their own spiritual director: "Those who have themselves for a spiritual director have a fool for a director." Another simply said, "You don't want to direct yourself. We need someone who is trained or 'degreed' in this, otherwise we fall to our own devices." It seems that in certain places there are people of such spiritual maturity that other lay people are interested in receiving direction from them instead of their priest, or perhaps in some cases, in addition to the direction they receive from their priest. This was a rare response, and many of these responses came from the same parish, which was uniquely steeped in spiritually mature adults trained in spiritual matters.

One unique answer claimed to prefer spiritual direction because it had been done with a layperson. "Most priests don't offer what I need in spiritual direction. The clergy need to incorporate more of the devout and educated laity to support these needs." Here we find an echo if the previous comments which called for the support of the educated or spiritually mature laity to be sources of spiritual direction.

Spiritual direction versus confession

The laity were also asked to compare the value of spiritual direction versus confession. Overall, most of the responses indicated that the option of spiritual direction versus confession was a choice based on the penitent's comfort and the subject of their confession. One might say that this is a matter of "length of stay." It seems as if they feel like they need to have a long conversation, they prefer spiritual direction, but if they want to simply confess in a shorter or more "to the point" mode, then the confessional is preferred. "It depends on what I want to talk about. I've used both depending on what kind of guidance I need." Here, it seems that in the minds of some of the people, the last two modes of confession, while being quite different from the general confession, are somewhat interchangeable, and perhaps equally as rare as the other, if not slightly more rare on the spiritual direction side of the matter.

At the other end of the spectrum, four people indicated that they "preferred spiritual direction over confession," and all of these respondents had varying reasons for why they preferred spiritual direction to confession, yet they shared a common thread. Three out of the four said that their preference had to do with comfort, although on different levels. For one it was about the setting. Another indicated that sometimes casual conversations simply pointed them toward confession unexpectedly. Yet another said it was about availability: "I'd rather 'drop in' for spiritual direction. I'm more comfortable that way." Although one in particular preferred the casual setting, they conceded that the confessional was also a source for good spiritual direction, and asserted that having confessions in the church somehow made them more important, yet they still preferred the casual setting based on their personality.

Among these four responses, the tone seems to be centered upon the personal comfort of the individual based on conditions we have already addressed. Perhaps this has to do with their personality to some degree, while there is also a possibility that in their context, the setting is simply more comfortable for spiritual direction than it is in the confessional.

Benefits of spiritual direction from those who practice it over confession

When asked about the benefits of spiritual direction, the answers fell into four major categories: "guidance," "emotional support and encouragement," "anonymity," and "I'm unfamiliar with the practice." The vast majority, eighteen (50%) of the answers to this question leaned toward positively claiming that the greatest benefit of spiritual direction was "guidance." One said, "It's like getting a splinter pulled out." Another indicated that it "seemed more open-ended than confession." Some claimed it had great value to their lives, and many, nine in total, said that it put them back on the right path, or led them in a better direction. Two of the respondents addressed the differences they see between confession and spiritual direction: "Where confession helps you deal with the past, spiritual direction focuses on your future." The other said, "Confession is about coming to grips with bad decisions already made." Overall, the majority of the people who responded to this question about the third common mode of confession in the Anglican Church said that it was the good direction they received in spiritual direction that benefitted them the most. It is interesting that the people themselves have come to make a distinction, although to a limited extent, that confession is about getting the bad out, and spiritual direction is about restoring the good. Or rather, confession was about addressing deeds already done, while spiritual direction focuses more on their future behavior. This, I think, is a helpful distinction, and could probably be promulgated more among the parishes, although this distinction makes these two separate modes: (confession and spiritual direction) less distinguishable, and more of a hand-in-hand process of spiritual growth. While there is some truth to the potential for an inter-connection, we have also seen that both seem to work equally as well autonomously, rather than one pointing to and being dependent upon the other.

Three people (8.33%) said that the greatest benefit of spiritual direction was the emotional support and encouragement brought about by the practice. In all three cases, the clergy were the supportive parties. One said, "It usually confirms what I already know, but it's nice to have someone encourage me and keep me committed." Another said, "I find the same relief and comfort as confession. I think it is important to know that my priest cares, and that he's not just 'going through the drill.'" These emotional responses are important, in that the people demonstrate a keen awareness of the distinction of whether or not the clergy seem to be attentive to their personal spiritual needs, or whether they are simply just another number in the confessional. While this emotional perception is not dependent upon the nature of the confessional or spiritual direction processes themselves, it is important to note that the people are positively affected when they feel as though the confessor is concerned, compassionate, and eager to help them by offering positive encouragement, and by attentively responding to their needs spoken of during the session as opposed to having the same "cookie cutter" response to everything.

In summary, people seem to return to spiritual direction because it has in fact been helpful to them, and they feel encouraged by the time spent with a director who offers them guidance, and who helps them move in a positive direction beyond merely unloading the sin and returning to it again and again.

The Best Advice Of The Laity

At the end of the study the laity were asked, "What, in your eyes, is the biggest problem with the modern confessional? What could be improved?" The participants were encouraged to give their best advice to the clergy on how to improve the quality and frequency of use in the "modern confessional." Some people gave a single focused response, while others had a number of suggestions that have already been integrated into the previous sections. As such, these responses will not be reported by percentage of respondents, as many people indicated answers in more than one category. This section also serves as an adequate summary of the people's responses to the use of the confessional and spiritual direction, from their perspectives.

There were six different response categories that will be presented in order from most frequent or prevalent, to least. The responses fell into the following categories: "more teaching," "more availability or better advertisement," "bring back the confessional booths," "better education for the clergy," "offer a face-to-face encounter," and "change nothing."

Twenty-five people suggested as their number one piece of advice to the clergy was: more teaching on confession was needed at the parish level. Within this category, there were several sub-points as to the suggested nature or focus of the teaching. Seven of the responses suggested that the "positive aspect" of confession be taught and emphasized more, saying things such as: "Stress the relief you feel afterwards," or, "Teach the people that it's not a scary thing, and that there are many benefits." In the same vein, two people suggested emphasis on the positive guidance to be reaped from making a confession: "It brings a lot of relief and people should hear that it can lead you in a much better direction." Another said, "There needs to be an understanding that this is a step on the road to improving yourself." Eight people, who desired to emphasize the positive added comment about trying to remove the fear, stigma, or threat factor from the people's perception of confession. Two people had almost identical comments pertaining to fear in light of the clergy component: "Address the stigma that the priest is going to judge people. He doesn't." Others simply emphasized that teaching the positive, and the 'how-to' of confession helps to put away the fear. One peculiar comment focused on the fear aspect, saying that the respondent had, in their youth, been regularly threatened with confession as a punishment. This, of course, goes along with the previous comments concerning the teaching of confession in a positive tone. If confession is considered or treated as a punishment for when people, particularly children, are behaving badly, then they will only ever look on it from a negative perspective of fear. One other unique comment addressed fear with "vulnerability" as a part of the confessional process: "Teach the people that there is a level of vulnerability to this. And it's a good thing, because you're open, you've laid it out there, and you're ready to receive guidance. People have got to get over that sense of self-sufficiency, admit that they need others, and get over their fear of being vulnerable." This is most interesting in that it approaches the confessional practice with a level of fear, yet holy fear. If we teach that the confessional will always come with some level of personal anxiety or trepidation, but that it is a good and natural thing to be somewhat afraid of change, even in the positive, then when the people are met with those feelings the teaching process affirms their fears, and supports their decision to move forward.

A few smaller suggestions were made in the positive realm. Four of the participants suggested making manuals or handouts on the "how-to" aspect of confession that should include the process itself, an examination of conscience, and some instruction on what level or depth to make a confession such as how many details to provide or when to speak of their frequency. The general theme of these comments was: if the people know what to expect and how to prepare, they will be more acquainted with the process before going into it for the first time. Finally, for the positive teaching aspect, two people suggested utilizing more laity in the process of spiritual direction, while making sure that they function under the authority of the resident clergy. Furthermore, two individuals commented on teaching about the general confession from two different standpoints: "Offer a better teaching on confession to the people. Why do we need to go? Is the general confession enough? What sins belong to which practice?" The other suggested that we teach a better use of the general confession itself: "[The general confession] can be a good thing too, if we use it well and not just say the words." Here we see that the people are open to teaching all three modes of common Anglican confession, and to instruct them better on when each mode is appropriate to their needs.

The second major response to this request for advice from the laity to clergy related in some way to "more opportunity or better advertisement." Nine people addressed the availability issue, saying that confession hours needed to be made more available, advertised, and posted, and two additional comments within this section also stressed a need for a variety of confessional times, such as evenings in addition to the most prevalent current times in the morning, so as not to prevent those who are already accustomed to making confessions from coming at the regularly scheduled time(s). This comment is important as it teaches us that the old model of offering confession on Saturday mornings may not be sufficient in a world where Saturdays are not as much of a day of rest or leisure as they used to be for previous generations. We live in a much busier world, and as such, a variety of opportunities might better serve our people's needs.

Two responses also appeared here, although they have appeared several times elsewhere in this study, pertaining to making an appointment. Both participants said, "I'll never make an appointment [to make my confession]." This is most important to note, as a vast majority of the clergy (67.4%) in the study indicated that this was the most popular way in which they offered to hear confessions. The same group of clergy also offered comments such as: "I hear them by appointment, but no one has made an appointment in over five years." These data should be telling us something, and that "something" is: the people are highly unlikely to make an appointment, so it is the responsibility of the clergy to offer to hear confessions at regular times, even if the participants are few. They will be even fewer if not offered at all, or only by appointment.

Six respondents made comment about the clergy under this heading of availability, asking for other clergy to be made available to them, just as many people throughout this study have commented that they are very unlikely to make a confession to their own priest. Some have commented as to "why," stating a fear that they must see their priest on a regular basis and are afraid of encountering a confessor outside of the confessional, as they are concerned about the priest's future perceptions of them (the penitent), or for other more detailed reasons, such as, "I don't want to confess to a married priest." One in particular suggested: "Maybe if there was a 'diocesan confession guy' or a rotation, I would be more likely to go." Another suggested, "Partner with another Church to hear confessions." These are all fine ideas, and are also ideas which free up the clergy from having to offer regular confession hours, particularly when they serve a parish that is without confessional facilities, or are not as capable in the confessional as their neighboring clergy. The clergy should deduce from this study that there is a spiritual need among the people, whether or not they are trained to address it, and that there are alternative solutions to this problem beyond simply learning more and sitting more often to hear confessions. If parishes could partner together much time could be better utilized and the comfort of the people may increase in the confessional.

The third major response to this question had repeating themes related to the venue of confessions. Many people desire to see a return of the confessional booth. In this case, five respondents addressed the confessional booth in a positive way, but for varying reasons. Three of the five addressed the privacy issue, with such comments as: "Even if you do it in the Priest's office, you never know who's around the corner." Another addressed the open-church venue, "We need better facilities for confession. The church isn't private enough. You never know who's walking in." Another echoed this, but added, "I wonder if the people in the back of the church can hear me." These concerns are important, particularly if the people hang their expectations of the confessional on privacy issues. Offering the people a context in which to hear confessions in comfort and privacy is, and should be, a major concern for the confessor.

Two of the five aforementioned participants responded with concerns about how they encountered the clergy in the confessional process. One simply said, "There's a 'thing' to those confessionals, when you're in your little box, and no one knows. I don't want to see the priest's face." Another said, "I like the old confessionals. I have a certain discomfort with face-to-face encounters." If the teaching of the Church is to be that the confession is offered to God, and that the priest is a conduit of that grace, then perhaps a confessional booth is the ideal place for the penitent to receive guidance in a way that supports the idea that the identity of the confessor is not as important as the content of their guidance. If the people perceive a danger of being judged, recognized, or otherwise tainted in some way in the eyes of their priest, then removing the identity or privacy issue may be a simple fix to a deep emotional hindrance for some penitents.

One comment on this part of the process added another word about the use of the general confession: "If we had the 'hot box,' I would likely use it. The general confession seems to have phased out the use of the confessional and private confession." Even here we see an acknowledgement that the general confession has become the popular means of confessing for most parishioners, to the point of nearly "phasing out" the other two modes entirely. While this perception is statistically very valid, we also witness from other responses in this study that there is a real need for the confessional, and that even this respondent has stated, "If we had the hot box, I'd use it." Which begs the question, if we do not offer confession in any context, what are the people going to do? If we offer no alternatives, we should not be surprised when the people default to what is simply available.

The final three categories of responses to this question of advice from laity to clergy are minimal, but worthy of outlining briefly. The first, with two comments, suggested "better training for the clergy." One commented: "Teach the clergy to better sell the practice, and teach them in some manner of psychological training, or people-relations." This comment can be helpful in light of the world we live in, where professional counseling is prevalent and popular. It would probably benefit the clergy to have a basic awareness of basic counseling practices so to comment on them when they come up in the confessional, but also to recognize patterns of behavior, and to be prepared to refer people to proper counseling when our confessional training cannot meet their spiritual and psychological needs. The second comment here simply suggested that the clergy be more supportive of the practice: "If the priest doesn't embrace confession, neither will the people." This concern has already been rehearsed, but it is of note that this participant chose this as their final word to the clergy.

The second of the smaller categories, which only had one response, suggested a change in venue: "I'd just prefer to sit in the office." While many seem to prefer the sacred space in which to make a confession, there was one who preferred the face-to-face encounter. While this viewpoint was minimal in comparison to others in the study, it is likely there are others in the parishes that share this perspective, and some leeway could be made to allow for those who seek this kind of an encounter as well, such as asking the penitent whether they seek a face-to-face encounter, and having the ability to "drop the screen" as desired. Some confessionals even offer screens that can be lowered for this purpose. If the people knew that they had options, even within the context of a convertible confessional booth, they would likely be just as comfortable to lower the screen themselves, and have a conversation in the confessional booth.

Finally, a lone commenter said, "Keep it just as it is. Our priest is always available. We even have a back-up priest when ours is not available." Here we see that in one place where confession is regularly offered, one person's needs are being met adequately. Of course, this sort of comment also appeared earlier in the study, which simply demonstrates that in some places the confessional practice is active and doing good work. It also teaches us that those who are regular penitents are quite happy to be such and do not in any way feel as though they are being oppressed, but rather, that they are spiritually fed by the auricular confessional process in their Church.

In summary, it appears that the positive teaching on confession needs to cover several aspects of confession, from the "how-to," to "what to expect." Overall, people have stressed the need for more positive teaching, working to eliminate the negative stigma or fears surrounding confession. We, as clergy, could probably be doing a better job of explaining that confession is a good thing, and that there is some fear to be encountered, but that the fear will likely be alleviated by the relief of making a good confession once sin and guilt are replaced by good spiritual direction. Manuals would be a large help for the people, as they can easily read-up on the practice in-between offerings of classes within the Church. There is no need to "re-invent the wheel" here, as many neighboring clergy already use such manuals in their parishes, and a few examples will be provided at the end of this text. People also want to see regular and varied confession hours, and a variety of confessors made available to them, perhaps from other Churches, to remove any fears of having to regularly encounter their confessor outside of the confessional. The people also seem to have a real interest in confessional spaces, which they desire to be private, discrete, and in which the clergyman is heard and not seen. Not many of our churches have these, but they are a small construction for those interested in building a designated space for confession, or a "confessional on wheels." Keep in mind that they should be comfortable, sound-proofed, and would be best suited if they had a separate entrance and exit. Finally, the clergy could also always benefit from more learning, and further education on the needs of their people. While we function primarily in the spiritual realm, psychology does have something to offer in the diagnosis of certain patterns, and the awareness of those patterns can only serve to better equip the clergy to guide their penitents to wholeness of mind, body, and spirit. In short, the clergy have some work to do, but the people who participated in this study are encouraging of improvement, open to better confessional availability, and eager to see others benefit from the use of the confessional.

The historical study demonstrated to us a three-fold mode of confessional practice within the Anglican context:

1. The general confession in the communal context of the eucharist or morning prayer;

2. Auricular confession closely resembling the Catholic rites

3. Confession to a spiritual counselor or other mature Christian either in the context of a community, or sometimes to a monastic where available.

Here, the lay study supports the use of all three modes in the praxis of the diocese in which this study was conducted, but also the interest of the people whom desire to see an increase in the use of the second two modes, rather than a full dependence on the general confession to provide their confessional needs. If we can teach our people about these patterns, and how they may best take advantage of what they have to offer, these modes will be productive in meeting the spiritual needs of our penitents.

PART III: HEARING CONFESSIONS

CHAPTER NINE
Pastoral Reflection & Moving Forward

Now that we have studied the history of confession and atonement from the Bible to now, and evaluated the historic practices in light of the modern culture's response to confession as it is currently being implemented, or not implemented, in our parishes in the twenty-first century, we must take the time reflect on how to make this ministerial practice of hearing confession move forward. Here we will evaluate what worked, what did not work, what could be improved, and suggest future action for the people for whom this study was conducted, as well as for those who are not of the Anglican Diocese of Fort Worth. Finally, we will suggest areas of potential future study that arose from this research.

What worked?

Any study of history usually teaches us that we are not the first to consider certain precepts, nor the first to fail at implementing them. This historical study was quite helpful to the author in demonstrating that the struggle over the confessional is not something new, and the arguments both for and against it have not changed, but have remained fairly constant from the Reformation to now. The modern Church is one that has global influences on her spirituality, praxis, and theology, all of which carry the baggage of generations from before. If we are to look at the history of the confessional from a perspective of "what worked" we can see that the period of confessional development which most shined was the late patristic period when the rise of monastic asceticism nurtured the practices of spiritual direction and private confession into very useful practices. Where confessional practice seems to have lost its energy was following the fourth Lateran Council, when the Church imposed mandatory requirements on penitents to not only make a confession annually, but to make one to their own priest, and furthermore to take the confessional out of the hands of the monastic realm. This asceticism, which was once optional yet quite popular, produced dozens if not hundreds of penitentials, all of which nourished generations of penitents without having to be required. Perhaps if we returned to this "optional" view of confession, stopped stressing it as a requirement, but offering teaching on the old penitentials, people would gather the benefit from the practice itself— rather than from being told that they simply have to do it—and follow the priest's instruction, trusting that he has read these things.

As we have already exhaustively demonstrated, Anglicanism today, rather than following one trend or another, seems to encompass several levels of spirituality by utilizing one of three modes for atonement or confession: first, and seemingly most popular, the general confession in the communal context of the Eucharist or morning prayer; secondly, in some places auricular confession is practiced which closely resembles the Roman Catholic rites; and finally, confession to a spiritual counselor or other mature Christian either privately or in the context of a community. In one sense, this works because the general confession has been widely implemented into the life of the Church's liturgy, and the people in any Anglican realm are very likely to encounter the general confession in any liturgy of the Church, whether they are in the daily office or the Eucharist. However, we can say that the Anglican Church has also not been as successful in implementing the use of the latter two modes of confessional practice to any significant degree, although our liturgies now contain rites for auricular confession, and the clergy and people seem to have a vague awareness of spiritual direction, but no clear picture of how it is done, nor of how to integrate it successfully into the life of the Church. So, while the church has succeeded in some respect, and it has allowed for the other modes to exist, it has not been successful at implementing them consistently into the full life of the Church.

From the focus groups, we can clearly see that many people have been positively affected by the practice of making a confession, and the vast majority of them do indeed commend it to others for the edification of their souls. We can also see that very small portions of the clergy in this diocese support this practice with regular confessional hours although the bishop of the diocese is supportive of the practice, and of extended teaching on this practice. There are healthy pockets of confessional practice in all demographic segments of the diocese. The study itself was not only successful in the lay and clergy participation and in the interest among the study participants, but also in the subsequent excitement for confessional practice that has now been fostered by an open discussion among other clergy and lay-people as a result of their participation in this study. Several lay-people have reported a "re-kindling" of their confessional discipline since their participation in this study, and the clergy who have assisted the study have also fostered a positive stimulation or inspiration by offering better opportunities to hear confessions, to teach on the subject, and to improve their reading and education on confessional practice. The bishop also commissioned a newsletter article of me for the Lenten edition of our diocesan newsletter on the subject, which has been well received by people across the diocese, some of whom have offered positive correspondence since its publication.

What did not work?

Before going into depth on what did not work within the study, we should probably begin with what the study showed us was not working in the practice itself. From the study of the lay-people, we learn that they are not hearing much from the clergy about sacramental confession, if anything. There also seems to be a large lapse in offering regular confessional hours, and—seeing that only three out of the forty-seven parishes have confessional booths or spaces—the practice has largely fallen to dis-use, outside of a few particular parishes, and is usually restricted elsewhere to the "penitential" seasons of Advent and Lent (although most parishes do not offer confession during Advent either). There does not seem to be much harm done to confession by the clergy of the diocese, in that those participants who said that they were traumatized in their youth by confession being offered as a threat were not of this Diocese, nor of this tradition. However there is not much being done by the clergy to promote the practice either. As already addressed in the chapter on the clergy study, a significant number of the clergy were not trained in confessional practice, and many more have not been taught in the discipline of spiritual direction. Overall, there seems to be a large need for continued education for the clergy, so that they can then educate the laity, and be better stewards of these practices for their parishes.

As for the study itself, the greatest difficulty was getting the youth and the senior parishioners to participate in the study at the same time. It was also difficult for the clergy to gather people who had at one time made a confession and were willing to talk about confession. There is probably a wealth of data to be collected from those who were in some way disgruntled by the confessional practice to the point that they refused to participate in this study. They may have something to offer which goes beyond the scope of this study. In short, the majority of those who participated in this study were fairly positive toward the practice, but were willing to offer constructive criticism. It was expected that some of these parishes would bias the information if they were "confessional parishes" where the practice is well in hand, or that some more Protestant parishes would bias the material due to their ignorance of, or contempt for, the practice. However, this was not really the case—although, as stated, there may be some silence on this issue that we are not hearing due to pre-conceived biases among those who refused to participate. A more thorough study could probably be done in order to extract these more anti-confessional perspectives of the more Protestant wing of our diocese.

As for the pre-suppositions of this study that were not confirmed— it was assumed by the author that the practice of confessions being heard only in the church, or in a confessional booth, was an antiquated process, and that people no longer sought to participate in confession due to the fearsome context of the Church. The result from the study was quite the opposite of this. The people, amazingly, actually called for a return of the confessional booths, and for there to be a comfortable, sanctuary-oriented place, which is to say not the priest's office, for hearing confessions. Along with this presupposition, it was assumed that people are more likely to want to make a confession in the priest's office, or in some public space. This pre-supposition was based on the myriad experiences this priest has found to hear confessions in public. Part of the point of this study was to give the clergy a new outlook on hearing confessions, and being more available to the public, as a result of the findings of this study. However, this study produced a far different result, in that this study pointed out where we can be better confessors and spiritual directors within the context of our existing ministerial venues, as that is truly the desire of the people who are in our churches. The "failure" in this study was in producing any evidence that people want to make confessions more in any public place. The overwhelming response confirmed a desire for private confession: make a booth, and make it more available. Now, perhaps a separate study could be done to address this portion of the need for public confession, as this study failed to produce these results. There is no point of contention being made to argue that clergy should not continue to make themselves available for these public moments, and to be prepared to hear confessions in public as they arise. However it seems the process is very much the same, only the context is different. If clergy are prepared to be better confessors, and seek to be better about helping people who ask for advice to truly make a change in their lives by abandoning sin and seeking better things, then these public confessions will likely be even more effective than they are currently, while still allowing for regularly-scheduled confessional hours in the parish setting. The clergy really do need to make a better study of the confessional process, and to be more aware of those moments when people ask for "advice," but are really seeking to make a confession of their faults and asking for spiritual direction from someone who they view as an authority on the subject.

Finally, the clergy study could have been done in a better way, so as to directly associate demographic information with the practice of the clergy. Perhaps a focus group would have been a better means of studying the quality of confessional experience and education among the clergy, to compare this with the quantitative data of how often they offer confessions, in what seasons they taught, and how often they are teaching this material in the parishes. In this case, the qualitative study of the lay-people has been contrasted to a quantitative study of the practices offered by the clergy. Perhaps a more thorough study of both, with similar quantitative and qualitative data points would more precisely pinpoint which clergy and parishes have a greater need for education in their confessional practices. However, as this study was a survey, the material gathered was useful, and did render useful results from the data collected. Although, it would have been helpful if the quantitative study done as a follow-up to the lay focus-groups was more thorough, and then it would have answered decisively whether these points were a factor at all in the results.

What changes are to be made?

The previous chapters have addressed pastoral responses to this question, given the specific data gathered; however to summarize, the following suggestions might be helpful:

1. Build or offer a better confessional space—This space is not to be the priest's office, and it should hopefully be in, or adjacent to, the sacramental worship space of the church. The people have responded in specific detail that they want their confessions to be made privately, in a sacramental space, where no one else can hear them, and where they cannot be seen, nor can they see the priest's face. It would also be a good idea to have a separate entrance and exit for people who are coming out, to not have to encounter those coming into the confessional. Also,

these spaces need to be quite comfortable, with good chairs, padded kneelers, plenty of air getting in so as not to be too hot nor too cold. Also, if one were to build a confessional, make the screen in such a way as it can be dropped for a face-to-face encounter, should the penitent desire such a meeting. The desire for a more "face-to-face" encounter was the minority in the study, but it was present, if only to a minimal level of interest. The space should also offer some sense that they are confessing to God through the priest, and as such a cross (preferably a crucifix) or an icon, or other such decoration should be added to orient the penitent's thoughts in the matter.

2. Learn more to teach more—The people and clergy have spoken of a hunger for more knowledge on how to live better spiritual lives, and a neglect of the Church to provide them with anything of real substance, or with any frequency. Perhaps there is room for more diocesan-wide education on these subjects, with continuing education offered from experts in the field. Seminaries could also gather from this material that there is a need to better teach future clergy in the practices of confession or reconciliation, and spiritual direction. As there is a large hunger, those teaching the clergy should also increase curriculum offerings on these particular subjects. Although there will be a subsequent chapter in this text on the "how-to" of confessional practice for beginners, a suggested bibliography will also be appended to the end of this book. The books listed there are in order of what this author sees as most critical reading, to least critical reading. It is also suggested that the clergy continually revive their practices through regular reading and re-reading of the most helpful penitential texts, to stay fresh in their remembrance of these fine materials. It is most difficult for any one priest to remain an expert in all things sin related without continual study, even after the confession is over. This is not to say that one should bring up the confession at a later time, but rather that if a priest is stumped by a penitent's problem, they should seek to have a remedy the next time they hear a similar confession.

Among the materials offered in the suggested bibliography at the end of this text, pay special attention to Annemarie Kidder's book

Making Confession, Hearing Confession: A History of the Cure of Souls, particularly chapter fifteen on "The Decline of Confession in the Church." While this text departed from the historical narrative after the Reformation to focus specifically on the Anglican context of confession, Kidder goes into greater detail on the aftermath of the Reformation up to now in the Roman Catholic tradition, especially after the Second Vatican Council, and in light of the rise of modern psychology. Her analysis of the influence of secular or "clinical confessors" on confessional practice is marvelous, and quite fascinating. Her assertion, which she supports with quotes from Carl Jung and Sigmund Freud, demonstrates that the rise of the professional counselor came about as a result of a need for better preparation for the confessional, and yet modern psychology does not tend to point people back towards the confessional. In brief, she says,

> According to Carl Gustav Jung, one of the founders of modern psychotherapy and psychiatry, "The first beginnings of all analytical treatment are to be found in its prototype, the confessional." Even though no "causal connection" may exist, there is a close relationship "between the groundwork of psychoanalysis and the religious institution of the confessional."[187]

Her analysis of the perspective of the laity in the midst of the world where professional counseling is prevalent and expensive, while the confessional is free and yet scarce, may be of some importance to clergy who might wonder why their people are more likely to pay vast amounts of money to seek the advice of a secular counselor rather than the holy guidance of their parish priest who charges nothing.

Kidder also contributes a great deal of statistical data on confessional practice in the Roman Catholic Church since the Second Vatican Council. These data are fascinating, and are of paramount importance to those who want to make a deeper study in the decline of confession, even within Anglican tradition. Many people in Anglicanism have come to us from a Roman Catholic Church, and

---

[187] Kidder, Making confession, Hearing Confession, 231.

this chapter might help you understand some of the reasons why some of their people have abandoned their place in Roman Catholicism to seek refuge in the Anglican Church, having been reared for decades in the Roman tradition. This chapter pinpoints a period of history which deeply influenced those who are of age in the Anglican Church to be in leadership, and may offer the reader even more insights into the perspective of those whom we serve who may not have come out of that tradition, but grew up around those same people, and have been indirectly influenced by the shifts in confession in the more modern Roman tradition.

Interestingly, her conclusions closely mirror the results of this study. Her conclusive suggestions could be summarized in the following four points: first, a need for an increased theological understanding of confession; second, to provide a venue for people to meet Jesus; third, to encourage one another to confess to each other; and finally, to increase in the church a perspective of "inter-connectedness versus individuality." While she is writing from a more Protestant Presbyterian perspective (which is her tradition), it is most interesting that her conclusions very closely resemble the conclusions found in this study.

3. Understand the tendency for entropy—There is a need for continual repetitive teaching, quarterly at a maximum, seasonally as befits the penitential seasons of Advent and Lent, but consistently throughout all seasons, and in all ages, of educational offerings in the life of the local church. If we do not teach regularly and consistently about, not only confession, but also about sin or virtue in general, we should not assume that the people will retain anything we teach, let alone maintain their disciplines. There is a sense from the focus group question on the frequency of teaching on confession, that more than quarterly teaching on confession specifically would be too much, and yet less than twice annually expresses, indirectly, that this practice is not important enough to be taught or encouraged, and therefore, not important enough to be practiced. Albert Einstein described entropy with a thought experiment using the image of a perfume bottle. Einstein

posited that while perfume sprayed from a bottle will naturally diffuse throughout an entire room or space in a short amount of time, the same perfume will never naturally gather itself back into a concentrated form within the bottle. We can take from this illustration the simple idea that our classes, Bible studies, and sermons, once spoken, will spread throughout churches, through Bible study groups, casual discussions, and the common memory of the congregation, but will eventually fade or diffuse unless repeated at a comfortable or reasonable interval. Furthermore, our people have reported that they will not assume confession to be a regular offering of the Church in a vacuum of teaching, amidst other pressing concerns, and they will almost never make an appointment to make a confession, nor will they make discipline a matter for themselves, if not gently and consistently encouraged to do so by the clergy and other faithful laity. This is to say that we need to be regularly teaching the sacraments as necessary bearers of grace, particularly among those sacraments which we teach may be repeated: confession, unction, and the eucharist. We repeat the eucharist at the Lord's command for communal worship, and for participation in the passion of our Lord. We repeat confession, as we continue to sin after confessing our sins and have a great need for continual atonement. And likewise, we can repeat unction as we expect that it will indeed heal us and bring us into greater physical and spiritual health, and yet it is likely that we will become ill once again at a later time. But if we just assume people remember everything they were taught in a newcomer's class, or in confirmation class, we are assuming too much.

4. Variety is important—Offer a variety of times to make a confession, from mornings to evenings, and on weekends, and offer a variety of clergy with whom to make a confession. This is not to say that you have to hear confessions four times a week. But perhaps if you are already offering it on Saturday mornings, or one Saturday a month, perhaps you could add: Thursdays after evening prayer, or simply an advertisement that you will be staying after your weekly Wednesday mass for thirty minutes to hear confessions for those who are interested.

It is also important to have a variety in how confession is presented to the people. Preaching the same sermon every quarter will not get the people to the confessional. However, if you offer a sermon before Lent, an newsletter article before Advent, a Sunday school class on the history of atonement, and then a weekend retreat on "getting closer to God," the people will experience the suggestion of the confessional through a variety of opportunities which all seem different, and yet support the one and same conclusion: that confession brings us closer to God. Also consider bringing in others who are good at this, and have them teach a class for you. There are good retreat leaders who can have a positive effect upon your people because they are speaking with a voice that is not yours. While the people often depend on the clergy to guide them on certain subjects, it seems they respond better to the voices of strangers and lay people on the subjects of confession, tithing, and fasting. So take advantage of a variety of advertisement "voices" when speaking on this subject, and do not be afraid to seek the help of faithful laity, especially when you get a sense that the people are ignoring the message from you.

5. "Designated drivers"—To save the souls of your people, put them in the hands of good confessors, particularly if you are not a good confessor or spiritual director yourself. One of the most common refrains of the study was "I don't want to make a confession to my home priest." This is not the case everywhere, but it is the case in most places. If this is the case where you are, find a priest near your parish who is a good confessor, and offer to trade booths once in a while, or refer your people to other clergy nearby who offer regular confession hours. If the people know this is going to be even more anonymous than usual, you, or your neighbor cleric, might see a little more participation in the confessional.

Also, while auricular confession or private spiritual direction may not be within the preferred spirituality of some priests, clergy should be aware of a variety of needs within their parishes, and should be humble enough to admit that they cannot be the only source of teaching and healing for their people on all subjects uniformly. More simply said, if you are a more Protestant minister, understand that your people may not all be like you, and may need to partake of some more Catholic practices based on their personal history and spiritual needs. The same is true in reverse: if you are a more Catholic or Anglo-Catholic priest, know that not all of your people have this heritage, and may need a more casual means of making their confession to God, or more teaching on what this other half of our faith looks like. There are many stigmas that come from family histories, which seem to be on the decline in the younger generations, although there are plenty of older folks in our midst who grew up being told either, "We're Baptists, and all of those Catholics are going to hell!" or, "We're Catholics, and those Protestants are all going to hell!" While this seems like a joke, it is a reality that many people have been indoctrinated to think that all those who do things contrary to "what we do" are somehow just flat wrong, and so we should have nothing to do with them. But we all have the same heritage, to a certain point, and teaching them the history of the Church on this subject can help to put many of these deep-rooted biases to rest. Therefore, we should utilize each other's assets, and refer our people to experts when we are not as personally attuned to a certain practice.

In the time just prior to St. John Chrysostom, the Church had a system of designated confessors within the diocese. We find this in the writing of St. Basil who said:

> Confession of sin in analogous to confession of bodily ailments. Men do not tell their bodily ailments to everybody, but to men skilled at healing— so confession of sin should be made in the presence of those who have the power to heal.[188]

At Constantinople certain priests were designated to preside over penance, to hear confessions, and to prescribe penance just as a doctor would prescribe medicine for an illness. Everyone chose from among these designated confessors their own spiritual director, and the authorized confessors were designated and licensed by the bishop. This

---

[188] Penitential Discipline, Hastlehurst, 104.

is still true in some of the Eastern Churches, and even in some Roman Catholic dioceses. What if each diocese assigned two able confessors to be responsible to hear confessions regularly in each deanery? This way, every person in the diocese would have two choices of anonymous confessors, except of course, those who belonged to one of the parishes led by one of these confessors, in which case they would likely make their confession to the other confessor. One of the comments made among the focus groups was an inclination to confess to a priest who was not the penitent's own, for an added sense of anonymity in the confession. This would also allow for parish priests who are not as able in hearing confessions to direct their people to a regular confessor within their geographical vicinity. While these additional confessions might tax the time of the two regular confessors, one might find that they could also shift some responsibilities away from themselves toward others who are more gifted in administration, youth ministry, spiritual direction, or other natural spiritual gifts, and thus share the gifts of the clergy evenly across the diocese.

What should have been done differently?

As for the things this author would have changed about this study, it would be nice to have interviewed a separate sample of those who have never made a confession to ascertain their fears, apprehensions, or lack of knowledge over the practice. However, it is suspected that such a study would likely reveal many of the same results, although probably more fears than not, of the confessional practice. As for the studies themselves, it would have been better to gather demographic information at the sessions. An attempt was made to gather this material anonymously by computer survey after the participants completed their study. Each participant was given a small piece of paper with a website to visit so to answer just a few questions about their demographics and confessional practice. Less than half of the participants actually did the follow-up survey, so the data have been largely inconclusive. This was due to the fact that most of the people who responded were younger and more adept at "computer things." A short anonymous paper-questionnaire offered at the end of each focus group study would have been better to gather the demographic information of the participants. Furthermore, a cross-reference of demographics with this material may have been helpful, although it appears from the whole study that age, residence, and sex were of no consequence to the practice of the confessional. The common denominators were the lack of education and opportunity for the practice. So this portion of the study, although it would have been interesting, cannot be said to have been truly inconclusive.

CHAPTER TEN
A Brief "How-To" for Novice Confessors

While it may seem daunting to hear a private confession for the first time, having never been through the practice before now, this chapter will orient the reader to the practice, and how to manage the many fears the penitents will be bringing into in the confessional. So to set up this chapter properly, we will discuss the praxis of confession in the following order: first, we will talk about the mental preparation and necessary academic training for the confessor, some basic information about the process of hearing auricular confessions, and we will then equip you with the best resources to be a better confessor and physician of souls; secondly, we will review several means of hearing confessions in various contexts; and finally, we will review one classic model of diagnosing sin in the course of a confession so to equip the reader with enough information to get started as a confessor. Experience and further study will then continue to hone the skills begun in this chapter.

Preparing Yourself

On my first week as a curate, one of my parishioners asked me, "Father, now that you're officially a priest, how are you going to handle hearing the problems of people who might be three times older than you and have more collective knowledge than you?" My response was simple—I said, "Even though I may be young (I was twenty-seven at the time), and they may be older, the problems we typically have as people are well under way by the time we're seventeen years old. So their problems probably aren't all that new, it's just that they've moved in and made a home. The trouble, at any age, is getting them to move out." The parishioner nodded, and accepted this answer, and I was off the hook. But now, having spent a lot more time studying this subject, I can say that I think my answer would be the same today. Psychologists say that almost all of our habitual behaviors, for good or for worse, are typically indoctrinated by the time we are roughly seventeen years old, as are our patterns of behavior. The trouble is getting people to change a deeply rooted behavior pattern, and that begins from the inside out.

Understanding this so-called "human condition" is the beginning of preparing yourself to be a good confessor. The likelihood that someone will come to you for a small sin is miniscule. If they do, it is usually just the tip of the iceberg, and they are testing you to see if you are trustworthy to share anything deeper than their smallest sin. In my experience, people typically come to confession either because the pain of their sin has grown so much that it is pouring out of them in a way that makes them seek help, or they come to confession because someone talked them into the idea of being free of a burden that has been welling up inside of them for a while, possibly even for years. Knowing this, a confessor must learn to be merciful as God is merciful. In their eyes, whether they identify this phenomenon or not, they are coming to you as the physician of their souls. They are sick, they believe you have the cure, and they are coming to be relieved of pain, fear, anxiety, guilt, and a host of other things that sin brings out in their lives.

The role of a confessor is to bring people back into atonement with God. As such, confessors must also be those who have practiced this behavior themselves. After all, how can you introduce someone to another whom you yourself do not know? Being a good confessor has everything to do with a living participation in the Christian life with God, and our study has shown that the prayer life, empathy, love, and pastoral care that a confessor brings into the confessional really does come across in the course of the confession to the penitent. Anyone could read the books prescribed here, learn a few formulas for finding sin, attach a contrary virtue as a remedy, and do the technical work of a confessor in terms of diagnosis, attacking the sin, and prescribing a remedy. However, the missing component is the conveyance of God's mercy, the love God has for us, and the gentle assuring forgiveness that comes from a confessor who has known this mercy themself, and the experience of a pastor who has guided others over what will become a lifetime of ministry.

Therefore, preparing to hear confessions is not merely a matter of sharpening the knives and preparing for surgery. It is a matter of humbling oneself, making a confession prior to hearing a confession, and setting the tone of the confessional for the benefit of the penitents so that they may know forgiveness and be assured of the love God has for them despite their sin before they go in peace to pray for us. This is something the confessors can only learn by practicing themselves. No amount of teaching will prepare the soul to be merciful. It is by receiving mercy that we become merciful, as someone said somewhere, "Forgive us our trespasses, as we forgive those who trespass against us."

Now, to address briefly a few texts that will help the confessor—Evelyn Underhill gave an address to the clergy of the Worcester Diocesan Clergy Convention at Oxford in September of 1936, which was subsequently re-printed as an article entitled *The Parish Priest and the Life of Prayer*. In the opening paragraphs of this lecture, Underhill addresses this primary concern of the parish priest, which has everything to do with their role as a confessor:

> The man whose life is coloured by prayer, whose loving communion with God comes first, will always win souls; because he shows them in his own life and person the attractiveness of reality, the demand, the transforming power of the spiritual life. His intellectual powers and the rest will not, comparatively speaking, matter much. The point is that he stands as a witness to that which he proclaims. The most persuasive preacher, the most devoted and untiring social worker, the most up-to-date theologian—unless loving devotion to God exceeds and enfolds these activities—will not win souls. It follows from this, that the priest's life of prayer, his communion with God, is not only his primary obligation to the Church; it is also the only condition under which the work of the Christian ministry can be properly done. He is called, as the Book of Wisdom says, to be a 'friend of God, and prophet': and will only be a good prophet in so far as he is really a friend of God. For his business is to lead men out towards

eternity; and how can he do this, unless it is a country in which he is at home? He is required to represent the peace of God in a troubled society; but that is impossible, if he has not the habit of resorting to those deeps of the spirit where His Presence dwells.[189]

Once we have this under way, there are some technical and theological concerns within the confessional that can equip the confessor with necessary knowledge for guiding souls. One of the best texts to this end is *A Manual for Confessors* by Francis George Belton. This text covers the nature of the sacrament, the essential parts of the sacrament, the seal of the confession, the duties of a confessor, the treatment of various classes of penitents, and finally, the care of the sick and dying. As most confessions seem to come when people are in dire need of cleansing their souls, Belton's chapter on the *sick and dying* is one of the greatest expositions on the Church's teaching of the use of confession at the time of death, and in the use of viaticum and holy oils in this context. If a novice confessor were to study this book, and even take it into the confessional to read while waiting to hear confessions, the time will not have been ill spent, and in the course of preparing to hear confessions, the confessor will continue to hone their skills. Such continuous reading is tremendously helpful to the confessor, as there is quite a broad scope of material on the subject, and much to keep in mind. But with time, this learning becomes more readily accessible to the mind of the confessor, and will eventually become almost second nature.

The third suggested book for the novice confessor, to aid in their study of diagnosing sin and applying a remedy, is *The Elements of the Spiritual Life* by F.P. Harton. Describing the structure of his own book, Harton states:

> The plan of the book is simple. Part I deals with the action of God by grace; Part II with the human resistance to the divine will and the means whereby that resistance may be overcome; Part III is a brief outline of the divine economy of the sacraments; Part IV is concerned with the life of prayer, and

---

[189] The Parish Priest and the Life of Prayer by Evelyn Underhill. Little Gidding Press, Morningside Heights, New York. 1937. 2.

in Part V we consider the end of the spiritual life and the ways by which that end may be reached, concluding with a chapter on the guidance of souls with some consideration of the qualities of the ideal director. [190]

In his text, Harton saved the best teaching for the final chapter on *The Guidance of Souls*, which we would suggest might be read first, prior to the remainder of the book. This text is ideal for addressing the nature of sin, and the ways in which we can prayerfully learn to conquer them by knowing the true nature of the sin, and then applying a contrary virtue to crush the work of the sin in the life of the penitent.

Context: Where to Hear Confessions

By now, it is assumed that the previous pages of this text have been read and internalized, but as a brief summary in regards to context, the lay people who were interviewed in the focus groups on the study of confession and spiritual direction reported the following key results: almost unanimously, that they prefer to make a confession in a church setting, and that they want that experience to be as private as possible; they will almost never make an appointment to make a confession; and they are willing to hear more about confession in sermons and Bible studies; and furthermore, that they desire regular offerings for confessional hours. As such, we will address the location confessions are likely to be best heard, the times people say that they might come, and some suggestions on how to establish a confessional practice in a parish that has none.

Beginning with *where*, this might seem difficult, as most parishes outside of the Roman Catholic Church do not have confessional booths, or if they do, these have fallen out of use, or have become storage spaces. But there is a way to hear confessions in the Church, and a few signs properly paced can keep the practice private. Beginning with confessional booths: if your parish has one, it might be in need of a cleaning. As an anecdote here, I have a hobby I have maintained over

---

[190] The Elements of the Spiritual Life by F.P. Harton. S.P.C.K., London. 1957. v.

the last few years: when I travel to a new town for vacation or business, I frequently visit churches, and when they have confessional booths, I open the door and simply take a picture of whatever is in there. The vast majority of the time I discover cleaning supplies, a mop and bucket, old books stacked to the ceiling, offering baskets, and in one Episcopal cathedral I even found a sound system for their microphones. If your parish is in this habit, simply clean out the booth, with the following considerations: the space should be clean, comfortable (perhaps buy a new cushion or chair), suitably lighted, and it should have some means of separation between the clergy and the penitent. In some places this is done simply with a piece of cloth, while in others there are metal screens dividing the people from the clergy. While these apparatuses were invented in the Medieval period to keep the clergy from abusing the people in the confessional by exacting money, or passing anything else between the two rooms, the people have said very clearly that they are willing and eager to make a confession in a confessional booth, but they do not want to see the face of the clergy. This space should also be heated, cooled, or otherwise vented in a way that assures it does not become a sauna or meat locker, but also allows for baffling of sound. Some clergy have come to running a box-fan outside of the confessional, which creates just enough noise to muffle the sounds within the booth itself. Others have taken measures to sound-proof the confessional booths with carpet, professional sound-baffling materials, or simply by placing them in remote spaces. If there is to be a queue of people waiting in line to make confessions, have this queue begin somewhere a reasonable distance from the entrance to the confessional door to allow for maximum privacy, particularly if the confessional is not soundproofed, then start the line further back in the Church. Another good idea, where applicable, is to have an exit where people can depart the confessional without having to be seen by someone on the way out. Psychologists, professional counselors, and even medical doctors' offices often provide for this, in that they have a waiting room for patients who are waiting to see the doctor, and a separate exit room, or side door for those who have already seen the doctor. While this might seem counter-intuitive, as you might think that people are generally more skittish going into the confessional than coming out of one, the people have reported a sense of fear over who sees them leaving the confessional, but made no such comments about those seeing them waiting to make the confession. So if you have the box, use it, clean it out, or upgrade it and let people know it is open for business.

In many more modern churches and worship spaces, there is no confessional booth. In fact, many modern churches look more like auditoriums, which make this desire to make confessions in the worship space a difficult task to complete, but it is possible. In a few places, churches have built confessional boxes on wheels or on a low trolley that can be wheeled in for confessional hours, and then remotely stored when not in use. This is a very practical means of providing a space without having to build a permanent structure. Anyone could seemingly find a craftsman in or near a parish to build a rectangular box with two doors and two chairs, and a screen or cloth in between to serve this purpose. One clergyman reported privately to the clerical survey adding, "I built my own confessional on wheels, and since implementing it, my confessional activity has skyrocketed. The people want a private space for confession."

However, if there is no confessional booth, or if you happen to be offering confessions in an irregular context, such as while on a retreat, or at a camp, or in another place where you have a little time to prepare a confessional space, here are a few suggestions for how to arrange that space. Arrange a kneeler and a chair, or two separate chairs in such a way that the penitent sits or kneels behind the confessor, although not facing the confessor—they should be facing a cross, tabernacle, icon, or some other visual sign of God's presence in the space. This can be as big as the main sanctuary cross, or as simple as a small cross on the wall, or placed on the reading table of a prie dieu (prayer desk). In any case, the idea is to have them oriented in such a way as though they are talking to God, while the confessor is there in-between as an intermediary. This is where the term *auricular* confession comes from: *auricula* meaning "in the ear." In a church, this could be achieved by placing a chair inside the altar rail (but not centered), allowing for a penitent to kneel slightly behind the confessor while facing the altar. As long as the confessor never turns around, this can give some sense of privacy, and allow for the confession to be easily heard. By the way, this also allows the confessor to hold a prayer book or bible in which to hold confessional resources, which usually cannot be seen by the penitent, particularly if the chair has a tall back. In one church surveyed, the rector developed a system in which he put a small veil, about the size of a small window (roughly twenty-four inches square), on a hinged pole on the right side of the sanctuary, immediately adjacent to the altar rail. The priest in that parish would swing the arm holding the veil out parallel with the altar rail, and then he sat behind the veil inside the altar rail. This was a simple yet elegant solution that allowed the penitent to make a confession without seeing his face, and it was easily put away when not in use, and did not require much construction. Some clergy have heard confessions while sitting in the pews: the confessor sitting one pew ahead of the penitent. In all of these cases mentioned thus far, the confessions were heard in a church setting, which is, according to the survey, the primary desired location for the laity. They want to do sacramental things in sacramental spaces, whenever possible.

Now, if you are outside of a church, there is a way to bring the sense of sacred space to any location. For starters, use the same arrangements listed above, only find as private a space as possible, such as a small room or office with a door, the library of a retreat house, or even a remote location in plain air can serve this need of privacy. As long as the penitent cannot be heard by anyone but the confessor, the setting can be very simple. Arrange two chairs, or a chair and a kneeler, again in such a way as to have the penitent sitting behind you, but slightly off center. Once again, the people have reported that they are usually terrified of seeing the confessor's face, so be sensitive to the fact that they want privacy from others, as well as from you. While some regular penitents have more courage to go to confession, and therefore less fear of sitting down face-to-face, the likelihood of someone wanting you to remember them or their confession is low. Of course, all of this goes out the window in emergency situations. The more eager someone is to make a confession, the less likely they are to care if they see your face, particularly when on the verge of death, or perceived danger of death. In fact, in those cases, they are usually more relieved to see your face and to know that their pastor is there for them.

Once you have the seating arranged, put a cross on the wall, or orient them in a way that they are not talking directly to your face, but rather in some sense, that they are talking to God. Even the open sky is better than looking straight at the confessor. In the absence of a cross or other holy symbol, something as simple as a bible or a prayer book can do the trick, particularly since most prayer books tend to have a cross on the cover. While this may seem strange to some, we suggest that clergy should have in their car at all times: a bible, a cross, an oil stock, a confessional stole (there are many reversible white/purple stoles available at most religious bookstores), and a book of prayers for the sick and dying. Just as you never know when you might be called on to visit the sick or the dying, you also never know when someone might call on you to make their confession. Another idea is to make a small laminated card exclusively for confessions, and stick it in your prayer book or bible, or even in your jacket pocket, should you wear clericals. It can be awkward to have to share your prayer book with a penitent when they are trying to make a confession. Whereas, if you had a small card you could set out, or hand them in the hospital bed, this equips them with the format or liturgy to make a confession, and leaves you in possession of your prayer book. Many clergy also keep a suit jacket in their car for pastoral calls, as they usually come unexpectedly. This jacket usually contains a stole, a book of prayers for the sick, and sometimes an oil stock or a pocket aspergillum (holy water sprinkler). All of these things prepare you to be ready to do pastoral care at all times, but particularly to hear confessions in strange places. Having the equipment of the craft readily available is something that not only assists the penitents in their comfort level, as familiar holy things bring a sense of comfort in traumatic situations, but it will also boost your confidence to know that you cannot be caught off-guard when called upon to guide a soul back to God.

Concerning the times to hear confession, these may vary. We have already addressed the need to be prepared at random times, but the majority of this study shows that people will not make an appointment, and they actually desire to know when the confessional hours are to be offered in a parish, and who is to be the confessor (if you are in a multi-cleric parish). For many years, it seems, confessions have been scheduled for Saturday mornings. However, in modern times it seems Saturdays are not what they used to be, and most people have family activities on the weekends. As such, it may be a good idea to add a few alternative times to hear confessions. If a regular Saturday time is working for you, do not change your practices. But consider that there may be some who cannot make that time, and consider, not only a different day, but a different time of day. For example, offer to stay every day after evening prayer at say 5:30pm. Or if you have a weeknight mass, offer to hear confessions for a half hour before or after the mass. In any case, make these times regular, and see that they are posted in your announcements, calendar, or even on the parish sign. Many clergy who have posted their confessional hours on their sign have reported that complete strangers stop in from time to time to make a confession. This could be for one of several reasons: they wanted to confess immediately, they wanted to confess to a confessor who was not their priest or pastor, or they simply had nowhere else to go, since most places do not post confessional hours. Every successful business posts very clear signs on their door or sign indicating when they are open. Why should the confessional be any different? If we are in the business of saving souls, why not tell people we are "open for business"?

As a conclusion to this section, we will reiterate a few points that have already been covered in this study, but are worthy of repeating within this section on praxis: if you are not a good confessor, point your people toward those who are. If you are opposed to the idea of confession, consider that some of the people in your parish may not share your piety, and may consider it an essential part of their walk with God. If you are still learning to hear confessions, that is great, but continue to sit for confessions, even while you are learning. If you post regular hours, it is highly unlikely that you will be busy every minute, let alone every week you sit to hear confessions. Buy one or more of the "books for further study" mentioned within this text, and read a chapter each time you sit in the confessional. It is likely that by the time you have heard your fifth confession, you will have become an expert, or at least be well on your way. Finally, consider swapping confessional booths with a local confessor from time to time, and announce it in your parish. Those who are afraid to come and see you might be very eager to come if a certified clergyman is there who they know they never have to see again. The ultimate goal here is to provide a safe, private, and pastoral means to guide our people back to the Lord. Why not tap into the resources around you, and offer your people the very best in pastoral care, even if it is not your cup of tea?

Diagnosing sin, and prescribing a remedy

There are plenty of ethical and moral theologians who will say that changing the behavior of a sinner is not enough—which is true. Jesus teaches as much to the Scribes and Pharisees:

> Woe unto you, scribes and Pharisees, hypocrites! For ye make clean the outside of the cup and of the platter, but within they are full of extortion and excess. Thou blind Pharisee, cleanse first that which is within the cup and platter, that the outside of them may be clean also.[191]

Earlier in the same Gospel, he teaches the same theme to his disciples, albeit within the context of eating presumed "unclean" foods:

---

[191] Matthew 23:25-26

And he called the multitude, and said unto them, "Hear, and understand: Not that which goeth into the mouth defileth a man; but that which cometh out of the mouth, this defileth a man." Then came his disciples, and said unto him, "Knowest thou that the Pharisees were offended, after they heard this saying?" But Jesus answered and said, "Every plant, which my heavenly Father hath not planted, shall be rooted up. Let them alone: they be blind leaders of the blind. And if the blind lead the blind, both shall fall into the ditch." Then answered Peter and said unto him, "Declare unto us this parable." And Jesus said, "Are ye also yet without understanding? Do not ye yet understand, that whatsoever entereth in at the mouth goeth into the belly, and is cast out into the draught? But those things which proceed out of the mouth come forth from the heart; and they defile the man. For out of the heart proceed evil thoughts, murders, adulteries, fornications, thefts, false witness, blasphemies: These are the things which defile a man."[192]

In both cases, Jesus teaches that sin originates from the hearts and desires of people. Outward appearances, pious practices, and other signs of holiness are of no value if the intentions and thoughts behind them are corrupt and lead only to death. In fact, Jesus follows up the first reading by calling the Scribes and Pharisees "whitewashed sepulchers" or otherwise said, newly painted graves—the outside might be clean, but they contain nothing more than death and corruption. We all know that people can behave a certain way when they know they are being watched. Even the vilest sinner can behave long enough to be attend a Thanksgiving supper or a child's birthday party, just as the average speedy driver can easily slow down when a police car is on their bumper, however, changing a behavior permanently requires more than a temporary break from the sin. It requires, in addition, true sorrow and genuine repentance. As we have already read in the historical study, a classic model for discerning whether a confession is "valid" is three-fold, following the pattern of discerning: contrition, confession, and amendment of life. Using this model as an outline, we will discuss this mode of handling a confession.[193]

---

[192] Matthew 15:10-20

[193] Note: The intention of using this model is purely to provide a structure in which to guide novice confessors toward successfully hearing confessions. It is not intended to say that the predominant Catholic model is the only model. Furthermore, this is

First, begin your confessional hour(s) by sitting alone in the confessional, or before the cross, a tabernacle, or even an icon, or whatever suits your particular spirituality, and make a confession to God. Pour out your sins, and pray that God will assist your sorrow, grant you an honest acknowledgement of your sin, true forgiveness and absolution, and ask that he send His Holy Spirit to help you conquer the desire to sin the next time it arises. Conclude your prayers with a petition to be a conduit for God's grace, as you prepare to serve as a mediator between the penitents who come to you, and God to whom they desire to make their humble confession. While it is the belief of many clergy that the authority to forgive sins was granted to the Priesthood through "the keys" aforementioned in the scriptural study, when Jesus breathed on his disciples and said, "Whosoever sins ye remit, they are remitted unto them; and whosoever sins ye retain, they are retained"[194], yet even the most protestant minister believes that God is the forgiver of all sins—so, if you are of this belief, then serve in that capacity—as an intermediary between God and the penitent, and do your best to guide them to the throne of grace, that God may forgive them. But do help them along. If you do not believe clergy are ordained by God to forgive and remit sins, simply augment the absolution to say "Almighty God forgive you your sins" instead of "By the authority given by God to his ministers, I forgive you ...", or whatever your tradition's formularies or liturgies allow.

The next step, in the classical form of the confessional, is to diagnose contrition. As a reminder, contrition (Lat. *contritio*) means "sorrow" or "a rubbing against" (in the sense of a grinding feeling). This means that foremost, a penitent should be truly irritated and sorry for their sins. We diagnose sorrow by listening for certain queues to hear whether this person is truly sorry that they have hurt someone, or that

---

a model which predates any denominational distinctions, and although the Western Catholic Church has adopted this as the only valid model for making and hearing confessions, the Eastern Church has used similar models, and the Anglican church likewise has maintained some semblance of this model in the theological teaching on confession.

[194] John 20:23

their relationship with God is out of order, or whether it is actually false-contrition which is called attrition. Attrition is sorrow for sin, but not because they feel bad or have any true regret. Attrition is the feeling expressed by someone who is sad they got caught, or because they now face the consequences of what they have done.

Contrition is very difficult to diagnose, and one can never perfectly diagnose whether a penitent it truly contrite enough. This was, in fact, one of John Calvin's strongest arguments against auricular confession. He argued that if one cannot truly diagnose contrition, how is one to then prescribe a remedy? Simply answered, you just have to use your best judgment, and listen for signs of sorrow, irritation, and an inclination toward humility and a desire to "put things right." We may never know for sure whether someone is truly contrite, or as Calvin argued, "contrite enough" in measure to the gravity of their sin. We have to depend on the mercy of God to cover the gap. The Catholic answer to Calvin's argument is roughly this: that the confessor, working God's grace through the penitent in the confession, leads them to true contrition by the end of the confession. And this is truly sometimes the case. Sometimes confessors really do have to help the penitent figure out why they should have sorrow. Sometimes penitents only come into the confessional with a vague or veiled sense of guilt, but have not as yet figured out where to place the blame, how to humble themselves, or how to grow in sorrow for a sin that they are in fact, most of the time, quite fond of committing. This is the biggest trouble with our sins: we usually like them. It is relatively easy to give up doing something you hate. It is, however, quite difficult to give up something that we love, even if it causes us (and/or those around us) great harm, particularly when we have become comfortable living in the sin for a long time. A large part of teaching contrition to a penitent is in teaching them to conquer not only the action of their sins, but ultimately the desire for their sins. For a deeper understanding of this part of the process, read *Introduction to the Devout Life* by Francis deSales, who addressed this problem directly with some specific suggestions for conquering desire. In what he calls "The Second Purgation," de Sales addresses the purgation of affection for sin:

Although the Israelites left Egypt in effect, not all of them left it in affection, and hence in the wilderness many of them regretted their lack of the onions and fleshpots of Egypt. In like manner, there are penitents who leave sin in effect, but do not leave it in affection ...

> ... since you wish to live a devout life you must not only cease to sin, but you must also purify your heart of all affection for sin. In addition to the danger of falling again, such base affections so lastingly weaken and weigh down your spirits that it will be impossible to do good works promptly, diligently, and frequently, and it is in this that the very essence of devotion consists....such souls do good but with such spiritual weariness that it robs their good deeds of all grace and the deeds themselves are few in number, and of small effect.[195]

Accordingly, the role of the confessor, at times, is to teach the penitent to hate or have disgust for their desire to sin, and their affection for the things that take them away from God. This process of contritional diagnosis itself can bring much healing to the penitent through developing a sense of self-awareness of their sin through careful guidance toward replacing their affection for sin with affection for a holier life. For example, a smoker may not quit smoking because they are told it is bad for them. Most smokers like the fact that they are smokers, enjoy the act of smoking, and are under no delusion that smoking somehow good for them, and may even argue the benefits or why it is good for them. But they might be swayed from smoking because it is harming their relationship with another, or because their actions are physically harming someone dear to them, or even because the smoking will prevent them from spending time doing something else they love more than smoking. Appetite and desire for one thing can usually only be conquered replacing the desire or appetite with a desire for something greater or more enjoyable. Cutting out the bad is not enough. It must be replaced with a contrary good.

---

[195] Introduction to the Devout Life by Francis de Sales, trans. By John K. Ryan. Image Books, Doubleday, New York. 1989. 50-51.

As such, a confessor must be prepared to help their penitents determine why the have affection for their sins, and at times may have to convince them why they should feel sorry, all the while inquiring of them whether they really are feeling contrite, or if they in fact just feel guilty. Guilt is a large motivator for confession, both of the contrite, and of those that are only expressing attrition. One must be very discerning as to whether a penitent is coming to confession to have the confessor simply take the guilt away, or whether they are really interested in healing and making reconciliation with those they have hurt, including God. Perhaps a good "litmus" test is to ascertain whether this person is willing to make amends, or to seek reconciliation with those they have hurt. If the answer is no, then it is more likely that they want to conquer their guilt without actually remedying the source of the guilt, which is the desire to sin, or to satisfy only their own feelings. Even if you were to grant them absolution in this case, it is very likely that the guilt would remain, because the root cause of the sin, the desire, remains. To this point, Jesus says:

> When an unclean spirit goes out of a man, it passes through waterless places looking for rest, but finds none. Then it says, "I will return to the home I left." When it returns, it finds the house clean, swept, and in order. Then it goes and brings with it seven other spirits, worse than itself, and they go in and live there, so the last state of the man is worse than the first.[196]

Offering a penitent a superficial confession, without much diagnosis and guidance toward contrition and a change of heart, may in fact rid them of the sin and grant them absolution, but the danger is that the house which has been swept and cleaned out is just as ready to be re-inhabited by many worse spirits, unless we teach them to replace the tenants with more virtuous behaviors, attitudes, and remedies. Always be wary of quick confessions.

This leads us to the second attribute of a good confession, the confession. Confession (Latin *confessio*) means "to acknowledge" one's culpability. As already stated, sometimes the confessor has to help the

---

[196] Matthew 12: 43-45

penitent establish this before contrition is possible. Sometimes, in diagnosing the sin, the idiom, "The apple doesn't fall far from the tree," is quite true. Sometimes the root cause of the sin is quite obvious— for example: "I stole the food because I was hungry and didn't have any money." This is usually true of one-time sins, sins of opportunity, or sins committed out of a sense of urgency or necessity. But at other times, the root of the sin can be far from the fruit on the branches. A simple thought experiment to illustrate this point is to pretend someone came in confessing gluttony. "Father, I'm eating too much." This confession is pretty vague, is it not? Let us just try to imagine or identify the myriad reasons an individual might over-eat—here are a few cursory motives: guilt, depression, boredom, self-indulgence, fear, to feel better, to celebrate, and etc. There are dozens if not hundreds of reasons people eat, many of which have nothing to do with the actual cravings of the stomach, although there are those too. In helping guide a penitent toward acknowledging their sin, you might have to ask some deeper questions, such as: "Why do you think you overeat? Is it really about the food? Is there something else going on I should know about?" There is one school of thought about the confessional that came out during the early Medieval period, in which the confessor was to ask every possible question in determining this sort of thing: "Who were you with? Was this done in a Church? Are you a priest or a layman? Are you in a position of power over the person you harmed? What was the frequency of the sin? How often has this occurred?"[197] The potential litany goes on. While these questions do help us to determine the depth of the sin, the questions asked by the confessor must be pinpointed to the specific confession made by the penitent. Rather than subjecting them to the inquisition, the confessor should listen clearly to what the penitent says, and then ask probing questions as necessary to gain a

---

[197] For more texts such as these, see Medieval Handbooks of Penance trans. by John T. McNeill and Helena M. Gamer. Columbia University Press, New York. 1938. or Pastors and the Care of Souls in Medieval England ed. by John Shinners and William J. Dohar, University of Notre Dame Press, Notre Dame, Indiana. 1998.

reasonable amount of clarity. Most of the time, people will try to hold something back, as though they are "dipping a toe in the pool" to see whether the temperature is right for a full immersion. But this is usually quite obvious to the confessor.

As we can see from this brief example, helping someone get to the heart of their confession can also be difficult. This is where a confessional inventory, or an *Examination of Conscience* is helpful to the penitent to help bring some of this material to the confessor in a clearer way. An Examination of Conscience is an inventory conducted by the penitent in private before they come to the confessional. A sample copies will be included in the appendix to this text, although samples may be found in other places, including the St. Augustine Prayer Book. It is suggested that an Examination of Conscience handout or flyer should be readily available in a parish, and structured in such a way so to help the penitents understand what it is that they are doing, according to several diagnostic tools. The two most popular diagnostic tools for sin in an Examination of Conscience inventory are: the *Ten Commandments* and The *Seven Deadly Sins*. The good confessor should be very well versed in these diagnostic tools, as they are a tremendous help in filtering the dross out of murky confessions. When someone makes a confession, one good way to manage the litany of things penitents tend to bring to the confessional is to mentally put them into categories according to one of these tools, particularly the seven deadly sins. If someone lists fifteen sins, but ten of them seem to all center around one particular sin, then it is important to spend more time addressing the root of that one particular sin. At other times, a penitent will try to hide a major sin in a stack of other fairly mundane sins, as though we might not notice. Both situations require the confessor to have a good filter or triage process for handling a litany of sins. A good resource for developing this specific skill is the aforementioned *Elements of the Spiritual Life* by F.P. Harton. This text teaches us, as confessors, how to triage such litanies into specific categories so to recognize a pattern of behavior, and subsequently, to prescribe a suitable remedy. For every sin, there is a contrary virtue. But a confessor cannot prescribe the medicine, if they cannot identify the illness. One suggestion that may be helpful here is to have the penitents perform an Examination of Conscience on a piece of paper prior to coming to the confessional, and ask them to circle all of the sins they struggle with in a bright colored pen, such as a red pen, or a highlighter. By the end of the inventory, one portion of the paper will probably be far more colorful than the rest. This is likely where they should focus their first confession. But in the course of time, the other portions, or those that seem to come up again and again, are worthy of further care in the confessional, and may also be addressed in private spiritual direction. This is where regular penitents glean the most from the confessional—when they make this a discipline of regularly addressing the details, rather than dumping a litany into the confessional once every ten years. It is very difficult to handle a decade's worth of sins in ten minutes, although a confessor may grant them absolution, and suggest that they continue to make a confession on a regular basis so to conquer the big things first, and move on to the smaller sins in due course. Habitual sins, or problems that are beyond the skill-set of the confessor might be best handled by suggesting that the penitent consider professional counseling, or perhaps a few private sessions of spiritual direction outside of the confessional. Such suggestions should not be made contingencies for absolution, but may be great tools to assist the penitent into greater healing and spiritual progress. Furthermore, although the confessor may not bring up the confession again at a later time, particularly when they did not have a suitable answer and later discovered something that would have been helpful during the first confession. But the confessor may add this bit of knowledge to their library of knowledge, so not to be "bitten by the same dog twice."

This brings us to the final stages of the confessional process, which is broadly called amendment of life, but may also include penances, acts of charity, or other continued spiritual direction. To begin, amendment of life has to start with the will or the desire to not sin again. It does the soul no good to put out the fire of sin, only to leave behind the fuel, the kindling, and the matches for a future bonfire. When people come to make a confession, this is the part that may excite them, or cause them further grief. The role of a good confessor in guiding a penitent toward true amendment of life is to build up the penitent, reassure them of God's gift of the Holy Spirit which will help them conquer their sin, and equip them with suggestions to guide their desires back to their love of God and neighbor. This can begin in the opening words the confessor speaks after hearing a confession. Begin by thanking the penitent for being brave enough to come to confession and to desire to heal their souls. Congratulate them on taking the first step towards reconciliation, and assure them of God's love for them, and His desire to restore them to good graces. Confession is scary enough by itself. If the confessor can make the penitent feel good about making a confession right off the bat, then the remainder of the words spoken will be received with much more receptive ears than even the penitent thought was possible. Secondly, address the content of the sins. Show them where certain patterns exist in their behavior, inquire as necessary for clarity where needed, and help reflect back to them the image they have given in the confession. Nervous penitents are not always the best communicators, so after you talk to them about their troubles, conclude by asking them, "Am I hearing you right?" or "Does this seem to be on the right track toward helping you?" People will typically be quite willing to discuss things to a greater depth, and to offer more clarity, if they know that the confessor is interested in understanding them and healing them. Quite often it is the case that murky or vague confessions can be brought to the surface through some simple questions asking them to verify whether we are addressing their actual problem or not. And no matter where you conversation leads, always conclude every confession by asking, "Is there anything else you want to address today?" The confessor will likely be amazed at the answers that will follow this question. Sometimes, as already stated, people will spend a lot of their time in the confessional seeking to test our abilities, or our responses. Once you build them up, encourage them, and gain a bit more of their trust, you will often discover the grizzly bear that was hiding behind the clean white sheet they were showing you thus far. As we can see, this process is not so much of a linear progression, as a cyclical means of churning the cream of their guilt-ridden emotions and motives into a more solid confession. While we have been speaking with a lot of metaphors here, it should be clear that once the confessor has done this work, and has arrived at a clear picture of what is being confessed, the confessor can then guide the penitent toward a more lasting moment of atonement.

Another way of leading penitents toward a true amendment of life is to simply ask, "What do you think you should do about this?" It is often the case that they have something in mind, or rather that they are coming to you for advice on how to "make this right." For some sins, there are actual tangible means of atonement, such as restoring things that were stolen or offering a replacement for those things that were damaged, or apologies for hurt feelings, and etc. However, there are many sins for which there is no physical remedy. One cannot replace lost lives, remedy the pain of another's body or soul, or seek forgiveness of someone who is out of touch, or possibly even dead. In these latter cases, some of the remedy will likely simply be teaching the penitent to prevent the opportunity for sin from happening again, and growing spiritually in the process.

The church has long been in the practice of offering penances for this portion of the process, but this is also where much of the damage to the unity of the Church has its pedigree. Penances should be about the penitent, and should accomplish the following goals: adjust the attitude of the penitent towards a better line of thinking, re-orient the desires for the sin towards their contrary virtues, be an act of thanksgiving to God for the forgiveness received, and when possible, to serve as an opportunity to bless others. Penances were originally derived in the late Patristic period as a means of offering the penitent the means to practice the virtues they were taught in the confessional, and to restore their trust to the community. For those who were greedy, or selfish, acts of charity were intended to not just be a means of repayment to the community, but also a way for the penitent to practice, in real terms, a change of heart. Sometimes there is an act of charity or hospitality to be done, while many times, particularly for sins that have harmed someone emotionally, a penance can be something as simple as a Psalm that re-orients the thoughts of the penitent towards a more holy outlook, serving as preventative medicine. Prescribing "Our Fathers" or "Hail Marys" might be a good practice if the penitent has a more meditative or prayerful discipline in their lives, such as praying the rosary, but such penances can be quite arbitrary to those for whom such a remedy does no real good, particularly when they do not know these prayers. We now live in an age where the confessor cannot assume that the people know any prayers or ritual practices, as this has become far less mainstream. In the appendix, we will offer a chart of Psalms that correlate to the various sins prescribed in the examination of conscience (the Seven Deadly Sins and the Ten Commandments), which may be of use to the confessor. Some confessors have even been of the practice of printing a small version of this list to put in the back of a prayer book to be used by the confessor when they cannot remember the Psalms associated with each sin. Such tools can be quite handy to the confessor as they hear confessions and may be a useful reference tool to leave in or near the confessional space.

The end of the amendment of life process, which some consider to be a separate fourth and final step, is absolution. After listening for contrition, guiding the penitent through their confession to be as specific as necessary or possible, prescribing a remedy in the penances or with other spiritual guidance, the confession is concluded with an assurance of absolution. Prayer books that contain liturgies for confession, absolution of a penitent, or any other various titles given to this process, also usually contain at least one, but more likely several option for absolving sin. Modern liturgies have recognized the theological rift between those who claim that the clergy bear the authority to pronounce forgiveness in the first person, i.e. "I absolve you..." versus the more passive, "God absolves you..." formulary. In some liturgies, Deacons or lay people are permitted to hear confessions and to pronounce forgiveness following this latter pattern, saying something such as, "Almighty God forgive *us* our sins...", thus including themselves in the formulary and allowing God to be the bearer of this grace, rather than the confessor or celebrant of the liturgy. In short, read over the options before you begin, mark it in the prayer book as a reminder to yourself of your preferred absolution, and use whatever is in sync with your theological beliefs. The ultimate goal here is to relieve souls of sin, and arguments over the absolution tend to be fairly arbitrary or utterly moot.

Spiritual direction, which has been referenced here, is a separate discipline. Spiritual direction is a process that involves an extended relationship between the cleric and parishioner, and as such, does not necessarily carry with it the seal of the confession, unless, of course, a penitent makes their confession while in spiritual direction. In some places, the confessor and spiritual director are separate individuals. In certain churches, seminaries, or other ministerial contexts, this is required, as it is suspected that students, colleagues, or employees should not be in a confessional relationship as it may affect the professor-student relationship, or the same if a curate were to confess to their rector, or employee to boos, or anywhere where the confessor maintains a certain element of secular power over the penitent. Purely speaking, the confession is intended to stand alone, and to remain completely private, even to the moment itself—which is to say, even in the confessional space, previous confessions may only be brought up by the penitent, and never the confessor. As such, the content of the confession should never permeate the life outside of the confessional session as it stands alone. But if this were to be a fear, this is where having guest confessors, or a neighboring confessor-chaplain as a choice of confessor might be recommended. However, that being said, it also seems that confession and spiritual direction are intended to work hand-in-hand, or at least one should point to another, and vice versa. The process of healing a soul is usually not a one-stop-shopping experience. Although absolution may be granted, really conquering a long history of spiritual illness usually requires more than the confession alone can heal in a short amount of time. As such, spiritual direction may be of great benefit to such souls, as spiritual direction allows for a longer diagnostic period, and a means of measuring spiritual progress, where confessional moments stand alone, and do not continue outside of the singular confessional sitting. While some might think there to be a conflict of interest where the confessor is also someone in authority over their penitents, this would still be the case in spiritual direction, only without the seal of the confessional. But is this fear real? A confessor always has to bear, within themselves, a deep level of humility, which includes submitting their own secular power to the seal of the confessional. However, from personal experience, such situations do not tend to create more tension, but rather usually lead to the confessor having more love and mercy for their penitents, even for those under their authority. Remember, the goal of a confessor, as well as a spiritual director, is to bring the penitent back to God. It is not about our own relationships, and as such, such relational boundaries really do have to be sacrificed under the role of confessor, and even pastor. Furthermore, as regards the confessor-spiritual director relationship: a spiritual director is just as likely, if not more likely to hear more about a person's sins than the confessor sitting in a booth. Spiritual direction tends to be more invasive, more diagnostic, and longer in terms of length of time spent addressing certain sins with a spiritual director. As such, it appears that the confessor can be, and probably should be, the same person as the confessor. This is not to say that they have to be the penitent's exclusive confessor, or in cases where a layman is the spiritual director, the spiritual director may direct the penitent to make a confession after using spiritual direction as a diagnostic or a follow-up to a previous confession—particularly where a spiritual direction session has unearthed a sin previously not confessed. In either case, the conflict should not arise, and there are many ways to assure that a conflict could not arise. Simply saying that at confessor-penitent relationship in one instance is inappropriate due to authority structures, while not seeking an alternative solution to this situation, seems to be merely a scapegoat to get someone out of confession. If they really want to confession, provisions could be made.

For those who would desire to study more on spiritual direction, F.P. Harton's aforementioned *Elements of the Spiritual Life* is a good start, but a novice director might also consider *Spiritual Direction* by Martin Thornton, or any of Thornton's other books on Spiritual Direction themes. With the continuing prevalence of professional counselors, and even professional Christian counselor, this practice has waned. But there are some practitioners, and some good resources available to those who would make a study of the practice.

CHAPTER ELEVEN
Conclusion

As a summary conclusion to this study, we can see from history that our relationship with God will always be hindered by sin, and as such, we will always need a means of putting away sin, and reconciling ourselves to God.

The historical study began by showing us that God prescribes specific means of atoning with him over time, and that this reconciliation began on a communal level, but has evolved over time into reconciling both the sins of a community, and the sins of an individual. The most important shift came in the transition from atonement by sacrificial signs, to the atonement made once and for all by Jesus Christ on the cross. Our atonement with God is now grounded firmly in the ministry and mediation of Jesus. The historical study then showed us the transition from the older biblical model, to the more stringent early patristic practices in which penitents were admitted to the community over very long periods of time, under much scrutiny, and with a goal of maintaining the holiness of the Christian community. While these practices were not universally held, they were prevalent in the first four centuries following the crucifixion.

The late patristic period saw a shift in praxis, and in the understanding of personal spiritual direction through the life of the Church, the increased awareness of scripture, the codification of Church law, and in the rise of monasticism. These spiritual fathers did much to increase the opportunities for spiritual growth in the 4th through 9th centuries, and the penitentials which flourished largely in Ireland and Wales also led to a widespread use of penitential texts, and the increase of spiritual guidance in the centuries to follow.

The Medieval period witnessed a significant shift in the life of the Church, particularly in the Western Church, in which these practices were codified into sacramental practices, and confessional responsibility was placed solely in the hands of local priests. This shift, along with the abuses of the confessional in obtaining money for absolution, masses for the dead, and in the selling of indulgences to release souls from purgatory, all led to widespread dissention within the whole Church, including the Western Church which gave rise to these practices.

The Reformation sought to remedy some of these problems, and yet did not succeed to the level expected, but rather led to a further splintering of the Church into factions, which process was largely related to the subject of confessional practice, and the selling of indulgences. From the Reformation, the birth of mainline denominations led to various perspectives on how confessions were to be made, and Anglicanism, which also owes its origins to the Reformation, seems to have encapsulated three main modes of confessional practice: the general confession, resembling the more protestant traditions; auricular confession, resembling the more Roman Catholic traditions; and private spiritual direction, which seems to be minimal, but resembling an amalgamation between the more monastic practices of the late patristic period and modern psychology.

From the Reformation to now Anglicanism has witnessed a shift in confessional practices through the liturgies of the Church, and has now come to a place which is more supportive of auricular confession than allowed in previous centuries. The mixture of foundational sources in Anglican thought from very Protestant to very Catholic, have left us with a Church that is very much a hybrid of so many practices that it is difficult to identify Anglicanism with any one single tradition. Still, Anglicanism maintains these three modes of confessional practice, although the more Protestant perspectives seem to dominate the praxis of the Church.

This study sought to obtain the modern picture of the confessional from the perspective of both clergy and lay sources within the sample taken from a traditional Anglo-Catholic diocese, and as such has produced an image of the confessional which seems to fall right in line with the perspective painted by the study of the Anglican Church's liturgy and history over the last six centuries. Even in a diocese that is largely considered Anglo-Catholic in its outlook, sacramental confession is one of those realms of theology where the more Protestant perspectives have dominated, and left the Church with a vacuum of auricular confession and spiritual direction praxis. While the clergy have reported that the people simply do not seem to have much interest in confession, the people actually report the opposite, saying that it does not seem to be of much importance to the clergy, and it has not been made available to them either by teaching or opportunity. This study has sought to identify where the problem lies, and it seems to be in the education of the clergy, and the willingness to offer regular teaching on the subject. While this is not positive news, it is a place where the clergy can make some adjustments, and possibly make room for more teaching, now that the people have expressed an interest in the practice, and we have offered here at least one working model of confessional practice as a starting point for those who deem themselves undereducated in the practice and theology of the confessional.

In conclusion, auricular confession can, in fact, return to importance in the life of the Church, but also in the public sphere, if the clergy would make an earnest effort to teach and preach about confession, to offer confessional hours, and to be prepared to hear more confessions in the church and publicly. These clergy also need the support of their bishops, who for better or worse, are seen as the "Chief Shepherd" by the people in their dioceses. If the bishops encourage the practice in the dioceses, the clergy are probably more apt to act in favor of the practice, or at least to steer their people towards others who are keener on the confessional practices. There is a real interest among the laity in remedying their sin, and working to come closer to God. The next task is for the clergy to bridge this gap by making this practice accessible, while also doing so in a positive way that shines light on the great benefits of putting away our sins, and seeking help to become better children of God. This is where the laity desire to be, and it is now our job, as clergy to make this opportunity available to the people.

Future Action and Research

Perhaps there is room for another study to be offered outside of the context of a single diocese, from random strangers on the street, as to what their understanding of confession truly is. This study only encompassed the practice within a single diocese, and one that is thought to be more traditional or Anglo-Catholic. A similar study could be done in several dioceses, as to the nature, understanding, and practice of confession across The Episcopal Church, or the Anglican Communion. Then, if one so desired, there could be a study done with similar implications, across various traditions, including those who purport to practice confession, as well as those who do not.

Another avenue of further study would be, in the same contexts just described, a comprehensive qualitative study of clergy from all branches of the Church, both Protestant and Catholic. If we are to believe that the forgiveness of sins is paramount to our eternal destination, then we should probably be very serious about providing ourselves, and those in our spiritual care, with the best and most efficient means of removing sins, and furthermore leading our people in the paths of peace and righteousness, through the practice of virtues, through sermons, lectures, and private spiritual direction.

It seems our tradition as a whole has "given up the ghost" on the confessional, which is a shame. It has made such a large impact on a few of our people, some of whom have become active in ministry as a result of the guidance given in confession, and others who have come to know the healing power of confession and the power of forgiving others, as they have been forgiven. I have often found that a lot of people out there have in fact given up on themselves and conceded that their sin is just their own personal curse. But I have also encountered some of these people who once thought this way, and who have made a total life change after making a good confession, and, as such, became new people. Why wouldn't we want to make opportunities like these more prevalent by offering to hear confessions in our churches, in youth camps, in local prisons, or while sitting at a table at Starbucks? There are probably just as many, if not more sinners in Starbucks, or at the local bar, than in the prisons. The people all around us need to know that God is in the resurrection business, and so are we! Why not "hang a shingle" and tell people you're open for business?

Finally, although it has been stated that clergy could indeed point their people in the direction of good spiritual directors and confessors, it should be important to all clergy and serious disciples of Jesus Christ, clergy and lay, to make an effort to become masters of their souls. If we can embrace the need for mutual accountability in the context of healing our souls, life on earth will be greatly improved, and more souls will adjust their trajectories toward Heaven. We only achieve this through the encouragement of continual study, repeated practice, and gradual improvement into walking in the ways of Jesus Christ. AMEN

BIBLIOGRAPHY

Works Cited

Ancrene Wisse: A Guide for Anchoresses trans. by. Hugh White. Penguin Books, London, 1993.

Anglicanism ed. by Paul E. More and Frank L. Cross. Morehouse Publishing Co., Milwaukee, Wisconsin. 1935

Anti-Nicene Fathers, Vol. 2, eds. Alexander Roberts and James Donaldson. Peabody, Massachusetts. 1999.

An Apology of the Church of England by John Jewell, ed. by J.E. Booty. Cornell University Press, Ithica, New York, 1963.

The Book of Common Prayer Church Publishing Co. New York, 1979.

The Book of Common Prayer, 1549. Accessed March 12th, 2013. http://justus.anglican.org/resources/bcp/1549/BCP_1549.htm

The Book of Common Prayer, 1552. Accessed March 12th, 2013. http://justus.anglican.org/resources/bcp/1549/BCP_1549.htm

The Book of Common Prayer 1789, Accessed March 12th, 2013. http://justus.anglican.org/resources/bcp/1789/BCP_1789.htm

The Book of Common Prayer 1892, Accessed March 12th, 2013. http://justus.anglican.org/resources/bcp/1892/BCP_1892.htm

The Book of Common Prayer 1928, Accessed March 12th, 2013. http://justus.anglican.org/resources/bcp/1928/BCP_1928.htm

Catechism of the Catholic Church Doubleday, New York. 1995.

The Cloud of Unknowing ed. by. William Johnson. Doubleday/Image Books, New York, 1973.

Commentary on the American prayer Book By Marion J. Hatchett. The Seabury Press, New York. 1981.

Conferences by John Cassian, trans. by Colm Luibheid. Paulist Press, New York. 1985.

Counsels on the Spiritual Life by Mark the Monk, trans. by Tim Tivian and Augustine Casiday. St. Vladimir's Seminary Press, New York. 2009.

The Decrees of the Ecumenical Councils ed. by Norman P. Tanner S.J.. Georgetown University Press, Washington D.C.. 1990.

Defense of the Seven Sacraments by Henry VIII, re-ed. by Rev. Louis O'Donovan. Benziger Brothers, New York, 1908.

Documents of the English Reformation ed. by Gerald Bray. James Clarke & Co. Cambridge. 1994.

"Entire Absolution of a Penitent." Accessed March 9th, 2013.   http://www.anglicanhistory.org/pusey/pusey6.html

An Examination into the Doctrine and Practice of Confession by Edward William Jelf. Longmans, Green, and Co. London, 1875.

Formulations of Faith Put Forth During the Reign of Henry VIII ed. by Charles Lloyd. Oxford University Press, Oxford. 1856.

"Hints on Making a First Confession." Accessed March 9th, 2013. http://www.anglicanhistory.org/pusey/pusey1.html

The History of the Confessional by John Henry Hopkins. Harper & Brothers Publishers, New York. 1855.

Institutes of Christian Religion by John Calvin, trans. by. Henry Beveridge. Eerdmans, Michigan, 1972.

The Life and Times of St. Leo the Great by Trevor Jalland. S.P.C.K., New York. 1941.

Jeremy Taylor: Selected Works ed. by Thomas K. Carroll. Paulist Press, New York. 1990.

Liturgies and Offices of the Church by Edward Burbridge. Thomas Whittaker, New York. 1886.

Making Confession, Hearing Confession: A History of the Cure of Souls by Annemarie S. Kidder. Minnesota, Liturgical Press, 2010.

A Manual for Priests of the American Church. Society of St. John the Evangelist. Lorell Press, Avon Massachusetts. 1978

Martin Luther: Selections from His Writings ed. by John Dillenberger, Anchor Books Doubleday, New York, 1961.

Medieval Handbooks of Penance by John T. McNeill and Helena M. Gamer. Columbia University Press, New York. 1938.

Of the Laws of Ecclesiastical Polity by Richard Hooker, ed. by P.G. Stanwood. Harvard University Press, Cambridge, Massachusetts. 1981.

The Oxford Guide to the Book of Common Prayer Ed. by Charles Hefling and Cynthia Shattuck. Oxford University Press, Oxford. 2006.

The Parish Priest and the Life of Prayer by Evelyn Underhill. Little Gidding Press, Morningside Heights, New York. 1937.

Richard Rolle: The English Writings trans. and ed. by Rosamund Allen. Paulist Press, New York, 1988.

St. Augustine's Prayer Book ed. by The Rev. Loren Gavitt. Holy Cross Publications. West Park, New York. 1965.

The Scale (or Ladder) of Perfection by Walter Hilton. Art and Book Company, Westminster, 1901.

Select Documents of English Constitutional History ed. by George B. Adams and H. Morse Stephens. The Macmillan Company, London. 1939.

Showings by Julian of Norwich, trans. by Edmund College and James Walsh. Paulist Press, New York, 1978.

Some Account of the Penitential Discipline of the Early Church in the First four Centuries by R.S.T. Haslehurst. London, S.P.C.K., London. 1921

Spiritual Direction and the Care of Souls by Gary Moon and David Benner, Intervarsity Press, Downers Grove, Illinois. 2004.

Summa Theologica, by Thomas Aquinas. Benzinger Brothers. New York, 1952.

Thomas Cranmer's Doctrine of Repentance By Ashley Null. Oxford University Press, Oxford. 2000.

"Tract 71." Accessed March 9th, 2013. http://www.anglicanhistory. org/tracts/tract71.html

"Tract 90." Accessed March 9th, 2013. http://www.anglicanhistory. org/tracts/tract90/fulltext.html

Works Consulted

Absolution by Matthew Woodward. Folkestone, London. 1869.

Alcoholics Anonymous Ed. by Alcoholics Anonymous World Services, Inc. New York, 2001.

The Anglican Spiritual Tradition by John H. Moorman. Templegate Publishers, Springfield Illinois, 1983.

Auricular Confession and Penance by Charles Mercer Hall. St. Mary's, Asheville, North Carolina. 1916.

Auricular confession and Private Absolution by William Bacon Stevens. McCalla and Stavely, Philadelphia. 1880.

The Bishop's Call to Uniformity by Cecil Wray. Adam Holden, Liverpool. 1868.

Body and Soul by Percy Dearmer. E.P. Dutton & Co., New York, 1909.

The Book of Pastoral Rule by St. Gregory the Great, translated by Goerge . Demacopulos. St. Vladimir's Seminary Press, New York. 2007.

Celtic Penitentials by John Thomas McNeill. Librarie Ancienne, Paris. 1923.

The Celtic Penitentials and their Influence on Continental Christianity by John Thomas McNeill. Librairie Ancienne Honore Champion, Paris. 1923.

The Christian Faith by Claude B. Moss. S.P.C.K., New York, 1943.

Christian Proficiency by Martin Thornton, S.P.C.K., London, 1959.

Commentary on the Seven Penitential Psalms by The Right Reverend A.P. Forbes. Joseph Masters, London. 1853.

Confess Your Sins by John Stott. Westminster Press, Philadelphia, 1964.

Confession and Absolution by Alfred Mortimer. Longmans, Green, and Co. New York, 1906.

Confession and Absolution ed. by Martin Dudley and Geoffrey Rowell. The Liturgical Press, Minnesota, 1990.

Confession and Absolution by Vernon W. Hutton. Longhurst, London. 1869.

Confession and Absolution in the Bible by Warwick Elwin. J.Y. Hays, London. 1883.

Confession in the Church of England Anonymous. The Church Press, London. 1868.

Confessionals Anonymous. S.W. Partridge, London. 1865.

Confessions of St. Augustine. Trans. By John K. Ryan. Image Books, Doubleday, New York. 1960.

The Confessional: An Appeal to the Primitive and Catholic Forms of Absolution in the East and West by M. Hobart Seymour. Seeley, Jackson, & Halliday, London. 1870.

The Confessor After the Heart of Jesus by Canon A. Guerra. St. Louis, Missouri. 1901.

A Confessor's Handbook by Kurt Stasiak, O.S.B.; Paulist Press, New York, 1999.

Commentary on the Seven Penitential Psalms by A.P. Forbes. Joseph Masters, London. 1853.

Conversion Through Penance in the Italian Church of the 4th and 5th Centuries by Allan Fitzgerald. Edward Mellen Press, Lampeter. 1988.

Counsels on the Spiritual Life by Mark the Monk, translated by Tim Vivian. St. Vladimir's Seminary Press, New York. 2009.

The Country Parson and Selected Poems by George Herbert; SCM Press Ltd. London, 1956.

The Cure' D'Ars by Abbe Francis Trochu. Tan Books and Publishers, Rockford, Illinois. 1977.

The Cure of Souls: A Manual for the Clergy by William Walter Webb. James Pott & Co. New York. 1892.

Decently and In Order by The Rev. William C. Dewitt. Morehouse, Milwaukee, 1914.

Dogmatic Theology by Francis J. Hall. Longmans, Green, and Co. New York. 1921.

Doors to the Sacred: A Historical Introduction to the Sacraments in the Catholic Church by Joseph Martos. Doubleday & Co. Inc. Garden City, New York. 1981.

Eight Reasons Why Those Who Receive The Blessed Sacrament Should Go to Confession Anonymous. Church Press, London. 1866.

Elements of the Spiritual Life by F.P.Harton, S.P.C.K., London, 1957.

The English Religious Tradition and the Genius of Anglicanism ed. by Geoffrey Rowell. Abingdon Press, Nashville, 1992.

The Enkindling of Love (The Triple Way) by St. Bonaventure, trans. By Regis J. Armstrong

Exploring Spiritual Direction by Alan Jones. The Seabury Press, New York, 1982.

Essays in Pastoral Reconstruction by Martin Thornton, S.P.C.K., London, 1960.

Ethics and the New Testament by J.L. Houlden. T&T Clark, Edinburgh, 1992.

The Evolving Church and the Sacrament of Penance by Ladislas Orsy.

Dimension Books, Denville, New Jersey. 1978.

An Examination into the Doctrine and Practice of Confession by William Edward Jelf. Longmans, Green, and Co., London. 1875.

Examination of Conscience by Gaduel, translated by The Rev. Eugene Grimm. Benziger Brothers, New York. 1885.

Examination of Conscience: For the Use of Priests Who are Making a Retreat trans. by Eugene Grimm. Benziger Brothers, New York. 1885.

The Fundamental Principles of the Metaphysics of Ethics by Immanuel Kant. D. Appleton-Century Co., New York, 1938.

The Good Confessor by Gerald Kelly. Dublin Clonmore & Reynolds Ltd., London. 1952.

Hearing Confessions by Kenneth Ross. S.P.C.K., London, 1975.

The History of Auricular Confession by Count C.P. De Lasteyrie. Richard Bentley, London. 1848.

The History of Britain, Vol. III by J. S. Brewer. Oxford University Press, Oxford. 1845.

The History of Penance by Oscar Watkins. Longmans, Green, & Co. London. 1920.

Hooker and the Anglican Tradition by John S. Marshall. The University Press of the University of the South, Sewanee, Tennessee. 1963.

The Humiliation of Sinners: Public Penance in 13th Century France by Mary C. Mansfield. Cornell University Press, Ithaca, New York. 1995.

The Illness and Cure of the Soul in the Orthodox Tradition by Metropolitan of Nafpaktos Hiertheos, trans. by Effie Mavromichali. Birth of Theotokos Monastery, Levadia, Greece. 1993.

Interior Castle by Teresa of Avila. trans. by Kieran Kavanaugh and Otilio Rodriguez. Paulist Press, New York. 1979.

Introduction to the Devout Life by Francis De Sales, trans. by John K. Ryan. Doubleday, New York. 1989.

The Irish Penitentials and their Significance for the Sacrament of Penance Today by Hugh Connolly. Four Courts Press, Portland, Oregon. 1995.

The Jurisdiction of the Confessor by James P. Kelly. Benziger Brothers, New York. 1929.

Letters of Spiritual Counsel and Guidance by John Keble, ed. by Robert Van de Weyer. Harper Collins, London. 1995.

The Life of Moses by Gregory of Nyssa, translated by Abraham J. Malherbe and Everett Ferguson. Paulist Press, New York. 1978.

The Literature of Penance in Anglo-Saxon England by Allen Frantzen. Rutgers University Press, New Brunswick, New Jersey. 1983.

Liturgies and Offices of the Church by Edward Burbidge. Thomas Whittaker, New York. 1886.

Lord, Have Mercy: The Healing Power of Confession by Scott Hahn. Doubleday, New York, 2003.

A Manual for Confessors by Francis George Belton, Mowbray & Co. Ltd. London, 1949.

A New Introduction to Moral Theology by Herbert Waddams. SCM Press, London, 1964.

The Nine Ways of Prayer of St. Dominic anonymous. c. 1260-1288

Notes on the Absolution of the Sick and Dying by E.C. Linton. Longmans, Green & Co. London. 1915.

Notes on the Seven Penitential Psalms by The Rev. Alfred G. Mortimer. E.&J.B. Young & Co. New York. 1889.

On the Incarnation by St. Athanasius. St. Vladamir's Seminary Press, Crestwood, New York, 1996.

Ordering Women's Lives: Penitentials and Nunnery Rules in the Early Medieval West by Julie Ann Smith. Ashgate, Burlington. 2001.

The Oxford American Prayer Book Commentary by Massey Shepherd Jr.; Oxford University Press, New York, 1959.

Pardon and Peace: A Sinner's Guide to Confession by Francis Randolph. Ignatius Press, San Francisco, 2001.

The Parson's Handbook by Percy Dearmer. Oxford University Press, London, 1932.

Pastors and the Care of Souls in Medieval England ed. by John Shinners and William J. Dohar, University of Notre Dame Press, Notre Dame, Indiana. 1998.

Pastoral Theology: A Reorientation by Martin Thornton. SPCK, London, 1964.

Penance and the Anointing of the Sick by Bernhard Poschmann, trans. by Francis Courtney. Herder & Herder, Freiberg, Germany. 1964

Penitence, With Rules for Guidance and Hints for a First Confession by Edward Bouverie Pusey. Walter Smith. London. 1884.

Penitential Prayer in Second Temple Judaism by Rodney Alan Werline. Scholars Press, Atlanta, Georgia. 1998.

"A Place for Spiritual Direction" by Jamin Goggin. Accessed September 26th, 2011. http://pastors.com/a-place-for-spiritual-direction-part-1/

The Practice of Penance 900-1050 by Sarah Hamilton. The Royal Historical Society. Suffolk, U.K. 2001.

The Priest as Confessor by A.H. Baverstock. Cope & Fenwick, London. 1873.

A Priest's Handbook by Dennis Michno. Morehouse-Barlow Co., Inc.; Connecticut, 1983.

The Priest's Service Book trans. by Father Evagoras Constantinines. Published by Author. Merrillville, Indiana. 1989.

Psalm Fifty-One in the Light of Ancient Near Easter Patternism by Edward Dalglish. E.J. Brill, Leiden. 1962.

Quality Research Papers for Students of Religion and Theology by Nancy Vyhmeister, Zondervan, Grand Rapids, Michigan. 2008

Research Design by John W. Cresswell. Sage Productions, Thousand Oaks, California. 2003.

The Rite of Reconciliation: Sacrament and Discipline by Hope Philips Koski. MTS Thesis, Nashotah House, Wisconsin. 1980.

Ritual Notes by E.C.R. Lamburn. 11th Edition. W. Knott & Son Ltd. London. 1964.

The Romance of Orthodoxy by Homer F. Rogers. Ed. by Mary P. Tuck. Taylor Publishing Co, Dallas, 1991.

The Rule of St. Benedict trans. by Anthony Meisel and M.L. del Mastro; Image Books Doubleday. New York, 1975.

Sacramental Confession by John Howson. W. Isbister & Co. London. 1874.

The Sacramentals of the Holy Catholic Church by A.A. Lambing. Benziger Brothers, New York. 1892.

The Sacrament of Penance by Urling Whelpton. The Young Churchman Co. Milwaukee, Wisconsin. 1917.

The Sacrament of Reconciliation by Andrew Cuschieri. University Press of America, New York. 1992.

Saint Anselm: Basic Writings translated by S.N. Deane, Open court Publishing, LaSalle, Illinois. 1962.

St. Cyprian: The Lapsed; Ancient Christian Writers Series, Vol. 25 trans. and ed. by Maurice Bevenot, S.J.. The Newman Press, New York. 1956.

St. Cyprian: The Letters of Cyprian of Carthage; Ancient Christian Writers Series, Vol. 44 trans. and ed. by G.W. Clarke. The Newman Press, New York.

Selections from: A Serious Call to a Devout and Holy Life by William Law. Ed. by Emilie Griffin, Harper Collins, San Francisco, 1978.

The Service Book of the Holy Orthodox-Catholic Apostolic Church by Isabel Florence Hapgood. Houghton, Mifflin, and Co. Boston. 1906.

Seven Penitential Psalms, Chiefly from Patristic Sources by Alfred Mortimer. E.&J.B. Young & Co, New York. 1889.

Sex and the New Medieval Literature of Confession, 1150-1300 by Pierre J. Payer. Pontifical Institute of Medieval Studies. 2009.

Sin and Confession on the Eve of the Reformation by Thomas N. Tentler. Princeton University Press, Princeton, New Jersey. 1977.

Sin and Society in Fourteenth-Century England: A Study of the Memoriale Presbiterorum by Michael Haren. Clarendon Press, Oxford. 2000.

Some Account of the Penitential Discipline of the Early Church by R.S.T. Haslehurst. S.P.C.K., London. 1921.

Some Principles of Moral Theology by Kenneth E. Kirk. Longmans, Green, and Company, Ltd. London, 1961.

Spiritual Care by Dietrich Bonhoeffer, trans. by Jay C. Rochelle. Fortress Press, New York. 1985.

Spiritual Counsel in the Anglican Tradition ed. by. David Hein and Charles R. Henery. Wiph & Stock, Eugene, 2010.

Spiritual Direction in the Orthodox Christian Tradition by F. Gregory Rogers. Journal of Psychology and Theology, December 22, 2002.

Spiritual Direction and Meditation by Thomas Merton. Liturgical Press, Collegevill, Minnesota, 1960.

The Spiritual Life by Evelyn Underhill. Hodder and Stoughton, London, 1938.

Spirituality for Everyday Living: An Adaptation of the Rule of St. Benedict by Brian C. Taylor. The Liturgical Press. Collegeville, Minnesota. 1989.

The Spiritual Exercises of St. Ignatius trans. by Anthony Mottola. Image Books, New York, 1964.

The Spiritual Life by Evelyn Underhill. Nodder & Stoughton Ltd. London. 1938.

The Study of Liturgy ed. by Jones, Wainwright, and Yarnold. Oxford University Press, New York, 1978.

Theory and Practice of the Confessional by Caspar E. Schieler. Benziger Brothers, New York. 1905.

Treatise on Law by St. Thomas Aquinas. Gateway Editions, Washington D.C., 1988.

The Untapped Power of the Sacrament of Penance by Christopher J. Walsh, Servant Books, Cincinnati, 1989.

What to Say to the Penitent by Charles Hugo Doyle. Roman Catholic Books, Harrison, New York. 1953.

Why I Don't Go to Confession Anonymous. S.W. Partridge and Co. London. 1868.

The Worship of the Church by Massey Shepherd Jr., Seabury Press, New York, 1963.

Suggested bibliography for those interested in deeper confessional study

For Clergy

Practical Texts

A Manual for Confessors by Francis George Belton, Mowbray & Co. Ltd. London, 1949.

Elements of the Spiritual Life by F.P.Harton, S.P.C.K., London, 1957.

The Cure of Souls: A Manual for the Clergy by William Walter Webb. James Pott & Co. New York. 1892.

A Confessor's Handbook by Kurt Stasiak, O.S.B.; Paulist Press, New York, 1999.

Hearing Confessions by Kenneth Ross. S.P.C.K., London, 1975.

Note: Novice confessors would be best served by reading Harton's chapter on offering spiritual direction, and then work your way through Belton and the rest of Harton, and then continue your studies through the other texts. The historical texts below are tremendously helpful for understanding, but in my opinion it is better to begin with a groundwork of praxis, and then work through motives and antiquity later. This will not hinder your progress, but rather give you a structure in which to later "feather your nest."

Historical Texts

Making Confession, Hearing Confession: A History of the Cure of Souls by Annemarie S. Kidder. Liturgical Press, Collegeville, Minnesota. 2010.

The History of the Confessional by John Henry Hopkins. Harper & Brothers, New York. 1855.

Spiritual Direction and the Care of Souls by Gary Moon and David Benner, Intervarsity Press, Downers Grove, Illinois. 2004.

Confession and Absolution ed. by Martin Dudley and Geoffrey Rowell. The Liturgical Press, Minnesota, 1990.

For Laity

Pardon and Peace: A Sinner's Guide to Confession by Francis Randolph. Ignatius Press, San Francisco, 2001.

Lord, Have Mercy: The Healing Power of Confession by Scott Hahn. Doubleday, New York, 2003.

For Both

Introduction to the Devout Life by Francis De Sales, trans. by John K. Ryan. Doubleday, New York. 1989.

Spiritual Counsel in the Anglican Tradition ed. by. David Hein and Charles R. Henery. Wiph & Stock, Eugene, 2010.

The Untapped Power of the Sacrament of Penance by Christopher J. Walsh, Servant Books, Cincinnati, 1989.

Letters of Spiritual Counsel and Guidance by John Keble, ed. by Robert Van de Weyer. Harper Collins, London. 1995.

11359382R00177

Made in the USA
San Bernardino, CA
15 May 2014